"CHALLENGING"

"POWERFUL"

"MAGNIFICENT"

". . . one of the most challenging books of the decade. . . ."
—Anatole Broyard, *The New York Times*

"A magnificent psychophilosophical synthesis which ranks among the truly important books of the year. Professor Becker writes with power and brilliant insight . . . moves unflinchingly toward a masterful articulation of the limitations of psychoanalysis and of reason itself in helping man transcend his conflicting fears of both death and life . . . his book will be acknowledged as a major work."
—*Publishers Weekly*

". . . to read it is to know the delight inherent in the unfolding of a mind grasping at new possibilities and forming a new synthesis. *The Denial of Death* is a great book—one of the few great books of the 20th or any other century. . . ."
—*Albuquerque Journal Book Review*

". . . a splendidly written book by an erudite and fluent professor. . . . He manifests astonishing insight into the theories of Sigmund Freud, Otto Rank, Soren Kierkegaard, Carl Jung, Erich Fromm, and other giants. . . . Becker has written a powerful book. . . ."
—*Best Sellers*

". . . a brilliant, passionate synthesis of the human sciences which resurrects and revitalizes . . . the ideas of psychophilosophical geniuses. . . . *The Denial of Death* fuses them clearly, beautifully, with amazing concision, into an organic body of theory which attempts nothing less than to explain the possibilities of man's meaningful, sane survival. . . ."
—*Minneapolis Tribune*

". . . magnificent . . . not only the culmination but the triumph of Becker's attempt to create a meaningful 'science of man' . . . a moving, important and necessary work that speaks not only to the social scientists and theologians but to all of us finite creatures."
—*Commonweal*

THE DENIAL
OF DEATH

Books by ERNEST BECKER

Angel in Armor (paper)

Escape from Evil

The Denial of Death (cloth and paper)

The Structure of Evil (paper)

All available from THE FREE PRESS,
A Division of Macmillan Publishing Co., Inc.

THE DENIAL
OF DEATH

Ernest Becker

THE FREE PRESS
A Division of Macmillan Publishing Co., Inc.
NEW YORK

Collier Macmillan Publishers
LONDON

The Free Press
A Division of Macmillan Publishing Co., Inc.
866 Third Avenue, New York, N.Y. 10022

Collier Macmillan Canada, Ltd.

First Free Press Paperback Edition 1975

Library of Congress Catalog Card Number: 73–1860

Printed in the United States of America

hardbound printing number
4 5 6 7 8 9 10

paperback printing number

1 2 3 4 5 6 7 8 9 10

Library of Congress Cataloging in Publication Data

Becker, Ernest.
    The denial of death.

    Includes bibliographical references.
    1. Death. 2. Kierkegaard, Søren Aabye, 1813–
1855. 3. Courage. I. Title. [DNLM: 1. Death.
BF789.D4 B395d 1973]
BD444.B36   128'.5   73–1860
ISBN 0-02-902310-6 pbk

To the memory of my beloved parents, who unwittingly gave me—among many other things—the most paradoxical gift of all: a confusion about heroism.

Non ridere, non lugere, neque detestari, sed intelligere. (Not to laugh, not to lament, not to curse, but to understand.)
—SPINOZA

Contents

	Preface	ix
CHAPTER ONE:	*Introduction: Human Nature and the Heroic*	1

PART I: THE DEPTH PSYCHOLOGY OF HEROISM — 9

CHAPTER TWO:	*The Terror of Death*	11
CHAPTER THREE:	*The Recasting of Some Basic Psychoanalytic Ideas*	25
CHAPTER FOUR:	*Human Character as a Vital Lie*	47
CHAPTER FIVE:	*The Psychoanalyst Kierkegaard*	67
CHAPTER SIX:	*The Problem of Freud's Character, Noch Einmal*	93

PART II: THE FAILURES OF HEROISM — 125

CHAPTER SEVEN:	*The Spell Cast by Persons— The Nexus of Unfreedom*	127
CHAPTER EIGHT:	*Otto Rank and the Closure of Psychoanalysis on Kierkegaard*	159
CHAPTER NINE:	*The Present Outcome of Psychoanalysis*	176
CHAPTER TEN:	*A General View of Mental Illness*	208

PART III: RETROSPECT AND CONCLUSION: THE DILEMMAS OF HEROISM — 253

CHAPTER ELEVEN:	*Psychology and Religion: What Is the Heroic Individual?*	255
	References	286
	Index	305

> *... for the time being I gave up writing—there is*
> *already too much truth in the world—an over-*
> *production which apparently cannot be consumed!*
> —OTTO RANK[1]

The prospect of death, Dr. Johnson said, wonderfully concentrates the mind. The main thesis of this book is that it does much more than that: the idea of death, the fear of it, haunts the human animal like nothing else; it is a mainspring of human activity—activity designed largely to avoid the fatality of death, to overcome it by denying in some way that it is the final destiny for man. The noted anthropologist A. M. Hocart once argued that primitives were not bothered by the fear of death; that a sagacious sampling of anthropological evidence would show that death was, more often than not, accompanied by rejoicing and festivities; that death seemed to be an occasion for celebration rather than fear—much like the traditional Irish wake. Hocart wanted to dispel the notion that (compared to modern man) primitives were childish and frightened by reality; anthropologists have now largely accomplished this rehabilitation of the primitive. But this argument leaves untouched the fact that the fear of death is indeed a universal in the human condition. To be sure, primitives often celebrate death—as Hocart and others have shown—*because* they believe that death is the ultimate promotion, the final ritual elevation to a higher form of life, to the enjoyment of eternity in some form. Most modern Westerners have trouble believing this any more, which is what makes the fear of death so prominent a part of our psychological make-up.

In these pages I try to show that the fear of death is a universal that unites data from several disciplines of the human sciences, and makes wonderfully clear and intelligible human actions that we have buried under mountains of fact, and obscured with endless back-and-forth arguments about the "true" human motives. The man of knowledge in our time is bowed down under a burden he never imagined he would ever have: the overproduction of truth that cannot be consumed. For centuries man lived in the belief that truth was slim and elusive and that once he found it the troubles of mankind would be over. And here we are in the closing decades of the 20th century, choking on truth. There has been so much brilliant writing, so many genial discoveries, so vast an extension and elaboration of these discoveries—yet the mind is silent as the world spins on its age-old demonic career. I remember reading how, at the famous St. Louis World Exposition in 1904, the speaker at the prestigious science meeting was having trouble speaking against the noise of the new weapons that were being demonstrated nearby. He said something condescending and tolerant about this needlessly disruptive play, as though the future belonged to science and not to militarism. World War I showed everyone the priority of things on this planet, which party was playing idle games and which wasn't. This year the order of priority was again graphically shown by a world arms budget of 204 billion dollars, at a time when human living conditions on the planet were worse than ever.

Why, then, the reader may ask, add still another weighty tome to a useless overproduction? Well, there are personal reasons, of course: habit, drivenness, dogged hopefulness. And there is Eros, the urge to the unification of experience, to form, to greater meaningfulness. One of the reasons, I believe, that knowledge is in a state of useless overproduction is that it is strewn all over the place, spoken in a thousand competitive voices. Its insignificant fragments are magnified all out of proportion, while its major and world-historical insights lie around begging for attention. There is no throbbing, vital center. Norman O. Brown observed that the great world needs more Eros and less strife, and the intellectual world needs it just as much. There has to be revealed the harmony that unites many different positions, so that the "sterile and ignorant polemics" can be abated.[2]

I have written this book fundamentally as a study in harmonization of the Babel of views on man and on the human condition, in the belief that the time is ripe for a synthesis that covers the best thought in many fields, from the human sciences to religion. I have tried to avoid moving against and negating any point of view, no matter how personally antipathetic to me, if it seems to have in it a core of truthfulness. I have had the growing realization over the past few years that the problem of man's knowledge is not to oppose and to demolish opposing views, but to include them in a larger theoretical structure. One of the ironies of the creative process is that it partly cripples itself in order to function. I mean that, usually, in order to turn out a piece of work the author has to exaggerate the emphasis of it, to oppose it in a forcefully competitive way to other versions of truth; and he gets carried away by his own exaggeration, as his distinctive image is built on it. But each honest thinker who is basically an empiricist has to have some truth in his position, no matter how extremely he has formulated it. The problem is to find the truth underneath the exaggeration, to cut away the excess elaboration or distortion and include that truth where it fits.

A second reason for my writing this book is that I have had more than my share of problems with this fitting-together of valid truths in the past dozen years. I have been trying to come to grips with the ideas of Freud and his interpreters and heirs, with what might be the distillation of modern psychology—and now I think I have finally succeeded. In this sense this book is a bid for the peace of my scholarly soul, an offering for intellectual absolution; I feel that it is my first mature work.

One of the main things I try to do in this book is to present a summing-up of psychology after Freud by tying the whole development of psychology back to the still-towering Kierkegaard. I am thus arguing for a merger of psychology and mythico-religious perspective. I base this argument in large part on the work of Otto Rank, and I have made a major attempt to transcribe the relevance of his magnificent edifice of thought. This coming-to-grips with Rank's work is long overdue; and if I have succeeded in it, it probably comprises the main value of the book.

Rank is so prominent in these pages that perhaps a few words of introduction about him would be helpful here. Frederick Perls once observed that Rank's book *Art and Artist* was "beyond praise."[3] I remember being so struck by this judgment that I went immediately to the book: I couldn't very well imagine how anything scientific could be "beyond praise." Even the work of Freud himself seemed to me to be praiseworthy, that is, somehow expectable as a product of the human mind. But Perls was right: Rank was—as the young people say—"something else." You cannot merely praise much of his work because in its stunning brilliance it is often fantastic, gratuitous, superlative; the insights seem like a gift, beyond what is necessary. I suppose part of the reason—in addition to his genius—was that Rank's thought always spanned several fields of knowledge; when he talked about, say, anthropological data and you expected anthropological insight, you got something else, something more. Living as we do in an era of hyperspecialization we have lost the expectation of this kind of delight; the experts give us manageable thrills—if they thrill us at all.

One thing that I hope my confrontation of Rank will do is to send the reader directly to his books. There is no substitute for reading Rank. My personal copies of his books are marked in the covers with an uncommon abundance of notes, underlinings, double exclamation points; he is a mine for years of insights and pondering. My treatment of Rank is merely an outline of his thought: its foundations, many of its basic insights, and its overall implications. This will be the pale Rank, not the staggeringly rich one of his books. Also, Ira Progoff's outline presentation and appraisal of Rank is so correct, so finely balanced in judgment, that it can hardly be improved upon as a brief appreciation.[4] Rank is very diffuse, very hard to read, so rich that he is almost inaccessible to the general reader. He was painfully aware of this and for a time hoped that Anaïs Nin would rewrite his books for him so that they would have a chance to have the effect they should have had. What I give in these pages is my own version of Rank, filled out in my own way, a sort of brief "translation" of his system in the hope of making it accessible as a whole. In this book I cover only his individual psychology; in another book I will sketch his schema for a psychology of history.

There are several ways of looking at Rank. Some see him as a brilliant coworker of Freud, a member of the early circle of psychoanalysis who helped give it broader currency by bringing to it his own vast erudition, who showed how psychoanalysis could illuminate cultural history, myth, and legend—as, for example, in his early work on *The Myth of the Birth of the Hero* and *The Incest-Motif*. They would go on to say that because Rank was never analyzed, his repressions gradually got the better of him, and he turned away from the stable and creative life he had close to Freud; in his later years his personal instability gradually overcame him, and he died prematurely in frustration and loneliness. Others see Rank as an overeager disciple of Freud, who tried prematurely to be original and in so doing even exaggerated psychoanalytic reductionism. This judgment is based almost solely on his 1924 book *The Trauma of Birth* and usually stops there. Still others see Rank as a brilliant member of Freud's close circle, an eager favorite of Freud, whose university education was suggested and financially helped by Freud and who repaid psychoanalysis with insights into many fields: cultural history, childhood development, the psychology of art, literary criticism, primitive thought, and so on. In short, a sort of many-faceted but not-too-well-organized or self-controlled boy-wonder—an intellectually superior Theodor Reik, so to speak.

But all these ways of summing up Rank are wrong, and we know that they derive largely from the mythology of the circle of psychoanalysts themselves. They never forgave Rank for turning away from Freud and so diminishing their own immortality-symbol (to use Rank's way of understanding their bitterness and pettiness). Admittedly, Rank's *Trauma of Birth* gave his detractors an easy handle on him, a justified reason for disparaging his stature; it was an exaggerated and ill-fated book that poisoned his public image, even though he himself reconsidered it and went so far beyond it. Not being merely a coworker of Freud, a broad-ranging servant of psychoanalysis, Rank had his own, unique, and perfectly thought-out system of ideas. He knew where he wanted to begin, what body of data he had to pass through, and where it all pointed. He knew these things specifically as regards psychoanalysis itself, which he wanted to transcend and did; he knew it roughly, as regards the philosophical implications of his own system of thought, but he was not given the time to work this out, as his life was cut short. He was certainly as complete a system-maker as were Adler and Jung; his system of thought is at least as brilliant as theirs, if not more so in some ways. We respect Adler for the solidity of his judgment, the directness of his insight, his uncompromising humanism; we admire Jung for the courage and openness with which he embraced both science and religion; but even more than these two, Rank's system has implications for the deepest and broadest development of the social sciences, implications that have only begun to be tapped.

Paul Roazen, writing about "The Legend of Freud,"[5] aptly observed that "any writer whose mistakes have taken this long to correct is . . . quite a figure in intellectual history." Yet the whole matter is very curious, because Adler, Jung, and Rank very early corrected most of Freud's basic mistakes. The question for the historian is, rather, what there was in the nature of the psychoanalytic movement, the ideas themselves, the public and the scholarly mind that kept these corrections so ignored or so separated from the main movement of cumulative scientific thought.

Even a book of broad scope has to be very selective of the truths it picks out of the mountain of truth that is stifling us. Many thinkers of importance are mentioned only in passing: the reader may wonder, for example, why I lean so much on Rank and hardly mention Jung in a book that has as a major aim the closure of psychoanalysis on religion. One reason is that Jung is so prominent and has so many effective interpreters, while Rank is hardly known and has had hardly anyone to speak for him. Another reason is that although Rank's thought is difficult, it is always right on the central problems, Jung's is not, and a good part of it wanders into needless esotericism; the result is that he often obscures on the one hand what he reveals on the other. I can't see that all his tomes on alchemy add one bit to the weight of his psychoanalytic insight.

A good many phrasings of insight into human nature I owe to exchanges with Marie Becker, whose fineness and realism on these matters are most rare. I want to thank (with the customary disclaimers) Paul Roazen for his kindness in passing Chapter Six through the net of his great knowledge of Freud. Robert N. Bellah read the entire manuscript, and I am very grateful for his general criticisms and specific suggestions; those that I was able to act on definitely improved the book; as for the others, I fear that they pose the larger and longer-range task of changing myself.

THE DENIAL OF DEATH

CHAPTER ONE

Introduction: Human Nature
and the Heroic

In times such as ours there is a great pressure to come up with concepts that help men understand their dilemma; there is an urge toward vital ideas, toward a simplification of needless intellectual complexity. Sometimes this makes for big lies that resolve tensions and make it easy for action to move forward with just the rationalizations that people need. But it also makes for the slow disengagement of truths that help men get a grip on what is happening to them, that tell them where the problems really are.

One such vital truth that has long been known is the idea of *heroism;* but in "normal" scholarly times we never thought of making much out of it, of parading it, or of using it as a central concept. Yet the popular mind always knew how important it was: as William James—who covered just about everything—remarked at the turn of the century: "mankind's common instinct for reality . . . has always held the world to be essentially a theatre for heroism."[1] Not only the popular mind knew, but philosophers of all ages, and in our culture especially Emerson and Nietzsche—which is why we still thrill to them: we like to be reminded that our central calling, our main task on this planet, is the heroic.*

One way of looking at the whole development of social science since Marx and of psychology since Freud is that it represents a massive detailing and clarification of the problem of human heroism. This perspective sets the tone for the seriousness of our discussion: we now have the scientific underpinning for a true understanding of the nature of heroism and its place in human life. If "mankind's

* In the following discussion I am obliged to repeat and sum up things I have written elsewhere (*The Birth and Death of Meaning,* Second Edition, New York: Free Press, 1971) in order to set the framework for the other chapters.

common instinct for reality" is right, we have achieved the remarkable feat of exposing that reality in a scientific way.

One of the key concepts for understanding man's urge to heroism is the idea of "narcissism." As Erich Fromm has so well reminded us, this idea is one of Freud's great and lasting contributions. Freud discovered that each of us repeats the tragedy of the mythical Greek Narcissus: we are hopelessly absorbed with ourselves. If we care about anyone it is usually ourselves first of all. As Aristotle somewhere put it: luck is when the guy next to you gets hit with the arrow. Twenty-five hundred years of history have not changed man's basic narcissism; most of the time, for most of us, this is still a workable definition of luck. It is one of the meaner aspects of narcissism that we feel that practically everyone is expendable except ourselves. We should feel prepared, as Emerson once put it, to recreate the whole world out of ourselves even if no one else existed. The thought frightens us; we don't know how we could do it without others—yet at bottom the basic resource is there: we could suffice alone if need be, if we could trust ourselves as Emerson wanted. And if we don't feel this trust emotionally, still most of us would struggle to survive with all our powers, no matter how many around us died. Our organism is ready to fill the world all alone, even if our mind shrinks at the thought. This narcissism is what keeps men marching into point-blank fire in wars: at heart one doesn't feel that *he* will die, he only feels sorry for the man next to him. Freud's explanation for this was that the unconscious does not know death or time: in man's physiochemical, inner organic recesses he feels immortal.

None of these observations implies human guile. Man does not seem able to "help" his selfishness; it seems to come from his animal nature. Through countless ages of evolution the organism has had to protect its own integrity; it had its own physiochemical identity and was dedicated to preserving it. This is one of the main problems in organ transplants: the organism protects itself against foreign matter, even if it is a new heart that would keep it alive. The protoplasm itself harbors its own, nurtures itself against the world, against invasions of its integrity. It seems to enjoy its own pulsations, expanding into the world and ingesting pieces of it. If you took a blind and dumb organism and gave it self-consciousness and a name, if you made it stand out of nature and know consciously that it was unique, then you would have narcissism. In man, physiochemical identity and the sense of power and activity have become conscious.

In man a working level of narcissism is inseparable from self-esteem, from a basic sense of self-worth. We have learned, mostly from Alfred Adler, that what man needs most is to feel secure in his self-esteem. But man is not just a blind glob of idling protoplasm, but a creature with a name who lives in a world of symbols and dreams and not merely matter. His sense of self-worth is constituted symbolically, his cherished narcissism feeds on symbols, on an abstract idea of his own worth, an idea composed of sounds, words, and images, in the air, in the mind, on paper. And this means that man's natural yearning for organismic activity, the pleasures of incorporation and expansion, can be fed limitlessly in the domain of symbols and so into immortality. The single organism can expand into dimensions of worlds and times without moving a physical limb; it can take eternity into itself even as it gaspingly dies.

In childhood we see the struggle for self-esteem at its least disguised. The child is unashamed about what he needs and wants most. His whole organism shouts the claims of his natural narcissism. And this claim can make childhood hellish for the adults concerned, especially when there are several children competing at once for the prerogatives of limitless self-extension, what we might call "cosmic significance." The term is not meant to be taken lightly, because this is where our discussion is leading. We like to speak casually about "sibling rivalry," as though it were some kind of by-product of growing up, a bit of competitiveness and selfishness of children who have been spoiled, who haven't yet grown into a generous social nature. But it is too all-absorbing and relentless to be an aberration, it expresses the heart of the creature: the desire to stand out, to be *the* one in creation. When you combine natural narcissism with the basic need for self-esteem, you create a creature who has to feel himself an object of primary value: first in the universe, representing in himself all of life. This is the reason for the daily and usually excruciating struggle with siblings: the child cannot allow himself to be second-best or devalued, much less left out. "You gave him the biggest piece of candy!" "You gave him more juice!" "Here's a little more, then." "Now *she's* got more juice than me!" "You let her light the fire in the fireplace and not me." "Okay, you light a piece of paper." "But this piece of paper is *smaller* than the one she lit." And so on and on. An animal who gets his feeling of worth symbolically has to minutely compare himself to those around him, to make sure he doesn't come off second-best. Sibling rivalry is a critical problem that reflects the basic human condition: it is not that children are vicious, selfish, or domineering. It is that they so openly express man's tragic destiny: he must desperately justify himself as an object of primary value in the universe; he must stand out, be a hero, make the biggest possible contribution to world life, show that he *counts* more than anything or anyone else.

When we appreciate how natural it is for man to strive to be a hero, how deeply it goes in his evolutionary and organismic constitution, how openly he shows it as a child, then it is all the more curious how ignorant most of us are, consciously, of what we really want and need. In our culture anyway, especially in modern times, the heroic seems too big for us, or we too small for it. Tell a young man that he is entitled to be a hero and he will blush. We disguise our struggle by piling up figures in a bank book to reflect privately our sense of heroic worth. Or by having only a little better home in the neighborhood, a bigger car, brighter children. But underneath throbs the ache of cosmic specialness, no matter how we mask it in concerns of smaller scope. Occasionally someone admits that he takes his heroism seriously, which gives most of us a chill, as did U.S. Congressman Mendel Rivers, who fed appropriations to the military machine and said he was the most powerful man since Julius Caesar. We may shudder at the crassness of earthly heroism, of both Caesar and his imitators, but the fault is not theirs, it is in the way society sets up its hero system and in the people it allows to fill its roles. The urge to heroism is natural, and to admit it honest. For everyone to admit it would probably release such pent-up force as to be devastating to societies as they now are.

The fact is that this is what society is and always has been: a symbolic action system, a structure of statuses and roles, customs and rules for behavior, designed to serve as a vehicle for earthly heroism. Each script is somewhat unique, each culture has a different hero system. What the anthropologists call "cultural relativity" is thus really the relativity of hero-systems the world over. But each cultural system is a dramatization of earthly heroics; each system cuts out roles for performances of various degrees of heroism: from the "high" heroism of a Churchill, a Mao, or a Buddha, to the "low" heroism of the coal miner, the peasant, the simple priest; the plain, everyday, earthy heroism wrought by gnarled working hands guiding a family through hunger and disease.

It doesn't matter whether the cultural hero-system is frankly magical, religious, and primitive or secular, scientific, and civilized. It is still a mythical hero-system in which people serve in order to earn a feeling of primary value, of cosmic specialness, of ultimate usefulness to creation, of unshakable meaning. They earn this feeling by carving out a place in nature, by building an edifice that reflects human value: a temple, a cathedral, a totem pole, a sky-scraper, a family that spans three generations. The hope and belief is that the things that man creates in society are of lasting worth and meaning, that they outlive or outshine death and decay, that man and his products count. When Norman O. Brown said that Western society since Newton, no matter how scientific or secular it claims to be, is still as "religious" as any other, this is what he meant: "civilized" society is a hopeful belief and protest that science, money and goods *make man count* for more than any other animal. In this sense everything that man does is religious and heroic, and yet in danger of being fictitious and fallible.

The question that becomes then the most important one that man can put to himself is simply this: how conscious is he of what he is doing to earn his feeling of heroism? I suggested that if everyone honestly admitted his urge to be a hero it would be a devastating release of truth. It would make men demand that culture give them their due—a primary sense of human value as unique contributors to cosmic life. How would our modern societies contrive to satisfy such an honest demand, without being shaken to their foundations? Only those societies we today call "primitive" provided this feeling for their members. The minority groups in present-day industrial society who shout for freedom and human dignity are really clumsily asking that they be given a sense of primary heroism of which they have been cheated historically. This is why their insistent claims are so troublesome and upsetting: how do we do such an "unreasonable" thing within the ways in which society is now set up? "They are asking for the impossible" is the way we usually put our bafflement.

But the truth about the need for heroism is not easy for anyone to admit, even the very ones who want to have their claims recognized. There's the rub. As we shall see from our subsequent discussion, to become conscious of what one is doing to earn his feeling of heroism is the main self-analytic problem of life. Everything painful and sobering in what psychoanalytic genius and religious genius have discovered about man revolves around the terror of admitting what one is doing to earn his self-esteem. This is why human heroics is a blind drivenness that burns people up; in passionate people, a screaming for glory as uncritical and reflexive as the howling of a dog. In the more passive masses of mediocre men it is disguised as they humbly and complainingly follow out the roles that society provides for their heroics and try to earn their promotions within the system: wearing the standard uniforms—but allowing themselves to stick out, but ever so little and so safely, with a little ribbon or a red boutonniere, but not with head and shoulders.

If we were to peel away this massive disguise, the blocks of repression over human techniques for earning glory, we would arrive at the potentially most liberating question of all, the main problem of human life: How *empirically true* is the cultural hero system that sustains and drives men? We mentioned the meaner side of man's urge to cosmic heroism, but there is obviously the noble side as well. Man will lay down his life for his country, his society, his family. He will choose to throw himself on a grenade to save his comrades; he is capable of the highest generosity and self-sacrifice. But he has to feel and believe that what he is doing is truly heroic, timeless, and supremely meaningful. The crisis of modern society is precisely that the youth no longer feel heroic in the plan for action that their culture has set up. They don't believe it is empirically true to the problems of their lives and times. We are living a crisis of heroism that reaches into every aspect of our social life: the dropouts of university heroism, of business and career heroism, of political-action heroism; the rise of anti-heroes, those who would be heroic each in his own way or like Charles Manson with his special "family", those whose tormented heroics lash out at the system that itself has ceased to represent agreed heroism. The great perplexity of our time, the churning of our age, is that the youth have sensed—for better or for worse—a great social-historical truth: that just as there are useless self-sacrifices in unjust wars, so too is there an ignoble heroics of whole societies: it can be the viciously destructive heroics of Hitler's Germany or the plain debasing and silly heroics of the acquisition and display of consumer goods, the piling up of money and privileges that now characterizes whole ways of life, capitalist and Soviet.

And the crisis of society is, of course, the crisis of organized religion too: religion is no longer valid as a hero system, and so the youth scorn it. If traditional culture is discredited as heroics, then the church that supports that culture automatically discredits itself. If the church, on the other hand, chooses to insist on its own special heroics, it might find that in crucial ways it must work against the culture, recruit youth to be anti-heroes to the ways of life of the society they live in. This is the dilemma of religion in our time.

Conclusion

What I have tried to do in this brief introduction is to suggest that the problem of heroics is the central one of human life, that it goes deeper into human nature than anything else because it is based on organismic narcissism and on the child's need for self-esteem as *the* condition for his life. Society itself is a codified hero system, which means that society everywhere is a living myth of the significance of human life, a defiant creation of meaning. Every society thus is a "religion" whether it thinks so or not: Soviet "religion" and Maoist "religion" are as truly religious as are scientific and consumer "religion," no matter how much they may try to disguise themselves by omitting religious and spiritual ideas from their lives. As we shall see further on, it was Otto Rank who showed psychologically this religious nature of all human cultural creation; and more recently the idea was revived by Norman O. Brown in his

Life Against Death and by Robert Jay Lifton in his *Revolutionary Immortality*. If we accept these suggestions, then we must admit that we are dealing with *the* universal human problem; and we must be prepared to probe into it as honestly as possible, to be as shocked by the self-revelation of man as the best thought will allow. Let us pick this thought up with Kierkegaard and take it through Freud, to see where this stripping down of the last 150 years will lead us. If the penetrating honesty of a few books could immediately change the world, then the five authors just mentioned would already have shaken the nations to their foundations. But since everyone is carrying on as though the vital truths about man did not yet exist, it is necessary to add still another weight in the scale of human self-exposure. For twenty-five hundred years we have hoped and believed that if mankind could reveal itself to itself, could widely come to know its own cherished motives, then somehow it would tilt the balance of things in its own favor.

PART I

THE DEPTH
PSYCHOLOGY
OF HEROISM

*I drink not from mere joy in wine nor to scoff
at faith—no, only to forget myself for a moment,
that only do I want of intoxication, that alone.*
—OMAR KHAYYAM

CHAPTER TWO

The Terror of Death

*Is it not for us to confess that in our civilized
attitude towards death we are once more living
psychologically beyond our means, and must
reform and give truth its due? Would it not be
better to give death the place in actuality and in
our thoughts which properly belongs to it, and to
yield a little more prominence to that unconscious
attitude towards death which we have hitherto
so carefully suppressed? This hardly seems indeed
a greater achievement, but rather a backward
step . . . but it has the merit of taking somewhat
more into account the true state of affairs. . . .*
—SIGMUND FREUD[1]

The first thing we have to do with heroism is to lay bare its underside, show what gives human heroics its specific nature and impetus.
Here we introduce directly one of the great rediscoveries of modern
thought: that of all things that move man, one of the principal ones
is his terror of death. After Darwin the problem of death as an
evolutionary one came to the fore, and many thinkers immediately
saw that it was a major psychological problem for man.[2] They also
very quickly saw what real heroism was about, as Shaler wrote just
at the turn of the century:[3] heroism is first and foremost a reflex of
the terror of death. We admire most the courage to face death; we
give such valor our highest and most constant adoration; it moves us

deeply in our hearts because we have doubts about how brave we ourselves would be. When we see a man bravely facing his own extinction we rehearse the greatest victory we can imagine. And so the hero has been the center of human honor and acclaim since probably the beginning of specifically human evolution. But even before that our primate ancestors deferred to others who were extrapowerful and courageous and ignored those who were cowardly. Man has elevated animal courage into a cult.

Anthropological and historical research also began, in the nineteenth century, to put together a picture of the heroic since primitive and ancient times. The hero was the man who could go into the spirit world, the world of the dead, and return alive. He had his descendants in the mystery cults of the Eastern Mediterranean, which were cults of death and resurrection. The divine hero of each of these cults was one who had come back from the dead. And as we know today from the research into ancient myths and rituals, Christianity itself was a competitor with the mystery cults and won out—among other reasons—because it, too, featured a healer with supernatural powers who had risen from the dead. The great triumph of Easter is the joyful shout "Christ has risen!", an echo of the same joy that the devotees of the mystery cults enacted at their ceremonies of the victory over death. These cults, as G. Stanley Hall so aptly put it, were an attempt to attain "an immunity bath" from the greatest evil: death and the dread of it.[4] All historical religions addressed themselves to this same problem of how to bear the end of life. Religions like Hinduism and Buddhism performed the ingenious trick of pretending not to want to be reborn, which is a sort of negative magic: claiming not to want what you really want most.[5] When philosophy took over from religion it also took over religion's central problem, and death became the real "muse of philosophy" from its beginnings in Greece right through Heidegger and modern existentialism.[6]

We already have volumes of work and thought on the subject, from religion and philosophy and—since Darwin—from science itself. The problem is how to make sense out of it; the accumulation of research and opinion on the fear of death is already too large to be dealt with and summarized in any simple way. The revival of interest in death, in the last few decades, has alone already piled up a formidable literature, and this literature does not point in any single direction.

The "Healthy-Minded" Argument

There are "healthy-minded" persons who maintain that fear of death is not a natural thing for man, that we are not born with it. An increasing number of careful studies on how the actual fear of death develops in the child[7] agree fairly well that the child has no knowledge of death until about the age of three to five. How could he? It is too abstract an idea, too removed from his experience. He lives in a world that is full of living, acting things, responding to him, amusing him, feeding him. He doesn't know what it means for life to disappear forever, nor theorize where it would go. Only gradually does he recognize that there is a thing called death that takes some people away forever; very reluctantly he comes to admit that it sooner or later takes everyone away, but this gradual realization of the inevitability of death can take up until the ninth or tenth year.

If the child has no knowledge of an abstract idea like absolute negation, he does have his own anxieties. He is absolutely dependent on the mother, experiences loneliness when she is absent, frustration when he is deprived of gratification, irritation at hunger and discomfort, and so on. If he were abandoned to himself his world would drop away, and his organism must sense this at some level; we call this the anxiety of object-loss. Isn't this anxiety, then, a natural, organismic fear of annihilation? Again, there are many who look at this as a very relative matter. They believe that if the mother has done her job in a warm and dependable way, the child's natural anxieties and guilts will develop in a moderate way, and he will be able to place them firmly under the control of his developing personality.[8] The child who has good maternal experiences will develop a sense of basic security and will not be subject to morbid fears of losing support, of being annihilated, or the like.[9] As he grows up to understand death rationally by the age of nine or ten, he will accept it as part of his world view, but the idea will not poison his self-confident attitude toward life. The psychiatrist Rhein-gold says categorically that annihilation anxiety is not part of the child's natural experience but is engendered in him by bad experiences with a depriving mother.[10] This theory puts the whole burden of anxiety onto the child's nurture and not his nature. Another psychiatrist, in a less extreme vein, sees the fear of death as greatly heightened by the child's experiences with his parents, by their hostile denial of his life impulses, and, more generally, by the antagonism of society to human freedom and self-expansiveness.[11]

As we will see later on, this view is very popular today in the widespread movement toward unrepressed living, the urge to a new freedom for natural biological urges, a new attitude of pride and joy in the body, the abandonment of shame, guilt, and self-hatred. From this point of view, fear of death is something that society creates and at the same time uses against the person to keep him in submission; the psychiatrist Moloney talked about it as a "culture mechanism," and Marcuse as an "ideology."[12] Norman O. Brown, in a vastly influential book that we shall discuss at some length, went so far as to say that there could be a birth and development of the child in a "second innocence" that would be free of the fear of death because it would not deny natural vitality and would leave the child fully open to physical living.[13]

It is easy to see that, from this point of view, those who have bad early experiences will be most morbidly fixated on the anxiety of death; and if by chance they grow up to be philosophers they will probably make the idea a central dictum of their thought—as did Schopenhauer, who both hated his mother and went on to pronounce death the "muse of philosophy." If you have a "sour" character structure or especially tragic experiences, then you are bound to be pessimistic. One psychologist remarked to me that the whole idea of the fear of death was an import by existentialists and Protestant theologians who had been scarred by their European experiences or who carried around the extra weight of a Calvinist and Lutheran heritage of life-denial. Even the distinguished psychologist Gardner Murphy seems to lean to this school and urges us to study *the person* who exhibits the fear of death, who places anxiety in the center of his thought; and Murphy asks why the living of life in love and joy cannot also be regarded as real and basic.[14]

The "Morbidly-Minded" Argument

The "healthy-minded" argument just discussed is one side of the picture of the accumulated research and opinion on the problem of the fear of death, but there is another side. A large body of people would agree with these observations on early experience and would admit that experiences may heighten natural anxieties and later fears, but these people would also claim very strongly that nevertheless the fear of death is natural and is present in everyone, that it is the basic fear that influences all others, a fear from which no one is immune, no matter how disguised it may be. William James spoke very early for this school, and with his usual colorful realism he called death "the worm at the core" of man's pretensions to happiness.[15] No less a student of human nature than Max Scheler thought that all men must have some kind of certain intuition of this "worm at the core," whether they admitted it or not.[16] Countless other authorities—some of whom we shall parade in the following pages—belong to this school: students of the stature of Freud, many of his close circle, and serious researchers who are not psychoanalysts. What are we to make of a dispute in which there are two distinct camps, both studded with distinguished authorities? Jacques Choron goes so far as to say that it is questionable whether it will ever be possible to decide whether the fear of death is or is not the basic anxiety.[17] In matters like this, then, the most that one can do is to take sides, to give an opinion based on the authorities that seem to him most compelling, and to present some of the compelling arguments.

I frankly side with this second school—in fact, this whole book is a network of arguments based on the universality of the fear of death, or "terror" as I prefer to call it, in order to convey how all-consuming it is when we look it full in the face. The first document that I want to present and linger on is a paper written by the noted psychoanalyst Gregory Zilboorg; it is an especially penetrating essay that—for succinctness and scope—has not been much improved upon, even though it appeared several decades ago.[18] Zilboorg says that most people think death fear is absent because it rarely shows its true face; but he argues that underneath all appearances fear of death is universally present:

For behind the sense of insecurity in the face of danger, behind the sense of discouragement and depression, there always lurks the basic fear of death, a fear which undergoes most complex elaborations and manifests itself in many indirect ways. . . . No one is free of the fear of death. . . . The anxiety neuroses, the various phobic states, even a considerable number of depressive suicidal states and many schizophrenias amply demonstrate the ever-present fear of death which becomes woven into the major conflicts of the given psychopathological conditions. . . . We may take for granted that the fear of death is always present in our mental functioning.[19]

Hadn't James said the same thing earlier, in his own way?

Let sanguine healthy-mindedness do its best with its strange power of living in the moment and ignoring and forgetting, still the evil background is really there to be thought of, and the skull will grin in at the banquet.[20]

The difference in these two statements is not so much in the imagery and style as in the fact that Zilboorg's comes almost a half-century later and is based on that much more real clinical work, not only on philosophical speculation or personal intuition. But it also continues the straight line of development from James and the post-Darwinians who saw the fear of death as a biological and evolutionary problem. Here I think he is on very sound ground, and I especially like the way he puts the case. Zilboorg points out that this fear is actually an expression of the instinct of self-preservation, which functions as a constant drive to maintain life and to master the dangers that threaten life:

Such constant expenditure of psychological energy on the business of preserving life would be impossible if the fear of death were not as constant. The very term "self-preservation" implies an effort against some force of disintegration; the affective aspect of this is fear, fear of death.[21]

In other words, the fear of death must be present behind all our normal functioning, in order for the organism to be armed toward self-preservation. But the fear of death cannot be present constantly in one's mental functioning, else the organism could not function. Zilboorg continues:

If this fear were as constantly conscious, we should be unable to function normally. It must be properly repressed to keep us living with any modicum of comfort. We know very well that to repress means more than to put away and to forget that which was put away and the place where we put it. It means also to maintain a constant psychological effort to keep the lid on and inwardly never relax our watchfulness.[22]

And so we can understand what seems like an impossible paradox: the ever-present fear of death in the normal biological functioning of our instinct of self-preservation, as well as our utter obliviousness to this fear in our conscious life:

Therefore in normal times we move about actually without ever believing in our own death, as if we fully believed in our own corporeal immortality. We are intent on mastering death. . . . A man will say, of course, that he knows he will die some day, but he does not really care. He is having a good time with living, and he does not think about death and does not care to bother about it—but this is a purely intellectual, verbal admission. The affect of fear is repressed.[23]

The argument from biology and evolution is basic and has to be taken seriously; I don't see how it can be left out of any discussion. Animals in order to survive have had to be protected by fear-responses, in relation not only to other animals but to nature itself. They had to see the real relationship of their limited powers to the dangerous world in which they were immersed. Reality and fear go together naturally. As the human infant is in an even more exposed and helpless situation, it is foolish to assume that the fear response of animals would have disappeared in such a weak and highly sensitive species. It is more reasonable to think that it was instead heightened, as some of the early Darwinians thought: early men who were most afraid were those who were most realistic about their situation in nature, and they passed on to their offspring a realism that had a high survival value.[24] The result was the emergence of man as we know him: a hyperanxious animal who constantly invents reasons for anxiety even where there are none.

The argument from psychoanalysis is less speculative and has to be taken even more seriously. It showed us something about the child's inner world that we had never realized: namely, that it was more filled with terror, the more the child was different from other animals. We could say that fear is programmed into the lower animals by ready-made instincts; but an animal who has no instincts has no programmed fears. Man's fears are fashioned out of the ways in which he perceives the world. Now, what is unique about the child's perception of the world? For one thing, the extreme confusion of cause-and-effect relationships; for another, extreme unreality about the limits of his own powers. The child lives in a situation of utter dependence; and when his needs are met it must seem to him that he has magical powers, real omnipotence. If he experiences pain, hunger, or discomfort, all he has to do is to scream and he is relieved and lulled by gentle, loving sounds. He is a magician and a telepath who has only to mumble and to imagine and the world turns to his desires.

But now the penalty for such perceptions. In a magical world where things cause other things to happen just by a mere thought or a look of displeasure, anything can happen to anyone. When the child experiences inevitable and real frustrations from his parents, he directs hate and destructive feelings toward them; and he has no way of knowing that malevolent feelings cannot be fulfilled by the same magic as were his other wishes. Psychoanalysts believe that this confusion is a main cause of guilt and helplessness in the child. In his very fine essay Wahl summed up this paradox:

. . . the socialization processes for all children are painful and frustrating, and hence no child escapes forming hostile death wishes toward his socializers. Therefore, none escape the fear of personal death in either direct or symbolic form. Repression is usually . . . immediate and effective. . . .[25]

The child is too weak to take responsibility for all this destructive feeling, and he can't control the magical execution of his desires. This is what we mean by an immature ego: the child doesn't have the sure ability to organize his perceptions and his relationship to the world; he can't control his own activity; and he doesn't have sure command over the acts of others. He thus has no real control over the magical cause-and-effect that he senses, either inside himself or outside in nature and in others: his destructive wishes could explode, his parents' wishes likewise. The forces of nature are confused, externally and internally; and for a weak ego this fact makes for quantities of exaggerated potential power and added terror. The result is that the child—at least some of the time—lives with an inner sense of chaos that other animals are immune to.[26]

Ironically, even when the child makes out real cause-and-effect relationships they become a burden to him because he overgeneralizes them. One such generalization is what the psychoanalysts call the "talion principle." The child crushes insects, sees the cat eat a mouse and make it vanish, joins with the family to make a pet rabbit disappear into their interiors, and so on. He comes to know something about the power relations of the world but can't give them relative value: the parents could eat him and make him vanish, and he could likewise eat them; when the father gets a fierce glow in his eyes as he clubs a rat, the watching child might also expect to be clubbed—especially if he has been thinking bad magical thoughts.

I don't want to seem to make an exact picture of processes that are still unclear to us or to make out that all children live in the same world and have the same problems; also, I wouldn't want to make the child's world seem more lurid than it really is most of the time; but I think it is important to show the painful contradictions that must be present in it at least some of the time and to show how fantastic a world it surely is for the first few years of the child's life. Perhaps then we could understand better why Zilboorg said that the fear of death "undergoes most complex elaborations and manifests itself in many indirect ways." Or, as Wahl so perfectly put it, death is a *complex symbol* and not any particular, sharply defined thing to the child:

. . . the child's concept of death is not a single thing, but it is rather a composite of mutually contradictory paradoxes . . . death itself is not only a state, but a complex symbol, the significance of which will vary from one person to another and from one culture to another.[27]

We could understand, too, why children have their recurrent nightmares, their universal phobias of insects and mean dogs. In their tortured interiors radiate complex symbols of many inadmissible realities—terror of the world, the horror of one's own wishes, the fear of vengeance by the parents, the disappearance of things, one's lack of control over anything, really. It is too much for any animal to take, but the child has to take it, and so he wakes up screaming with almost punctual regularity during the period when his weak ego is in the process of consolidating things.

The "Disappearance" of the Fear of Death

Yet, the nightmares become more and more widely spaced, and some children have more than others: we are back again to the beginning of our discussion, to those who do not believe that the fear of death is normal, who think that it is a neurotic exaggeration that draws on bad early experiences. Otherwise, they say, how explain that so many people—the vast majority—seem to survive the flurry of childhood nightmares and go on to live a healthy, more-or-less optimistic life, untroubled by death? As Montaigne said, the peasant has a profound indifference and a patience toward death and the sinister side of life; and if we say that this is because of his stupidity, then "let's all learn from stupidity."[28] Today, when we know more than Montaigne, we would say "let's all learn from repression"—but the moral would have just as much weight: repression takes care of the complex symbol of death for most people.

But its disappearance doesn't mean that the fear was never there. The argument of those who believe in the universality of the innate terror of death rests its case mostly on what we know about how effective repression is. The argument can probably never be cleanly decided: if you claim that a concept is not present because it is repressed, you can't lose; it is not a fair game, intellectually, because you always hold the trump card. This type of argument makes psychoanalysis seem unscientific to many people, the fact that its proponents can claim that someone denies one of their concepts because he represses his consciousness of its truth.

But repression is not a magical word for winning arguments; it is a real phenomenon, and we have been able to study many of its workings. This study gives it legitimacy as a scientific concept and makes it a more-or-less dependable ally in our argument. For one thing, there is a growing body of research trying to get at the consciousness of death denied by repression that uses psychological tests such as measuring galvanic skin responses; it strongly suggests that underneath the most bland exterior lurks the universal anxiety, the "worm at the core."[29]

For another thing, there is nothing like shocks in the real world to jar loose repressions. Recently psychiatrists reported an increase in anxiety neuroses in children as a result of the earth tremors in Southern California. For these children the discovery that life really includes cataclysmic danger was too much for their still-imperfect denial systems—hence open outbursts of anxiety. With adults we see this manifestation of anxiety in the face of impending catastrophe where it takes the form of panic. Recently several people suffered broken limbs and other injuries after forcing open their airplane's safety door during take-off and jumping from the wing to the ground; the incident was triggered by the backfire of an engine. Obviously underneath these harmless noises other things are rumbling in the creature.

But even more important is how repression works: it is not simply a negative force opposing life energies; it lives on life energies and uses them creatively. I mean that fears are naturally absorbed by expansive organismic striving. Nature seems to have built into organisms an innate healthy-mindedness; it expresses itself in self-delight, in the pleasure of unfolding one's capacities into the world, in the incorporation of things in that world, and in feeding on its limitless experiences. This is a lot of very positive experience, and when a powerful organism moves with it, it gives contentment. As Santayana once put it: a lion must feel more secure that God is on his side than a gazelle. On the most elemental level the organism works actively against its own fragility by seeking to expand and perpetuate itself in living experience; instead of shrinking, it moves toward more life. Also, it does one thing at a time, avoiding needless distractions from all-absorbing activity; in this way, it would seem, fear of death can be carefully ignored or actually absorbed in the life-expanding processes. Occasionally we seem to see such a vital organism on the human level: I am thinking of the portrait of *Zorba the Greek* drawn by Nikos Kazantzakis. Zorba was an ideal of the nonchalant victory of all-absorbing daily passion over timidity and death, and he purged others in his life-affirming flame. But Kazantzakis himself was no Zorba—which is partly why the character of Zorba rang a bit false—nor are most other men. Still, everyone enjoys a working amount of basic narcissism, even though it is not a lion's. The child who is well nourished and loved develops, as we said, a sense of magical omnipotence, a sense of his own indestructibility, a feeling of proven power and secure support. He can imagine himself, deep down, to be eternal. We might say that his repression of the idea of his own death is made easy for him because he is fortified against it in his very narcissistic vitality. This type of character probably helped Freud to say that the unconscious does not know death. Anyway, we know that basic narcissism is increased when one's childhood experiences have been securely life-supporting and warmly enhancing to the sense of self, to the feeling of being really special, truly Number One in creation. The result is that some people have more of what the psychoanalyst Leon J. Saul has aptly called "Inner Sustainment."[30] It is a sense of bodily confidence in the face of experience that sees the person more easily through severe life crises and even sharp personality changes; it almost seems to take the place of the directive instincts of lower animals. One can't help thinking of Freud again, who had more inner sustainment than most men, thanks to his mother and favorable early environment; he knew the confidence and courage that it gave to a man, and he himself faced up to life and to a fatal cancer with a Stoic heroism. Again we have evidence that the complex symbol of fear of death would be very variable in its intensity; it would be, as Wahl concluded, "profoundly dependent upon the nature and the vicissitudes of the developmental process."[31]

But I want to be careful not to make too much of natural vitality and inner sustainment. As we will see in Chapter Six, even the unusually favored Freud suffered his whole life from phobias and from death-anxiety; and he came to fully perceive the world under the aspect of natural terror. I don't believe that the complex symbol of death is ever absent, no matter how much vitality and inner sustainment a person has. Even more, if we say that these powers make repression easy and natural, we are only saying the half of it. Actually, they get their very power from repression. Psychiatrists argue that the fear of death varies in intensity depending on the developmental process, and I think that one important reason for this variability is that the fear is transmuted in that process. If the child has had a very favorable upbringing, it only serves all the better to hide the fear of death. After all, repression is made possible by the natural identification of the child with the powers of his parents. If he has been well cared for, identification comes easily and solidly, and his parents' powerful triumph over death automatically becomes his. What is more natural to banish one's fears than to live on delegated powers? And what does the whole growing-up period signify, if not the giving over of one's life-project? I am going to be talking about these things all the way through this book and do not want to develop them in this introductory discussion. What we will see is that man cuts out for himself a manageable world: he throws himself into action uncritically, unthinkingly. He accepts the cultural programming that turns his nose where he is supposed to look; he doesn't bite the world off in one piece as a giant would, but in small manageable pieces, as a beaver does. He uses all kinds of techniques, which we call the "character defenses": he learns not to expose himself, not to stand out; he learns to embed himself in other-power, both of concrete persons and of things and cultural commands; the result is that he comes to exist in the imagined infallibility of the world around him. He doesn't have to have fears when his feet are solidly mired and his life mapped out in a ready-made maze. All he has to do is to plunge ahead in a compulsive style of drivenness in the "ways of the world" that the child learns and in which he lives later as a kind of grim equanimity—the "strange power of living in the moment and ignoring and forgetting"—as James put it. This is the deeper reason that Montaigne's peasant isn't troubled until the very end, when the Angel of Death, who has always been sitting on his shoulder, extends his wing. Or at least until he is prematurely startled into dumb awareness, like the "Husbands" in John Cassavetes' fine film. At times like this, when the awareness dawns that has always been blotted out by frenetic, ready-made activity, we see the transmutation of repression redistilled, so to speak, and the fear of death emerges in pure essence. This is why people have psychotic breaks when repression no longer works, when the forward momentum of activity is no longer possible. Besides, the peasant mentality is far less romantic than Montaigne would have us believe. The peasant's equanimity is usually immersed in a style of life that has elements of real madness, and so it protects him: an undercurrent of constant hate and bitterness expressed in feuding, bullying, bickering and family quarrels, the petty mentality, the self-deprecation, the superstition, the obsessive control of daily life by a strict authoritarianism, and so on. As the title of a recent essay by Joseph Lopreato has it: "How would you like to be a peasant?"

We will also touch upon another large dimension in which the complex symbol of death is transmuted and transcended by man— belief in immortality, the extension of one's being into eternity. Right now we can conclude that there are many ways that repression works to calm the anxious human animal, so that he need not be anxious at all.

I think we have reconciled our two divergent positions on the fear of death. The "environmental" and the "innate" positions are both part of the same picture; they merge naturally into one another; it all depends from which angle you approach the picture: from the side of the disguises and transmutations of the fear of death or from the side of its apparent absence. I admit with a sense of scientific uneasiness that whatever angle you use, you don't get at the actual fear of death; and so I reluctantly agree with Choron that the argument can probably never be cleanly "won." Nevertheless something very important emerges: there are different images of man that he can draw and choose from.

On the one hand, we see a human animal who is partly dead to the world, who is most "dignified" when he shows a certain obliviousness to his fate, when he allows himself to be driven through life; who is most "free" when he lives in secure dependency on powers around him, when he is least in possession of himself. On the other hand, we get an image of a human animal who is overly sensitive to the world, who cannot shut it out, who is thrown back on his own meagre powers, and who seems least free to move and act, least in possession of himself, and most undignified. Whichever image we choose to identify with depends in large part upon ourselves. Let us then explore and develop these images further to see what they reveal to us.

CHAPTER THREE

The Recasting of Some Basic
Psychoanalytic Ideas

From the child of five to myself is but a step. But
from the new-born baby to the child of five is an
appalling distance.
—LEO TOLSTOI

Now that we have outlined the argument in the first two chapters, it is time to fill in the details. Why exactly is the world so terrible for the human animal? Why do people have such trouble digging up the resources to face that terror openly and bravely? To talk about these things takes us right into the heart of psychoanalytic theory and what is now the existential rebirth in psychology; it lays bare the nature of man with a clarity and comprehensiveness that are truly amazing.

Man's Existential Dilemma

We always knew that there was something peculiar about man, something deep down that characterized him and set him apart from the other animals. It was something that had to go right to his core, something that made him suffer his peculiar fate, that made it impossible to escape. For ages, when philosophers talked about the core of man they referred to it as his "essence," something fixed in his nature, deep down, some special quality or substance. But nothing like it was ever found; man's peculiarity still remained a dilemma. The reason it was never found, as Erich Fromm put it in an excellent discussion, was that there was no essence, that the essence of man is really his *paradoxical* nature, the fact that he is half animal and half symbolic.[1] As we shall see in Chapter Five it was Kierkegaard who forcefully introduced the existential paradox into modern psychology, with his brilliant analysis of the Adam and Eve myth that had conveyed that paradox to the Western mind for all time. In recent times every psychologist who has done vital work has made this paradox the main problem of his thought: Otto Rank (to whom I want to devote special chapters later on) more consistently and brilliantly than anyone else since Kierkegaard, Carl Jung, Erich Fromm, Rollo May, Ernest Schachtel, Abraham Maslow, Harold F. Searles, Norman O. Brown, Laura Perls, and others.

We might call this existential paradox the condition of *individuality within finitude.* Man has a symbolic identity that brings him sharply out of nature. He is a symbolic self, a creature with a name, a life history. He is a creator with a mind that soars out to speculate about atoms and infinity, who can place himself imaginatively at a point in space and contemplate bemusedly his own planet. This immense expansion, this dexterity, this ethereality, this self-consciousness gives to man literally the status of a small god in nature, as the Renaissance thinkers knew.

Yet, at the same time, as the Eastern sages also knew, man is a worm and food for worms. This is the paradox: he is out of nature and hopelessly in it; he is dual, up in the stars and yet housed in a heart-pumping, breath-gasping body that once belonged to a fish and still carries the gill-marks to prove it. His body is a material fleshy casing that is alien to him in many ways—the strangest and most repugnant way being that it aches and bleeds and will decay and die. Man is literally split in two: he has an awareness of his own splendid uniqueness in that he sticks out of nature with a towering majesty, and yet he goes back into the ground a few feet in order blindly and dumbly to rot and disappear forever. It is a terrifying dilemma to be in and to have to live with. The lower animals are, of course, spared this painful contradiction, as they lack a symbolic identity and the self-consciousness that goes with it. They merely act and move reflexively as they are driven by their instincts. If they pause at all, it is only a physical pause; inside they are anonymous, and even their faces have no name. They live in a world without time, pulsating, as it were, in a state of dumb being. This is what has made it so simple to shoot down whole herds of buffalo or elephants. The animals don't know that death is happening and continue grazing placidly while others drop alongside them. The knowledge of death is reflective and conceptual, and animals are spared it. They live and they disappear with the same thoughtlessness: a few minutes of fear, a few seconds of anguish, and it is over. But to live a whole lifetime with the fate of death haunting one's dreams and even the most sun-filled days—that's something else.

It is only if you let the full weight of this paradox sink down on your mind and feelings that you can realize what an impossible situation it is for an animal to be in. I believe that those who speculate that a full apprehension of man's condition would drive him insane are right, quite literally right. Babies are occasionally born with gills and tails, but this is not publicized—instead it is hushed up. Who wants to face up fully to the creatures we are, clawing and gasping for breath in a universe beyond our ken? I think such events illustrate the meaning of Pascal's chilling reflection: "Men are so necessarily mad that not to be mad would amount to another form of madness." *Necessarily* because the existential dualism makes an impossible situation, an excruciating dilemma. *Mad* because, as we shall see, everything that man does in his symbolic world is an attempt to deny and overcome his grotesque fate. He literally drives himself into a blind obliviousness with social games, psychological tricks, personal preoccupations so far removed from the reality of his situation that they are forms of madness—agreed madness, shared madness, disguised and dignified madness, but madness all the same. "Character-traits," said Sandor Ferenczi, one of the most brilliant minds of Freud's intimate circle of early psychoanalysts, "are secret psychoses." This is not a smug witticism offered in passing by a young science drunk with its own explanatory power and success; it is a mature scientific judgment of the most devastating self-revelatory kind ever fashioned by man trying to understand himself. Ferenczi had already seen behind the tight-lipped masks, the smiling masks, the earnest masks, the satisfied masks that people use to bluff the world and themselves about their secret psychoses. More recently Erich Fromm[2] wondered why most people did not become insane in the face of the existential contradiction between a symbolic self, that seems to give man infinite worth in a timeless scheme of things, and a body that is worth about 98¢. How to reconcile the two?

In order to understand the weight of the dualism of the human condition, we have to know that the child can't really handle either end of it. The most characteristic thing about him is that he is precocious or premature; his world piles up on him and he piles up on himself. He has right from the beginning an exquisite sensory system that rapidly develops to take in all the sensations of his world with an extreme finesse. Add to it the quick development of language and the sense of self and pile it all upon a helpless infant body trying vainly to grab the world correctly and safely. The result is ludicrous. The child is overwhelmed by experiences of the dualism of the self and the body from both areas, since he can be master of neither. He is not a confident social self, adept manipulator of symbolic categories of words, thoughts, names, or places,— or especially of time, that great mystery for him; he doesn't even know what a clock is. Nor is he a functioning adult animal who can work and procreate, do the serious things he sees happening around him: he can't "do like father" in any way. He is a prodigy in limbo. In both halves of his experience he is dispossessed, yet impressions keep pouring in on him and sensations keep welling up within him, flooding his body. He has to make some kind of sense out of them, establish some kind of ascendancy over them. Will it be thoughts over body, or body over thoughts? Not so easy. There can be no clearcut victory or straightforward solution of the existential dilemma he is in. It is his problem almost right from the beginning of his life, yet he is only a child to handle it. Children feel hounded by symbols they don't understand the need of, verbal demands that seem picayune, and rules and codes that call them away from their pleasure in the straightforward expression of their natural energies. And when they try to master the body, pretend it isn't there, act "like a little man," the body suddenly overwhelms them, submerges them in vomit or excrement—and the child breaks down in desperate tears over his melted pretense at being a purely symbolic animal. Often the child deliberately soils himself or continues to wet the bed, to protest against the imposition of artificial symbolic rules: he seems to be saying that the body is his primary reality and that he wants to remain in the simpler physical Eden and not be thrown out into the world of "right and wrong."

In this way we realize directly and poignantly that what we call the child's character is a *modus vivendi* achieved after the most unequal struggle any animal has to go through; a struggle that the child can never really understand because he doesn't know what is happening to him, why he is responding as he does, or what is really at stake in the battle. The victory in this kind of battle is truly Pyrrhic: character is a face that one sets to the world, but it hides an inner defeat. The child emerges with a name, a family, a play-world in a neighborhood, all clearly cut out for him. But his insides are full of nightmarish memories of impossible battles, terrifying anxieties of blood, pain, aloneness, darkness; mixed with limitless desires, sensations of unspeakable beauty, majesty, awe, mystery; and fantasies and hallucinations of mixtures between the two, the impossible attempt to compromise between bodies and symbols. We shall see in a few pages how sexuality enters in with its very definite focus, to further confuse and complicate the child's world. To grow up at all is to conceal the mass of internal scar tissue that throbs in our dreams.

So we see that the two dimensions of human existence—the body and the self—can never be reconciled seamlessly, which explains the second half of Pascal's reflection: "not to be mad would amount to another form of madness." Here Pascal proves that great students of human nature could see behind the masks of men long before scientific psychoanalysis. They lacked clinical documentation but they saw that the coolest repression, the most convincing equanimity, or the warmest self-satisfaction were accomplished lies both toward the world and to oneself. With the clinical documentation of psychoanalytic thought, we got a fairly comprehensive picture of human character styles—what we can now call "styles of madness" after Pascal. We might say that psychoanalysis revealed to us the complex penalties of denying the truth of man's condition, what we might call *the costs of pretending not to be mad.* If we had to offer the briefest explanation of all the evil that men have wreaked upon themselves and upon their world since the beginnings of time right up until tomorrow, it would be not in terms of man's animal heredity, his instincts and his evolution: it would be simply in *the toll that his pretense of sanity takes,* as he tries to deny his true condition. But more of this vital idea later.

The Meaning of Anality

A sensitive thinker in the age of Freud has had to live a tortured intellectual life—at least this is an autobiographical reflection. There seems to be so much truth in the Freudian world view, and at the same time so much of it seems so wrong-headed. The ambiguities of Freud's legacy were not in the wrong ideas that he had, since it has been relatively easy to lay these aside; the problem has been in his brilliantly true insights, which were stated in a way that they fell just to one side of reality; and we needed an immense amount of work and clarification in order to bring the two into line. Actually what was needed was a framework into which to fit the corpus of psychoanalytic insight, so that the truth of it could emerge clearly and unambiguously, free of the nineteenth-century reductionism, instinctivism, and biologism that Freud fettered it with. This framework is the existential one; reinterpretations of Freud within an existential context give his insights their full scientific stature. This goal was recently achieved brilliantly by Norman O. Brown[3] in his reinterpretation of the idea of "anality" and its central role in psychoanalytic theory; probably the main value of that book historically is that it has reclaimed the most esoteric and inverted of the Freudian ideas and has made them the property of the human sciences.

I am tempted to quote lavishly from the analytic riches of Brown's book, but there is no point in repeating what he has already written. Let us just observe that the basic key to the problem of anality is that it reflects the dualism of man's condition—his self and his body. Anality and its problems arise in childhood because it is then that the child already makes the alarming discovery that his body is strange and fallible and has a definite ascendancy over him by its demands and needs. Try as he may to take the greatest flights of fancy, he must always come back to it. Strangest and most degrading of all is the discovery that the body has, located in the lower rear and out of sight, a hole from which stinking smells emerge and even more, a stinking substance—most disagreeable to everyone else and eventually even to the child himself.

At first the child is amused by his anus and feces, and gaily inserts his finger into the orifice, smelling it, smearing feces on the walls, playing games of touching objects with his anus, and the like. This is a universal form of play that does the serious work of all play: it reflects the discovery and exercise of natural bodily functions; it masters an area of strangeness; it establishes power and control over the deterministic laws of the natural world; and it does all this with symbols and fancy.* With anal play the child is already becoming a philosopher of the human condition. But like all philosophers he is still bound by it, and his main task in life becomes the denial of what the anus represents: that in fact, he is nothing *but* body so far as nature is concerned. Nature's values are bodily values, human values are mental values, and though they take the loftiest flights they are built upon excrement, impossible without it, always brought back to it. As Montaigne put it, on the highest throne in the world man sits on his arse. Usually this epigram makes people laugh because it seems to reclaim the world from artificial pride and snobbery and to bring things back to egalitarian values. But if we push the observation even further and say men sit not only on their arse, but over a warm and fuming pile of their own excrement—the joke is no longer funny. The tragedy of man's dualism, his ludicrous situation, becomes too real. The anus and its incomprehensible, repulsive product represents not only physical determinism and boundness, but the fate as well of all that is physical: decay and death.

We now understand that what psychoanalysts have called "anality" or anal character traits are really forms of the universal

---

* As anal play is an essential exercise in human mastery, it is better not interfered with. If the adult anxiously cuts it short, then he charges the animal function with an extra dose of anxiety. It becomes more threatening and has to be extra-denied and extra-avoided as an alien part of oneself. This extra-grim denial is what we mean by the "anal character." An "anal" upbringing, then, would be an affirmation, via intense repression, of the horror of the degrading animal body as the human burden *sans pareil.*

protest against accident and death. Seen in this way a large part of the most esoteric psychoanalytic corpus of insights achieves a new vitality and meaningfulness. To say that someone is "anal" means that someone is trying extra-hard to protect himself against the accidents of life and danger of death, trying to use the symbols of culture as a sure means of triumph over natural mystery, trying to pass himself off as anything but an animal. When we comb the anthropological literature we find that men everywhere have been anal in some basic levels of their cultural strivings; and we find that primitives have often shown the most unashamed anality of all. They have been more innocent about what their real problem is, and they have not well disguised their disguise, so to speak, over the fallibilities of the human condition. We read that men of the Chagga tribe wear an anal plug all their lives, pretending to have sealed up the anus and not to need to defecate. An obvious triumph over mere physicalness. Or take the widespread practice of segregating women in special huts during menstruation and all the various taboos surrounding menstruation: it is obvious that man seeks to control the mysterious processes of nature as they manifest themselves within his own body. The body cannot be allowed to have the ascendancy over him.[4]

Anality explains why men yearn for freedom from contradictions and ambiguities, why they like their symbols pure, their Truth with a capital "T." On the other hand, when men really want to protest against artificialities, when they rebel against the symbolisms of culture, they fall back on the physical. They call thoughts down to earth, mannerisms back to basic chemistry. A perfect example of this was in the recent "anal" film *Brewster McCloud*, where speeches, official badges, and shiny manufactured surfaces were pummeled from the sky with obliterating excrement. The message was one that the modern filmmakers are making with great daring: calling the world back from hypocrisy by stressing basic things about life and the body. Stanley Kubrick jarred audiences when he showed in *2001* how man stepped out into space like an ape dancing to schmaltzy Strauss waltz music; and again in *A Clockwork Orange* he showed how naturally and satisfyingly a man can murder and rape in tune with the heroic transcendence of Beethoven's Ninth.

The upsetting thing about anality is that it reveals that all culture, all man's creative life-ways, are in some basic part of them a fabricated protest against natural reality, a denial of the truth of the human condition, and an attempt to forget the pathetic creature that man is. One of the most stunning parts of Brown's study was his presentation of anality in Jonathan Swift. The ultimate horror for Swift was the fact that the sublime, the beautiful, and the divine are inextricable from basic animal functions. In the head of the adoring male is the illusion that sublime beauty "is all head and wings, with no bottom to betray" it.[5] In one of Swift's poems a young man explains the grotesque contradiction that is tearing him apart:[6]

Nor wonder how I lost my Wits;
Oh! Caelia, Caelia, Caelia shits!

In other words, in Swift's mind there was an absolute contradiction "between the state of being in love and an awareness of the excremental function of the beloved."[7]

Erwin Straus, in his brilliant monograph on obsession,[8] similarly earlier showed how repulsed Swift was by the animality of the body, by its dirt and decay. Straus pronounced a more clinical judgment on Swift's disgust, seeing it as part of the typical obsessive's worldview: "For all obsessives sex is severed from unification and procreation. . . . Through the . . . isolation of the genitals from the whole of the body, sexual functions are experienced as excretions and as decay."[9] This degree of fragmentation is extreme, but we all see the world through obsessive eyes at least part of the time and to some degree; and as Freud said, not only neurotics take exception to the fact that "we are born between urine and faeces."[10] In this horror of the incongruity of man Swift the poet gives more tormented voice to the dilemma that haunts us all, and it is worth summing it up one final time: Excreting is the curse that threatens madness because it shows man his abject finitude, his physicalness, the likely unreality of his hopes and dreams. But even more immediately, it represents man's utter bafflement at the sheer *non-sense* of creation: to fashion the sublime miracle of the human face, the *mysterium tremendum* of radiant feminine beauty, the veritable goddesses that beautiful women are; to bring this out of nothing, out of the void, and make it shine in noonday; to take such a miracle and put miracles again within it, deep in the mystery of eyes that peer out—the eye that gave even the dry Darwin a chill: to do all this, and to combine it with an anus that shits! It is too much. Nature mocks us, and poets live in torture.

I have tried to recapture just a bit of the shock of a scientific and poetic discussion of the problem of anality, and if I have succeeded in such an offhand way, we can understand what the existential paradox means: that what bothers people is really incongruity, life as it *is*. This view leads to a whole re-examination of Freudian theory, not only of the problem of anality, but also of Freud's central idea, the Oedipus complex. Let us now linger on this, again using Brown's brilliant reformulation.

The Oedipal Project

Freud often tended to understand human motives in what can be called a "primitive" way. Sometimes so much so that when disciples like Rank and Ferenzci pulled away from him they accused him of simple-mindedness. The accusation is, of course, ludicrous, but there is something to it—probably what they were driving at: the doggedness with which Freud stuck to his stark sexual formulas. No matter how much he changed later in life, he always kept alive the letter of psychoanalytic dogma and fought against a watering-down of the motives he thought he uncovered. We will understand better why in a later chapter.

Take the Oedipus complex. In his early work Freud had said that this complex was the central dynamic in the psychic life. In his view, the boy child had innate drives of sexuality and he even wanted to possess his mother. At the same time, he knew that his father was his competitor, and he held in check a murderous aggressiveness toward him. The reason he held it in check was that he knew the father was physically stronger than he and that the result of an open fight would be the father's victory and the castration of the son. Hence the horror of blood, of mutilation, of the female genitals that seemed to have been mutilated; they testified that castration was a fact.

Freud modified his views all through his life, but he never got a full distance away from them. No wonder: they kept being "confirmed" in some intimate way by the people he studied. There was indeed something about the anus and the genitals, the physicalness of the family, and its copulations that weighed on the psyche of neurotics like an age-old stone. Freud thought that such a heavy weight must date from time immemorial, from the first emergence of humans out of primate ancestors. He thought that the guilt we each feel deep down is connected with a primal crime of patricide and incest committed in the dim recesses of prehistory; so deep is guilt ingrained, so much is it confused with the body, with sex and excrement, and with the parents. Freud never abandoned his views because they were correct in their elemental suggestiveness about the human condition—but not quite in the sense that he thought, or rather, not in the framework which he offered. Today we realize that all the talk about blood and excrement, sex and guilt, is true not because of urges to patricide and incest and fears of actual physical castration, but because all these things reflect man's horror of his own basic animal condition, a condition that he cannot— especially as a child—understand and a condition that—as an adult —he cannot accept. The guilt that he feels over bodily processes and urges is "pure" guilt: guilt as inhibition, as determinism, as smallness and boundness. It grows out of the constraint of *the basic animal condition,* the incomprehensible mystery of the body and the world.

Psychoanalysts have been preoccupied since the turn of the century with the experiences of childhood; but, strangely enough, it is only since "just yesterday" that we are able to put together a fairly complete and plausible commonsensical picture of why childhood is such a crucial period for man. We owe this picture to many people, including especially the neglected Rank, but it is Norman O. Brown who has summed it up more pointedly and definitively than anyone else, I think. As he argued in his own reorientation of Freud, the Oedipus complex is not the narrowly sexual problem of lust and competitiveness that Freud made out in his early work. Rather, the Oedipus complex is the Oedipal *project,* a project that sums up the basic problem of the child's life: whether he will be a passive object of fate, an appendage of others, a plaything of the world or whether he will be an active center within himself—whether he will control his own destiny with his own powers or not. As Brown put it:

The Oedipal project is not, as Freud's earlier formulations suggest, a natural love of the mother, but as his later writings recognize, a product of the conflict of ambivalence and an attempt to overcome that conflict by narcissistic inflation. The essence of the Oedipal complex is the project of becoming God—in Spinoza's formula, *causa sui*. . . . By the same token, it plainly exhibits infantile narcissism perverted by the flight from death. . . .

If the child's major task is a flight from helplessness and obliteration, then sexual matters are secondary and derivative, as Brown says:

Thus again it appears that the sexual organizations, pregenital and genital, do not correspond to the natural distribution of Eros in the human body: they represent a hypercathexis, a supercharge, of particular bodily functions and zones, a hypercathexis induced by the fantasies of human narcissism in flight from death.[11]

Let us take these technical gems and spread them out a bit. The Oedipal project is the flight from passivity, from obliteration, from contingency: the child wants to conquer death by becoming the *father of himself*, the creator and sustainer of his own life. We saw in Chapter Two that the child has an idea of death by the age of three, but long before that he is already at work to fortify himself against vulnerability. This process begins naturally in the very earliest stages of the infant's life—in what is called the "oral" stage. This is the stage before the child is fully differentiated from his mother in his own consciousness, before he is fully cognizant of his own body and its functions—or, as we say technically, before his body has become an object in his phenomenological field. The mother, at this time, represents literally the child's life-world. During this period her efforts are directed to the gratification of the child's wishes, to automatic relief of his tensions and pains. The child, then, at this time, is simply "full of himself," an unflinchable manipulator and champion of his world. He lives suffused in his own omnipotence and magically controls everything he needs to feed that omnipotence. He has only to cry to get food and warmth, to point to demand the moon and get a delightful rattle in its place. No wonder we understand this period as characterized by "primary narcissism": the child triumphantly controls his world by controlling the mother. His body is his narcissistic project, and he uses it to try to "swallow the world." The "anal stage" is another way of talking about the period when the child begins to turn his attention to his own body as an object in his phenomenal field. He discovers it and seeks to control it. His narcissistic project then becomes the mastery and the possession of the world through self-control.

At each stage in the unfolding discovery of his world and the problems that it poses, the child is intent on shaping that world to his own aggrandizement. He has to keep the feeling that he has absolute power and control, and in order to do that he has to cultivate independence of some kind, the conviction that he is shaping his own life. That is why Brown, like Rank, could say that the Oedipal project is "inevitably self-generated in the child and is directed against the parents, irrespective of how the parents behave." To put it paradoxically, "children toilet train themselves."[12] The profound meaning of this is that there is no "perfect" way to bring up a child, since he "brings himself up" by trying to shape himself into an absolute controller of his own destiny. As this aim is impossible, each character is, deeply and in some way, fantastically unreal, fundamentally imperfect. As Ferenczi so well summed it up: "Character is from the point of view of the psychoanalyst a sort of abnormality, a kind of mechanization of a particular way of reaction, rather similar to an obsessional symptom."[13]

The Castration Complex

In other words, the narcissistic project of self-creation, using the body as the primary base of operations, is doomed to failure. And the child finds it out: *this* is how we understand the power and meaning of what is called the "castration complex," as Freud came to develop it in his later writings and as Rank[14] and Brown have detailed it. In the newer understanding of the castration complex it is not the father's threats that the child reacts to. As Brown so well says, the castration complex comes into being solely in confrontation with the mother. This phenomenon is very crucial, and we must linger a bit on how it happens.

It all centers on the fact that the mother monopolizes the child's world; at first, she *is* his world. The child cannot survive without her, yet in order to get control of his own powers he has to get free of her. The mother thus represents two things to the child, and it helps us understand why the psychoanalysts have said that ambivalence characterizes the whole early growth period. On the one hand the mother is a pure source of pleasure and satisfaction, a secure power to lean on. She must appear as the goddess of beauty and goodness, victory and power; this is her "light" side, we might say, and it is blindly attractive. But on the other hand the child has to strain against this very dependency, or he loses the feeling that he has aegis over his own powers. That is another way of saying that the mother, by representing secure biological dependence, is also a fundamental threat.

The child comes to perceive her as a threat, which is already the beginning of the castration complex in confrontation with her. The child observes that the mother's body is different from the male's—strikingly different. And this difference gradually comes to make him very uncomfortable. Freud never tried to ease the shock of the revelations of his theory, and he called this discomfort "horror at the mutilated creature," the "castrated mother," the sight of genitals "devoid of a penis." Freud's shock effect seemed to many people to partake of caricature. The horror in the child's perceptions seemed too contrived, too pat, too much designed to fit into Freud's own addiction to sexual explanations and biological reductionism. Others, too, saw Freud's way of thinking as a reflection of his own ingrained patriarchy, his strong sense of masculine superiority, which made the woman seem naturally inferior if she lacked male appendages.

The fact is that the "horror at the mutilated creature" is contrived, but it is the child who contrives it. Psychoanalysts reported faithfully what their neurotic patients told them, even if they had to pry just the right words into their expressions. What troubles neurotics —as it troubles most people—is their own powerlessness; they must find something to set themselves against. If the mother represents biological dependence, then the dependence can be fought against by focussing it on the fact of *sexual differentiation*. If the child is to be truly *causa sui*, then he must aggressively defy the parents in some way, move beyond them and the threats and temptations they embody. The genitals are a small thing in the child's perceptual world; hardly enough to be traumatic just because they lack protuberance. As Brown so well put it, the horror is the child's "own invention; it is a tissue of fantasy inseparable from his own fantastic project of becoming father of himself (and, as fantasy, only remotely connected with actual sight of the female genitalia)."[15] Or, put another way, we can say that the child "fetishizes" the mother's body as an object of global danger to himself. It is one way of cutting her down to size, depriving her of her primary place in creation. Using Erwin Straus' formula, we would say that the child splits the mother's genitals off from her totality as a love-object; they then come to be experienced as a threat, as decay.

Penis-Envy

The real threat of the mother comes to be connected with her *sheer physicalness*. Her genitals are used as a convenient focus for the child's obsession with the problem of physicalness. If the mother is a goddess of light, she is also a witch of the dark. He sees her tie to the earth, her secret bodily processes that bind her to nature: the breast with its mysterious sticky milk, the menstrual odors and blood, the almost continual immersion of the productive mother in her corporeality, and not least—something the child is very sensitive to—the often neurotic and helpless character of this immersion. After the child gets hints about the mother's having babies, sees them being nursed, gets a good look at the toiletful of menstrual blood that seems to leave the witch quite intact and unconcerned, there is no question about her immersion in stark body-meanings and body-fallibilities. The mother must exude determinism, and the child expresses his horror at his complete dependency on what is physically vulnerable. And so we understand not only the boy's preferance for masculinity but also the girl's "penis-envy." Both boys and girls succumb to the desire to flee the sex represented by the mother;[16] they need little coaxing to identify with the father and his world. He seems more neutral physically, more cleanly powerful, less immersed in body determinisms; he seems more "symbolically free," represents the vast world outside of the home, the social world with its organized triumph over nature, the very escape from contingency that the child seeks.†

Both the boy and girl turn away from the mother as a sort of automatic reflex of their own needs for growth and independence. But the "horror, terror, contempt"[17] they feel is, as we said, part of their own fantastic perceptions of a situation they can't stand. This situation is not only the biological dependency and physicalness represented by the mother, but also the terrible revelation of the problem of the child's own body. The mother's body not only

---

† Penis-envy, then, arises from the fact that the mother's genitals have been split off from her body as a focalization of the problem of decay and vulnerability. Bernard Brodsky remarks about his female patient: "Her concept of woman as fecal greatly stimulated her penis envy, since the lively erectile penis was the antonym of the dead, inert stool." (B. Brodsky, "The Self-Representation, Anality, and the Fear of Dying," *Journal of the American Psychoanalytic Association*, 1959, Volume 7, p. 102.) Phyllis Greenacre—outstanding student of the child's experiences—had already remarked on this same equation in the child's perception: penis = movement, therefore life; feces = inertia, therefore death. (P. Greenacre, *Trauma, Growth and Personality*, New York: Norton, 1952, p. 264.) This makes penis-envy very natural. Greenacre even used the apt idea of "penis-awe" to refer to the spell that the large male appendage can cast in the child's perceptions of the father. The child, after all, lives in a world of body-power predominantly—he doesn't understand abstract or symbolic power. So, more body equals more life. A grown woman might well experience a lingering of the same feeling. An indentation and lack of protuberance, with all that goes on inside, is different from an aggressive extension that must give less of a feeling of vulnerability.

Brodsky's patient, as we might expect, was in trouble because both dimensions of her ambivalence toward her mother were heightened, the patient's need of her mother and the mother's threat to the patient: "The mother's overprotection and hindrance of the patient's gaining motor skills contributed to the faulty development of the self-image. She had both intense separation anxiety and marked castration anxiety." In other words, her dependency was intensified, and at the same time it intensified her castration anxiety, as she could not break away from an object that represented decay. This is an almost sure formula for clinical neurosis.

reveals a sex that threatens vulnerability and dependency—it reveals much more: it presents the problem of two sexes and so confronts the child with the fact that his body is itself arbitrary. It is not so much that the child sees that neither sex is "complete" in itself or that he understands that the particularity of each sex is a limitation of potential, a cheating of living fulness in some ways— he can't know these things or fully feel them. It is again not a sexual problem; it is more global, experienced as the curse of arbitrariness that the body represents. The child comes upon a world in which he could just as well have been born male or female, even dog, cat, or fish—for all that it seems to matter as regards power and control, capacity to withstand pain, annihilation, and death. The horror of sexual differentiation is a horror of "biological fact," as Brown so well says.[18] It is a fall out of illusion into sobering reality. It is a horror of assuming an immense new burden, the burden of the meaning of life and the body, of the fatality of one's incompleteness, his helplessness, his finitude.

And this, finally, is the hopeless terror of the castration complex that makes men tremble in their nightmares. It expresses the realization by the child that he is saddled with an impossible project; that the *causa-sui* pursuit on which he is launched *cannot be achieved by body-sexual means*,[19] even by protesting a body different from the mother. The fortress of the body, the primary base for narcissistic operations against the world in order to insure one's boundless powers, crumbles like sand. This is the tragic dethroning of the child, the ejection from paradise that the castration complex represents. Once he used any bodily zone or appendage for his Oedipal project of self-generation; now, the very genitals themselves mock his self-sufficiency.

This brings up the whole matter of why sexuality is such a universal problem. No one has written about the problem of sexuality better than Rank in his stunning essay on "Sexual Enlightenment."[20] As I am going to talk about it in some detail in Chapter Eight, there is no point in repeating that discussion here. But we can anticipate it by showing how sexuality is inseparable from our existential paradox, the dualism of human nature. The person is both a self and a body, and from the beginning there is the confusion about where "he" really "is"—in the symbolic inner self or in the physical body. Each phenomenological realm is different. The inner self represents the freedom of thought, imagination, and the infinite reach of symbolism. The body represents determinism and boundness. The child gradually learns that his freedom as a unique being is dragged back by the body and its appendages which dicate "what" he is. For this reason sexuality is as much a problem for the adult as for the child: the physical solution to the problem of who we are and why we have emerged on this planet is no help—in fact, it is a terrible threat. It doesn't tell the person what he is deep down inside, what kind of distinctive gift he is to work upon the world. This is why it is so difficult to have sex without guilt: guilt is there because the body casts a shadow on the person's inner freedom, his "real self" that—through the act of sex—is being forced into a standardized, mechanical, biological role. Even worse, the inner self is not even being called into consideration at all; the body takes over completely for the total person, and this kind of guilt makes the inner self shrink and threaten to disappear.

This is why a woman asks for assurance that the man wants "me" and not "only my body"; she is painfully conscious that her own distinctive inner personality can be dispensed with in the sexual act. If it is dispensed with, it doesn't count. The fact is that the man usually does want only the body, and the woman's total personality is reduced to a mere animal role. The existential paradox vanishes, and one has no distinctive humanity to protest. One creative way of coping with this is, of course, to allow it to happen and to go with it: what the psychoanalysts call "regression in the service of the ego." The person becomes, for a time, merely his physical self and so absolves the painfulness of the existential paradox and the guilt that goes with sex. Love is one great key to this kind of sexuality because it allows the collapse of the individual into the animal dimension without fear and guilt, but instead with trust and assurance that his distinctive inner freedom will not be negated by an animal surrender.

The Primal Scene

This is the right place to discuss another psychoanalytic idea that always seemed to many to bypass credulity, the so-called "trauma of the primal scene." The orthodox psychoanalytic notion was that when the child witnessed sexual intercourse between the parents (the primal scene) it left him with a deep-seated trauma because he could not take part in it. Freud talked about the actual "stimulation of sexual excitement upon observation of parental coitus."[21] Put so bluntly the idea seems incredible enough, but we must remember that Freud prided himself above all on the discovery of *infantile* sexuality. In the minds of other psychoanalysts the idea is given a slightly different emphasis. Thus, as Roheim put it, the primal scene represents the child's wish for reunion with the mother fulfilled; but he sees his father in his place, and instead of a complete identification with the succoring mother he sees the "violent motion" of a struggle.[22] Finally, Ferenczi—who was a keen student of the effects of the parents on the child—gives the matter another slightly different twist from Freud's stark formulation:

If intimate parental intercourse is observed by the child in the first or second year of life, when its capacity for excitement is already there but it lacks as yet adequate outlets for its emotion, an infantile neurosis may result.[23]

Roheim and Ferenczi, then, are actually talking about quite different things from Freud's subject. Roheim is talking about identification with the mother, who represents the total support of the child, and the child's inability to understand the relation of his loved object with other objects like the father. Ferenczi is saying that the child is overwhelmed by emotions that he cannot yet organize. This is precisely where a more existential interpretation of the problem comes in. The child uses his body as his *causa-sui* project; he only definitely abandons this project when he learns the impossibility of it. Each of these alternatives is a life-and-death matter for him; and so, if we are going to talk about trauma, it must be because of a confusion of life-and-death matters. Even when we are grown, most of us experience some distaste and disillusionment at the idea of our parents having intercourse; it doesn't seem the "right" thing for them to do. I think the exact reason for our distaste is that their image is confounded in our eyes. The thing that the parents represent most of all is the discouragement of the body as a *causa-sui* project; they represent the castration complex, disillusionment with the body, and the fear of it. Even

more, they themselves are the living embodiment of the cultural
world view that the child has to internalize in order for him to get
out of his impasse with his body. When *they themselves* do not
transcend the body in their most intimate relations, the child must
experience some anxious confusion. How is his struggling ego to
handle these double messages and make sense out of them? Furthermore, one of these messages is given in concrete physical grunts,
groans, and movement that must be overwhelming, especially as it
is precisely the horror of the body that the child is trying to overcome. If he tries to fall back on the body role and imitate his
parents, they become anxious or furious. He can well feel betrayed
by them: they reserve their bodies for the closest relationship but
deny it to him. They discourage physicalness with all the powers
at their command, and yet they themselves practice it with an all-
absorbing vengeance. When we take all this together we can see
that the primal scene can truly be a trauma, not because the child
can't get into the sexual act and express his own impulses but rather
because the primal scene is itself a complex symbol combining the
horror of the body, the betrayal of the cultural superego, and the
absolute blockage of any action that the child can take in the situation or any straightforward understanding that he can have of it. It
is the symbol of an anxious multiple bind.

The body, then, is one's animal fate that has to be struggled
against in some ways. At the same time, it offers experiences and
sensations, concrete pleasure that the inner symbolic world lacks.
No wonder man is impaled on the horns of sexual problems, why
Freud saw that sex was so prominent in human life—especially in
the neurotic conflicts of his patients. Sex is an inevitable component
of man's confusion over the meaning of his life, a meaning split
hopelessly into two realms—symbols (freedom) and body (fate).
No wonder, too, that most of us never abandon entirely the early
attempts of the child to use the body and its appendages as a
fortress or a machine to magically coerce the world. We try to get
metaphysical answers out of the body that the body—as a material
thing—cannot possibly give. We try to answer the transcendent
mystery of creation by experiences in one, partial, physical product
of that creation. This is why the mystique of sex is so widely practiced—say, in traditional France—and at the same time is so dis-

illusioning. It is comfortingly infantile in its indulgence and its pleasure, yet so self-defeating of real awareness and growth, if the person is using it to try to answer metaphysical questions. It then becomes a lie about reality, a screen against full consciousness.[24] If the adult reduces the problem of life to the area of sexuality, he repeats the fetishization of the child who focusses the problem of the mother upon her genitals. Sex then becomes a screen for terror, a fetishization of full consciousness about the real problem of life.

But this discussion doesn't exhaust the reasons that sex is so prominent a part of the confusions of life. Sex is also a positive way of working on one's personal freedom project. After all, it is one of the few areas of real privacy that a person has in an existence that is almost wholly social, entirely shaped by the parents and society. In this sense, sex as a project represents a retreat from the standardizations and monopolizations of the social world. No wonder people dedicate themselves so all-consumingly to it, often from childhood on in the form of secret masturbations that represent a protest and a triumph of the personal self. As we will see in Part II of this book, Rank goes so far as to say that this use of sex explains all sexual conflicts in the individual—"from masturbation to the most varied perversions."[25] The person attempts to use his sex in an entirely individual way in order to *control* it and relieve it of its determinism. It is as though one tried to transcend the body by depriving it entirely of its given character, to make sport and new invention in place of what nature "intended." The "perversions" of children certainly show this very clearly: they are the true artists of the body, using it as clay to assert their symbolic mastery. Freud saw this and recorded it as "polymorphous perversity"—which is one way of talking about it. But he seems not to have realized that this kind of play is already a very serious attempt to transcend determinism, not merely an animal search for a variety of body-zone pleasures.

By the time the child grows up, the inverted search for a personal existence through perversity gets set in an individual mold, and it becomes more secret. It has to be secret because the community won't stand for the attempt by people to wholly individualize themselves.[26] If there is going to be a victory over human incompleteness and limitation, it has to be a social project and not an individual one. Society wants to be the one to decide how people are to transcend death; it will tolerate the *causa-sui* project only if it fits into the standard social project. Otherwise there is the alarm of "Anarchy!" This is one of the reasons for bigotry and censorship of all kinds over personal morality: people fear that the standard morality will be undermined—another way of saying that they fear they will no longer be able to control life and death. A person is said to be "socialized" precisely when he accepts to "sublimate" the body-sexual character of his Oedipal project.[27] Now these euphemisms mean usually that he accepts to work on becoming the father of himself by abandoning his own project and by giving it over to "The Fathers." The castration complex has done its work, and one submits to "social reality"; he can now deflate his own desires and claims and can play it safe in the world of the powerful elders. He can even give his body over to the tribe, the state, the embracing magical umbrella of the elders and their symbols; that way it will no longer be a dangerous negation for him. But there is no real difference between a childish impossibility and an adult one; the only thing that the person achieves is a practiced self-deceit—what we call the "mature" character.

CHAPTER FOUR

Human Character as a Vital Lie

*Take stock of those around you and you will . . .
hear them talk in precise terms about themselves
and their surroundings, which would seem to
point to them having ideas on the matter. But
start to analyse those ideas and you will find that
they hardly reflect in any way the reality to which
they appear to refer, and if you go deeper you
will discover that there is not even an attempt to
adjust the ideas to this reality. Quite the contrary:
through these notions the individual is trying to
cut off any personal vision of reality, of his own
very life. For life is at the start a chaos in which
one is lost. The individual suspects this, but he is
frightened at finding himself face to face with
this terrible reality, and tries to cover it over with
a curtain of fantasy, where everything is clear. It
does not worry him that his "ideas" are not true,
he uses them as trenches for the defense of his
existence, as scarecrows to frighten away reality.*
—José Ortega y Gasset[1]

The problem of anality and the castration complex already takes us
a long way toward answering the question that intrigues us all: if
the basic quality of heroism is genuine courage, why are so few
people truly courageous? Why is it so rare to see a man who can
stand on his own feet? Even the great Carlyle, who frightened many
people, proclaimed that he stood on his father as on a stone pillar

buried in the ground under him. The unspoken implication is that if he stood on his own feet alone, the ground would cave in under him. This question goes right to the heart of the human condition, and we shall be attacking it from many sides all through this book. I once wrote[2] that I thought the reason man was so naturally cowardly was that he felt he had no authority; and the reason he had no authority was in the very nature of the way the human animal is shaped: all our meanings are built into us from the outside, from our dealings with others. This is what gives us a "self" and a superego. Our whole world of right and wrong, good and bad, our name, precisely who we are, is grafted into us; and we never feel we have authority to offer things on our own. How could we?—I argued—since we feel ourselves in many ways guilty and beholden to others, a lesser creation of theirs, indebted to them for our very birth.

But this is only part of the story—the most superficial and obvious part. There are deeper reasons for our lack of courage, and if we are going to understand man we have to dig for them. The psychologist Abraham Maslow had the keenest sense for significant ideas, and shortly before his recent untimely death he began to attack the problem of the fear of standing alone.[3] Maslow used a broad humanistic perspective in his work, and he liked to talk about concepts like "actualizing one's potential" and one's "full humanness." He saw these as natural developmental urges and wondered what holds them up, what blocks them. He answered the question in existential language, using terms like the "fear of one's own greatness" and the "evasion of one's destiny." This approach throws a new light on the problem of courage. In his words:

We fear our highest possibility (as well as our lowest ones). We are generally afraid to become that which we can glimpse in our most perfect moments. . . . We enjoy and even thrill to the godlike possibilities we see in ourselves in such peak moments. And yet we simultaneously shiver with weakness, awe and fear before these very same possibilities.[4]

Maslow used an apt term for this evasion of growth, this fear of realizing one's own fullest powers. He called it the "Jonah Syndrome." He understood the syndrome as the evasion of the full intensity of life:

We are just not strong enough to endure more! It is just too shaking and wearing. So often people in . . . ecstatic moments say, "It's too much," or "I can't stand it," or "I could die". . . . Delirious happiness cannot be borne for long. Our organisms are just too weak for any large doses of greatness. . . .

The Jonah Syndrome, then, seen from this basic point of view, is "partly a justified fear of being torn apart, of losing control, of being shattered and disintegrated, even of being killed by the experience." And the result of this syndrome is what we would expect a weak organism to do: to cut back the full intensity of life:

For some people this evasion of one's own growth, setting low levels of aspiration, the fear of doing what one is capable of doing, voluntary self-crippling, pseudo-stupidity, mock-humility are in fact defenses against grandiosity . . .[5]

It all boils down to a simple lack of strength to bear the superlative, to open oneself to the totality of experience—an idea that was well appreciated by William James and more recently was developed in phenomenological terms in the classic work of Rudolf Otto. Otto talked about the terror of the world, the feeling of overwhelming awe, wonder, and fear in the face of creation—the miracle of it, the *mysterium tremendum et fascinosum* of each single thing, of the fact that there are things at all.[6] What Otto did was to get descriptively at man's natural feeling of inferiority in the face of the massive transcendence of creation; his real *creature feeling* before the crushing and negating miracle of Being. We now

---

* As we shall see in the pages that follow, other thinkers had their version of the "Jonah Syndrome" long before Maslow; I am thinking especially of Rank, who gave the idea no special name, and of Freud, who probably began our scientific approach to it with his famous discovery of the "Wrecked by Success" syndrome. He saw that certain people couldn't stand success after they had achieved it; as it was too much for them, they quickly gave it up or went to pieces. I am leaving Freud out here because Maslow so well represents the existential approach that I believe is a considerable expansion of the Freudian horizon—even though Freud himself developed far toward an existential framework, as we shall see in Chapter Six where we discuss this problem again.

understand how a phenomenology of religious experience ties into psychology: right at the point of the problem of courage.

We might say that the child is a "natural" coward: he cannot have the strength to support the terror of creation. The world as it *is,* creation out of the void, things as they are, things as they are not, are too much for us to be able to stand. Or, better: they *would be* too much for us to bear without crumbling in a faint, trembling like a leaf, standing in a trance *in response* to the movement, colors, and odors of the world. I say "would be" because most of us—by the time we leave childhood—have repressed our vision of the primary miraculousness of creation. We have closed it off, changed it, and no longer perceive the world as it is to raw experience. Sometimes we may recapture this world by remembering some striking childhood perceptions, how suffused they were in emotion and wonder—how a favorite grandfather looked, or one's first love in his early teens. We change these heavily emotional perceptions precisely because we need to move about in the world with some kind of equanimity, some kind of strength and directness; we can't keep gaping with our heart in our mouth, greedily sucking up with our eyes everything great and powerful that strikes us. The great boon of repression is that it makes it possible to live decisively in an overwhelmingly miraculous and incomprehensible world, a world so full of beauty, majesty, and terror that if animals perceived it all they would be paralyzed to act.

But nature has protected the lower animal by endowing them with instincts. An instinct is a programmed perception that calls into play a programmed reaction. It is very simple. Animals are not moved by what they cannot react to. They live in a tiny world, a sliver of reality, one neuro-chemical program that keeps them walking behind their nose and shuts out everything else. But look at man, the impossible creature! Here nature seems to have thrown caution to the winds along with the programmed instincts. She created an animal who has no defense against full perception of the external world, an animal completely open to experience. Not only in front of his nose, in his *umwelt,* but in many other *umwelten.* He can relate not only to animals in his own species, but in some ways to all other species. He can contemplate not only what is edible for him, but everything that grows. He not only lives in this moment, but expands his inner self to yesterday, his curiosity to centuries ago, his fears to five billion years from now when the sun will cool, his hopes to an eternity from now. He lives not only on a tiny territory, nor even on an entire planet, but in a galaxy, in a universe, and in dimensions beyond visible universes. It is appalling, the burden that man bears, the *experiential* burden. As we saw in the last chapter, man can't even take his own body for granted as can other animals. It is not just hind feet, a tail that he drags, that are just "there," limbs to be used and taken for granted or chewed off when caught in a trap and when they give pain and prevent movement. Man's body is a *problem* to him that has to be explained. Not only his body is strange, but also its inner landscape, the memories and dreams. Man's very insides—his self—are foreign to him. He doesn't know who he is, why he was born, what he is doing on the planet, what he is supposed to do, what he can expect. His own existence is incomprehensible to him, a miracle just like the rest of creation, closer to him, right near his pounding heart, but for that reason all the more strange. Each thing is a problem, and man can shut out nothing. As Maslow has well said, "It is precisely the godlike in ourselves that we are ambivalent about, fascinated by and fearful of, motivated to and defensive against. This is one aspect of the basic human predicament, that we are simultaneously worms and gods."[7] There it is again: gods with anuses.

The historic value of Freud's work is that it came to grips with the peculiar animal that man was, the animal that was not programmed by instincts to close off perception and assure automatic equanimity and forceful action. Man had to invent and create out of himself the limitations of perception and the equanimity to live on this planet. And so the core of psychodynamics, the formation of the human character, is a study in human self-limitation and in the terrifying costs of that limitation. The hostility to psychoanalysis in the past, today, and in the future, will always be a hostility against admitting that man lives by lying to himself about himself and about his world, and that character, to follow Ferenczi and Brown, is a vital lie. I particularly like the way Maslow has summed up this contribution of Freudian thought:

Freud's greatest discovery, the one which lies at the root of psychodynamics, is that *the* great cause of much psychological illness is the fear of knowledge of oneself—of one's emotions, impulses, memories, capacities, potentialities, of one's destiny. We have discovered that fear of knowledge of oneself is very often isomorphic with, and parallel with, fear of the outside world.

And what is this fear, but a fear of the reality of creation in relation to our powers and possibilities:

In general this kind of fear is defensive, in the sense that it is a protection of our self-esteem, of our love and respect for ourselves. We tend to be afraid of any knowledge that could cause us to despise ourselves or to make us feel inferior, weak, worthless, evil, shameful. We protect ourselves and our ideal image of ourselves by repression and similar defenses, which are essentially techniques by which we avoid becoming conscious of unpleasant or dangerous truths.[8]

The individual has to repress *globally*, from the entire spectrum of his experience, if he wants to feel a warm sense of inner value and basic security. This sense of value and support is something that nature gives to each animal by the automatic instinctive programming and in the pulsating of the vital processes. But man, poor denuded creature, has to build and earn inner value and security. He must repress his smallness in the adult world, his failures to live up to adult commands and codes. He must repress his own feelings of physical and moral inadequacy, not only the inadequacy of his good intentions but also his guilt and his evil intensions: the death wishes and hatreds that result from being frustrated and blocked by the adults. He must repress his parents' inadequacy, their anxieties and terrors, because these make it difficult for him to feel secure and strong. He must repress his own anality, his compromising bodily functions that spell his mortality, his fundamental expendability in nature. And with all this, and more that we leave unsaid, he must repress the primary awesomeness of the external world.

In his later years Freud evidently came to realize, as Adler had earlier, that the thing that really bothers the child is the nature of his world, not so much his own inner drives. He talked less about the power of the Oedipus complex and more about "human perplexity and helplessness in the face of nature's dreaded forces," "the terrors of nature," "the painful riddle of death," "our anxiety in the face of life's dangers," and "the great necessities of fate, against which there is no remedy."[9] And when it came to the central problem of anxiety, he no longer talked—as he had in his early work—about the child's being overwhelmed from within by his instinctual urges; instead, Freud's formulations became existential. Anxiety was now seen largely as a matter of the reaction to global helplessness, abandonment, fate:

I therefore maintain that the fear of death is to be regarded as an analogue of the fear of castration, and that the situation to which the ego reacts is the state of being forsaken or deserted by the protecting superego—by the powers of destiny—which puts an end to security against every danger.[10]

This formulation indicates a great broadening of perspective. Add to it a generation or two of psychoanalytic clinical work, and we have achieved a remarkably faithful understanding of what really bothers the child, how life is really too much for him, how he has to avoid too much thought, too much perception, too much *life*. And at the same time, how he has to avoid the death that rumbles behind and underneath every carefree activity, that looks over his shoulder as he plays. The result is that we now know that the human animal is characterized by two great fears that other animals are protected from: the fear of life and the fear of death. In the science of man it was Otto Rank, above all, who brought these fears into prominence, based his whole system of thought on them, and showed how central they were to an understanding of man. At about the same time that Rank wrote, Heidegger brought these fears to the center of existential philosophy. He argued that the basic anxiety of man is anxiety *about* being-in-the-world, as well as anxiety *of* being-in-the-world. That is, both fear of death and fear of life, of experience and individuation.[11] Man is reluctant to move out into the overwhelmingness of his world, the real dangers of it; he shrinks back from losing himself in the all-consuming appetites of others, from spinning out of control in the clutchings and clawings of men, beasts and machines. As an animal organism man senses the kind of planet he has been put down on, the nightmarish, demonic frenzy in which nature has unleashed billions of individual organismic appetites of all kinds—not to mention earthquakes, meteors, and hurricanes, which seem to have their own hellish appetites. Each thing, in order to deliciously expand, is forever gobbling up others. Appetites may be innocent because they are naturally given, but any organism caught in the myriad cross-purposes of this planet is a potential victim of this very innocence—and it shrinks away from life lest it lose its own. Life can suck one up, sap his energies, submerge him, take away his self-control, give so much new experience so quickly that he will burst; make him stick out among others, emerge onto dangerous ground, load him up with new responsibilities which need great strength to bear, expose him to new contingencies, new chances. Above all there is the danger of a slip-up, an accident, a chance disease, and of course of death, the final sucking up, the total submergence and negation.

The great scientific simplification of psychoanalysis is the concept that the whole of early experience is an attempt by the child to deny the anxiety of his emergence, his fear of losing his support, of standing alone, helpless and afraid. The child's character, his style of life, is his way of using the power of others, the support of the things and the ideas of his culture, to banish from his awareness the actual fact of his natural impotence. Not only his impotence to avoid death, but his impotence to stand alone, firmly rooted on his own powers. In the face of the terror of the world, the miracle of creation, the crushing power of reality, not even the tiger has secure and limitless power, much less the child. His world is a transcendent mystery; even the parents to whom he relates in a natural and secure dependency are primary miracles. How else could they appear? The mother is the first awesome miracle that haunts the child his whole life, whether he lives within her powerful aura or rebels against it. The superordinacy of his world intrudes upon him in the form of fantastic faces smiling up close through gaping teeth, rolling eery eyes, piercing him from afar with burning and threatening glances. He lives in a world of flesh-and-blood Kwakiutl masks that mock his self-sufficiency. The only way he could securely oppose them would be to know that he is as godlike as they, but he can never know this straightforwardly and unambiguously. There is no secure answer to the awesome mystery of the human face that scrutinizes itself in the mirror; no answer, at any rate, that can come from the person himself, from his own center. One's own face may be godlike in its miraculousness, but one lacks the godlike power to know what it means, the godlike strength to have been responsible for its emergence.

In these ways, then, we understand that if the child were to give in to the overpowering character of reality and experience he would not be able to act with the kind of equanimity we need in our non-instinctive world. So one of the first things a child has to do is to learn to "abandon ecstasy," to do without awe, to leave fear and trembling behind. Only then can he act with a certain oblivious self-confidence, when he has naturalized his world. We say "naturalized" but we mean unnaturalized, falsified, with the truth obscured, the despair of the human condition hidden, a despair that the child glimpses in his night terrors and daytime phobias and neuroses. This despair he avoids by building defenses; and these defenses allow him to feel a basic sense of self-worth, of meaningfulness, of power. They allow him to feel that he *controls* his life and his death, that he really does live and act as a willful and free individual, that he has a unique and self-fashioned identity, that he *is somebody*—not just a trembling accident germinated on a hothouse planet that Carlyle for all time called a "hall of doom." We called one's life style a vital lie, and now we can understand better why we said it was vital: it is a *necessary* and basic dishonesty about oneself and one's whole situation. This revelation is what the Freudian revolution in thought really ends up in and is the basic reason that we still strain against Freud. We don't want to admit that we are fundamentally dishonest about reality, that we do not really control our own lives. We don't want to admit that we do not stand alone, that we always rely on something that transcends us, some system of ideas and powers in which we are embedded and which support us. This power is not always obvious. It need not be overtly a god or openly a stronger person, but it can be the power of an all-absorbing activity, a passion, a dedication to a game, a way of life, that like a comfortable web keeps a person buoyed up and ignorant of himself, of the fact that he does not rest on his own center. All of us are driven to be supported in a self-forgetful way, ignorant of what energies we really draw on, of the kind of lie we have fashioned in order to live securely and serenely. Augustine was a master analyst of this, as were Kierkegaard, Scheler, and Tillich in our day. They saw that man could strut and boast all he wanted, but that he really drew his "courage to be" from a god, a string of sexual conquests, a Big Brother, a flag, the proletariat, and the fetish of money and the size of a bank balance.

The defenses that form a person's character support a grand illusion, and when we grasp this we can understand the full drivenness of man. He is driven away from himself, from self-knowledge, self-reflection. He is driven toward things that support the lie of his character, his automatic equanimity. But he is also drawn precisely toward those things that make him anxious, as a way of skirting them masterfully, testing himself against them, controlling them by defying them. As Kierkegaard taught us, anxiety lures us on, becomes the spur to much of our energetic activity: we flirt with our own growth, but also dishonestly. This explains much of the friction in our lives. We enter symbiotic relationships in order to get the security we need, in order to get relief from our anxieties, our aloneness and helplessness; but these relationships also bind us, they enslave us even further because they support the lie we have fashioned. So we strain against them in order to be more free. The irony is that we do this straining uncritically, in a struggle within our own armor, as it were; and so we increase our drivenness, the second-hand quality of our struggle for freedom. Even in our flirtations with anxiety we are unconscious of our motives. We seek stress, we push our own limits, but we do it with our *screen against despair* and not with despair itself. We do it with the stock market, with sports cars, with atomic missiles, with the success ladder in the corporation or the competition in the university. We do it in the prison of a dialogue with our own little family, by marrying against their wishes or choosing a way of life because they frown on it, and so on. Hence the complicated and second-hand quality of our entire drivenness. Even in our passions we are nursery children playing with toys that represent the real world. Even when these toys crash and cost us our lives or our sanity, we are cheated of the consolation that we were in the real world instead of the playpen of our fantasies. We still did not meet our doom on our own manly terms, in contest with objective reality. It is fateful and ironic how the lie we need in order to live dooms us to a life that is never really ours.

It was not until the working out of modern psychoanalysis that we could understand something the poets and religious geniuses have long known: that the armor of character was so vital to us that to shed it meant to risk death and madness. It is not hard to reason out: If character is a neurotic defense against despair and you shed that defense, you admit the full flood of despair, the full realization of the true human condition, what men are really afraid of, what they struggle against, and are driven toward and away from. Freud summed it up beautifully when he somewhere remarked that psychoanalysis cured the neurotic misery in order to introduce the patient to the common misery of life. Neurosis is another word for describing a complicated technique for avoiding misery, but reality is the misery. That is why from earliest times sages have insisted that to see reality one must die and be reborn. The idea of death and rebirth was present in shamanistic times, in Zen thought, in Stoic thought, in Shakespeare's *King Lear,* as well as in Judeo-Christian and modern existential thought. But it was not until scientific psychology that we could understand what was at stake in the death and rebirth: that man's character was a neurotic structure that went right to the heart of his humanness. As Frederick Perls put it, "To suffer one's death and to be reborn is not easy." And it is not easy precisely because so much of one has to die.

I like the way Perls conceived the neurotic structure as a thick edifice built up of four layers. The first two layers are the everyday layers, the tactics that the child learns to get along in society by the facile use of words to win ready approval and to placate others and move them along with him: these are the glib, empty talk, "cliché," and role-playing layers. Many people live out their lives never getting underneath them. The third layer is a stiff one to penetrate: it is the "impasse" that covers our feeling of being empty and lost, the very feeling that we try to banish in building up our character defenses. Underneath this layer is the fourth and most baffling one: the "death" or fear-of-death layer; and this, as we have seen, is the layer of our true and basic animal anxieties, the terror that we carry around in our secret heart. Only when we explode this fourth layer, says Perls, do we get to the layer of what we might call our "authentic self": what we really are without sham, without disguise, without defenses against fear.[12]

From this sketch of the complex rings of defense that compose our character, our neurotic shield that protects our pulsating vitality from the dread of truth, we can get some idea of the difficult and excruciatingly painful, all-or-nothing process that psychological rebirth is. And when it is through psychologically, it only begins humanly: the worst is not the death, but the rebirth itself—there's the rub. What does it mean "to be born again" for man? It means for the first time to be subjected to the terrifying paradox of the human condition, since one must be born not as a god, but as a man, or as a god-worm, or a god who shits. Only this time without the neurotic shield that hides the full ambiguity of one's life. And so we know that every authentic rebirth is a real ejection from paradise, as the lives of Tolstoy, Péguy, and others attest. It takes men of granite, men who were automatically powerful, "secure in their drivenness" we might say, and it makes them tremble, makes them cry—as Péguy stood on the platforms of Parisian busses with hot tears rolling down his cheeks while he mumbled prayers.

It was Rank who very early admitted that anxiety could not all be overcome therapeutically, and this is what he meant: that it is impossible to stand up to the terror of one's condition without anxiety. It was Andras Angyal who got to the heart of the matter of psychotherapeutic rebirth when he said that the neurotic who has had therapy is like a member of Alcoholics Anonymous: he can never take his cure for granted, and the best sign of the genuineness of that cure is that he lives with *humility*.[13]

Full Humans and Part Humans

This discussion brings up a basic contradiction of the whole therapeutic enterprise that has not been aired widely enough; we are going to be dwelling on it at the close of this book, but this is the right place to introduce it. It is simply this: what sense does it make to talk about "enjoying one's full humanness"—as Maslow urges along with so many others—if "full humanness" means the primary *mis-adjustment* to the world? If you get rid of the four-layered neurotic shield, the armor that covers the characterological lie about life, how can you talk about "enjoying" this Pyrrhic victory? The person gives up something restricting and illusory, it is true, but only to come face to face with something even more awful: genuine despair. Full humanness means full fear and trembling, at least some of the waking day. When you get a person to emerge into life, away from his dependencies, his automatic safety in the cloak of someone else's power, what joy can you promise him with the burden of his aloneness? When you get a person to look at the sun as it bakes down on the daily carnage taking place on earth, the ridiculous accidents, the utter fragility of life, the powerlessness of those he thought most powerful—what comfort can you give him from a psychotherapeutic point of view? Luis Buñuel likes to introduce a mad dog into his films as counterpoint to the secure daily routine of repressed living. The meaning of his symbolism is that no matter what men pretend, they are only one accidental bite away from utter fallibility. The artist disguises the incongruity that is the pulse-beat of madness but he is aware of it. What would the average man do with a full consciousness of absurdity? He has fashioned his character for the precise purpose of putting it between himself and the facts of life; it is his special *tour-de-force* that allows him to ignore incongruities, to nourish himself on impossibilities, to thrive on blindness. He accomplishes thereby a peculiarly human victory: the ability to be smug about terror. Sartre has called man a "useless passion" because he is so hopelessly bungled, so deluded about his true condition. He wants to be a god with only the equipment of an animal, and so he thrives on fantasies. As Ortega so well put it in the epigraph we have used for this chapter, man uses his ideas for the defense of his existence, to frighten away reality. This is a serious game, the defense of one's existence—how take it away from people and leave them joyous?

Maslow talks very convincingly about "self-actualization" and the ecstasy of "peak experiences" wherein a person comes to see the world in all its awe and splendor and senses his own free inner expansion and the miracle of his being. Maslow calls this state "being cognition," the openness of perception to the truth of the world, a truth concealed by the neurotic distortions and illusions that protect one against overwhelming experiences. This idea is fine and correct, this enjoinder to develop the capacity for "being cognition" in order to break out of the one-dimensionality of our lives, the cave of our imprisoning security. But like most things human it is a very paradoxical kind of triumph. This was already clearly seen by Maslow, when he talked about the *"dangers of being-cognition."*[14] Maslow was too broad-minded and sober to imagine that being-cognition did not have an underside; but he didn't go far enough toward pointing out what a dangerous underside it was—that it could undermine one's whole position in the world. It can't be overstressed, one final time, that to see the world as it really is is devastating and terrifying. It achieves the very result that the child has painfully built his character over the years in order to avoid: it *makes routine, automatic, secure, self-confident activity impossible.* It makes thoughtless living in the world of men an impossibility. It places a trembling animal at the mercy of the entire cosmos and the problem of the meaning of it.

Let us digress here for a moment in order to show that this view of character is not one put forth by morbid existentialists but instead represents the now-agreed merger of Freudian and post-Freudian psychology. A subtle but very profound change has come over our understanding of the early development of the child. It is a change that can be summed up briefly in the shifts from Freudian to post-Freudian psychology and now back again to a sobered Freudianism. Freud saw the child as an antagonist of his world, as someone who had drives of aggression and sexuality that he wanted to work on the world. But as he could not work them out as a child, he had to suffer frustration and develop substitute satisfactions. The thwarting of these drives in childhood led to such a residue of bitterness and antisociality that the world would always be peopled by a type of animal that resented what it had done to him, what it had deprived him of. He would be a mean animal, deep down, one who felt cheated, one who harbored choked-up feelings and desires. He might on the surface be pleasant enough, responsible, creative; but underneath it all was a residue of trashiness that threatened to burst out and that in any event would somehow work itself out on others or on himself.

Freud's theory of innate instincts was undermined very early in social-psychological quarters and very late within psychoanalysis itself, and a new view of the child came into vogue. It tended to see the child as neutral, instinct-free, basically malleable; apart from some unknown factors of hereditary constitution and temperament, the child was looked upon wholly as a creature shaped by his environment. In this view the parents were thought to be responsible for the child's repressions, for the character defenses that he developed, and for the kind of person he turned out to be, as they had provided him with an environment and molded him to it. Even more than that, as the parents had opposed the child's natural energetic and free expansion and had demanded his surrender to their world, they could be considered in some fundamental way as guilty for whatever warpings his character had. If the child had no instincts he at least had plenty of free energy and a natural innocence of the body. He sought continual activity and diversion, wanted to move about his world in its entirety, to bend it to his use and delight as much as possible. He sought to express himself spontaneously, feel the most satisfaction in his bodily processes, derive the most comfort, thrill, and pleasure from others. But as this kind of limitless expansion is not possible in the world, the child has to be checked for his own good; and the parents were the checkers of his activity. Whatever attitudes the child had toward himself, his body, and his world were considered to have been implanted by his experience with his trainers and with his immediate environment.

This was the post-Freudian view of character development, the reaction against Freud's instinctivism. Actually it is pre-Freudian, dating from the Enlightenment and Rousseau and Marx. In recent years the most biting and carefully thought-out critique of this view was given by Norman O. Brown.[15] The epithets he used against Fromm and the neo-Freudians were bitter indeed for a book that called us all back to Eros. But the gravamen of Brown's critique was a serious one that had been overlooked by many in recent decades: that the situation of the child was an impossible one and that he had to fashion his own defenses against the world, had to find a way of surviving in it. As we saw in Chapter Three, the child's own existential dilemmas gave him his task quite independently of the parents: his "attitudes" came to him from his need to adapt to the whole desperate human condition, not merely to attune himself to the whims of his parents.

The student of ideas is entitled to wonder what kind of book Brown would have fashioned out of his brilliance if he had digested Adler and Rank with the thoroughness with which he studied Freud.

It was Adler and Rank, after all, who understood the desperate situation of the child, without falling either into the Freudian trap of inner instincts or that of easy environmentalism. As Rank put it once and for all, for all future psychoanalysts and students of man:

every human being is . . . equally unfree, that is, *we . . . create* out of freedom, a prison. . . .[16]

Rank was criticizing Rousseau's vision of man as born free and then put into chains by training and by society. Rank understood that in the face of the overwhelmingness of the world the child could not out of himself muster the stamina and the authority necessary to live in full expansiveness with limitless horizons of perception and experience.

We have arrived at a unique stage in the development of psychoanalytic thought. By fully incorporating the work of Adler and Rank on an equal level with Freud, modern psychoanalysis has been able to keep the roundness and soberness of the master without the errors, extreme formulations, and dogma of strict Freudianism. As I see it, Brown's book represents a declaration that the circle has been closed fully between the psychoanalysis of the founders and the most recent theoretical and clinical work, without anything essential being lost. Even on the syndrome that in truth could most justifiably accuse the parents of failing to fashion an adequate human being—that of schizophrenia—there has been a marked change of emphasis, a new consciousness of the tragic dimensions of human life. No one has summed this up better than Harold Searles, and I would like to quote at length his sensitive and authoritative personal statement, which I think is a very important one historically:

At Chestnut Lodge, the twice-weekly, hour-long case presentations usually have to do with schizophrenic patients. . . . When the author went there, nearly 12 years ago, the therapists—including the author—presenting these cases often tended to paint a totally, or almost totally, black picture of the patient's childhood family relationships; the feeling-atmosphere of the presentation was one of blame of the parents more than anything else. As the years have gone on, the author has found that the presentations have come to convey less and less of such blame, and to convey more and more of the tragedy of the patients' lives—tragedy which is so much of a piece with the tragedy of life for all of us that the presentation is often a profoundly grief-laden experience for both the presenter and the listeners. One feels that the staff-presentation now gives a truer picture of a patient's life, but a picture which is much more deeply shaking than was the blame-colored picture previously often seen.[17]

The tragedy of life that Searles is referring to is the one we have been discussing: man's finitude, his dread of death and of the over-whelmingness of life. The schizophrenic feels these more than any-one else because he has not been able to build the confident defenses that a person normally uses to deny them. The schizo-phrenic's misfortune is that he has been burdened with extra anxieties, extra guilt, extra helplessness, an even more unpredictable and unsupportive environment. He is not surely seated in his body, has no secure base from which to negotiate a defiance of and a denial of the real nature of the world. The parents have made him massively inept as an organism. He has to contrive extra-ingenious and extra-desperate ways of living in the world that will keep him from being torn apart by experience, since he is already almost apart. We see again confirmed the point of view that a person's character is a defense against despair, an attempt to avoid insanity because of the *real* nature of the world. Searles looks at schizo-phrenia precisely as the result of the inability to shut out terror, as a desperate style of living with terror. Frankly I don't know any-thing more cogent that needs to be said about this syndrome: it is a failure in humanization, which means a failure to *confidently deny* man's real situation on this planet. Schizophrenia is the limiting test case for the theory of character and reality that we have been ex-pounding here: the failure to build dependable character defenses allows the true nature of reality to appear to man. It is scientifically apodictic. The creativity of people on the schizophrenic end of the human continuum is a creativity that springs from the inability to accept the standardized cultural denials of the real nature of ex-perience. And the price of this kind of almost "extra human" crea-tivity is to live on the brink of madness, as men have long known. The schizophrenic is supremely creative in an almost extra-human sense because he is furthest from the animal: he lacks the secure instinctive programming of lower organisms; and he lacks the secure cultural programming of average men. No wonder he appears to average men as "crazy": he is not in anything's world.†

Conclusion

Let us close our long discussion of the function of character by juxtaposing two great pieces of poetic writing and insight, separated by almost three centuries. The first, by Thomas Traherne, gives a beautiful description of the world as it appears to the perceptions of the child before he has been able to fashion automatic reactions. Traherne describes the pristine perceptions of the child:

All appeared new, and strange at first, inexpressibly rare and delightful and beautiful. . . . The corn was orient and immortal wheat, which never should be reaped, nor was ever sown. I thought it had stood from everlasting to everlasting. The dust and stones of the street were as precious as gold; the gates were at first the end of the world. The green trees when I saw them first through one of the gates transported and ravished me, their sweetness and unusual beauty made my heart to leap, and almost mad with ecstasy, they were such strange and wonderful things. The Men! O what venerable and reverend creatures did the aged seem! Immortal Cherubims! And young men glittering and sparkling Angels, and maids strange seraphic pieces of life and beauty! Boys and girls tumbling in the street, and playing, were moving jewels. I knew not that they were born or should die. . . . The city seemed to stand in Eden. . . .

We might call this the paradise of prerepression. But then, Traherne goes on to describe his fall from Eden; the development of cultural perceptions and denials of the pristine character of reality; and like a modern psychoanalyst in the early days of, say, Chestnut Lodge, he accuses the parents of this fall, makes his whole case against them:

Thoughts are the most present things to thoughts, and of the most powerful influence. My soul was only apt and disposed to great things; but souls to souls are like apples to apples, one being rotten rots another. When I began to speak and go, nothing began to be present to me, but

† For a fuller summing-up of the problem of schizophrenic failure see Chapter Ten.

what was present to me in their thoughts. Nor was anything present to me any other way, than it was so to them. . . . All things were absent which they talked not of. So I began among my play-fellows to prize a drum, a fine coat, a penny, a gilded book, & c.,. . . . As for the Heavens and the Sun and Stars they disappeared, and were no more unto me than the bare walls. So that the strange riches of man's invention quite overcame the riches of Nature, being learned more laboriously and in the second place.[18]

What is missing in this splendid portrayal of the child's fall from natural perception into the artificialities of the cultural world? Nothing less than what we have cited as the great post-Freudian merger on the human personality: Traherne's own complicity in the process, his *need* to fall from grace in order to grow, move about without anxiety, protect himself *against* the Sun, the Stars, the Heavens. Traherne doesn't record his other pristine reactions, say, to the piercing screams of his "play-fellows" as they cut their hands or smashed their noses and mouths and splashed him with globs of weird, warm red that sent terror into his bowels. He says that he knew not that they should die, that all seemed immortal—but did his parents introduce death into the world? This was the deep-lying rot that rubbed into his soul, and it rubbed in not from the parents but from the world, from the "riches of nature." In some complex ways death edged itself as a symbol into his perceptions and chilled his soul, and to banish the *facts* of life Traherne had to remold his paradise, even to lying about it in his memory as we all do. True, the earth was the place of mystical beauty that he painted it and that Carlyle later agreed to be "a mystic temple"; but it was at the same time "a hall of doom" that Traherne chose to deny in his memory of childhood.

The totality of the human condition is the thing that is so hard for man to recapture. He wants his world safe for delight, wants to blame others for his fate. Compare to Traherne a modern poet's consciousness of the full roundness of the human condition. Marcia Lee Anderson tells us with penetrating brilliance how we have to live in a hall of doom, what we need to do to protect ourselves:

We multiply diseases for delight,
Invent a horrid want, a shameful doubt,
Luxuriate in license, feed on night,

Make inward bedlam—and will not come out.
Why should we? Stripped of subtle complications,
Who could regard the sun except with fear?
This is our shelter against contemplation,
Our only refuge from the plain and clear.
Who would crawl out from under the obscure
To stand defenseless in the sunny air?
No terror of obliquity so sure
As the most shining terror of despair
To know how simple is our deepest need,
How sharp, and how impossible to feed.[19]

The irony of man's condition is that the deepest need is to be free of the anxiety of death and annihilation; but it is life itself which awakens it, and so we must shrink from being fully alive. Marcia Lee Anderson draws the circle not only on Traherne, but on Maslow, on humanistic psychoanalysis, and even on Freudian Norman O. Brown himself. What exactly would it mean on this earth to be wholly unrepressed, to live in full bodily and psychic expansiveness? It can only mean to be reborn into madness. Brown warns us of the full radicalness of his reading of Freud by stressing that he resolutely follows Ferenczi's insight that "Character-traits are, so to speak, secret psychoses."[20] This is shaking scientific truth, and we have also subscribed to it with Brown. If it has seemed hard for men to get agreement on such a truth during the age of Freud, one day it will be secure.

But the chilling reality behind this truth is even more upsetting, and there doesn't seem to be much that we can do with it or will ever be able to do with it: I mean that *without* character-traits there has to be full and open psychosis. At the very end of this book I want to sum up the basic contradictions of Brown's argument for new men without character defenses, his hope for a rebirth of mankind into a "second innocence." For now, it is enough to invoke Marcia Lee Anderson's complete scientific formula: "Stripped of subtle complications [i.e., of all the character defenses—repression, denial, misperception of reality], who could regard the sun except with fear?"

CHAPTER FIVE

The Psychoanalyst Kierkegaard

*The whole order of things fills me with a sense
of anguish, from the gnat to the mysteries of
incarnation; all is entirely unintelligible to me,
and particularly my own person. Great is my
sorrow, without limits. None knows of it, except
God in Heaven, and He cannot have pity.*
—Sören Kierkegaard[1]

Today we can call Kierkegaard a "psychoanalyst" without fear of
being laughed at—or at least with confidence that the scoffers are
uninformed. In the last few decades a new discovery of Kierkegaard
has been taking place, a discovery that is momentous because it
links him into the whole structure of knowledge in the humanities
in our time. We used to think that there was a strict difference between science and belief and that psychiatry and religion were
consequently far apart. But now we find that psychiatric and religious perspectives on reality are intimately related. For one thing
they grow out of one another historically, as we shall see in a later
section. Even more importantly for now, they reinforce one another.
Psychiatric experience and religious experience cannot be separated
either subjectively in the person's own eyes or objectively in the
theory of character development.

Nowhere is this merger of religious and psychiatric categories
clearer than in the work of Kierkegaard. He gave us some of the
best empirical analyses of the human condition ever fashioned by
man's mind. But ironically, it was not until the epoch of the
scientific atheist Freud that we could see the scientific stature of
the theologian Kierkegaard's work. Only then did we have the

clinical evidence to support it. The noted psychologist Mowrer summed it up perfectly two decades ago: "Freud had to live and write before the earlier work of Kierkegaard could be correctly understood and appreciated."[2] There have been several good attempts to show how Kierkegaard anticipated the data of modern clinical psychology. Most of the European existentialists have had something to say about this, along with theologians like Paul Tillich.[3] The meaning of this work is that it draws a circle around psychiatry and religion; it shows that the best existential analysis of the human condition leads directly into the problems of God and faith, which is exactly what Kierkegaard had argued.

I am not going to attempt to repeat and decode Kierkegaard's breathtakingly penetrating and often difficult-to-understand analysis of the human condition. What I want to do instead is to try to present a summing-up of the main argument contained in his psychological works, as pointedly and sparingly as possible, so that the reader can see "in a nutshell" what Kierkegaard was driving at. If I can do this without getting too involved because fascinated by Kierkegaard's genius, the reader should be struck by the result. The structure of Kierkegaard's understanding of man *is almost exactly a recap of the modern clinical picture of man that we have sketched in the first four chapters of this book.* The reader can then judge for himself how congruent the two pictures are at basic points (even though I don't present Kierkegaard in his stunning detail), why it is that we are today comparing Kierkegaard's stature in psychology to Freud's, and why I and others are prepared to call Kierkegaard as great a student of the human condition as was Freud. The fact is that, although writing in the 1840's he was really post-Freudian, which conveys the eternal uncanniness of genius.

The Existential Paradox as the Beginning of Psychology and Religion

The foundation stone for Kierkegaard's view of man is the myth of the Fall, the ejection of Adam and Eve from the Garden of Eden. In this myth is contained, as we saw, the basic insight of psychology for all time: that man is a union of opposites, of self-consciousness and of physical body. Man emerged from the instinctive thoughtless action of the lower animals and came to reflect on his condition. He was given a consciousness of his individuality and his part-divinity in creation, the beauty and uniqueness of his face and his name. At the same time he was given the consciousness of the terror of the world and of his own death and decay. This paradox is the really constant thing about man in all periods of history and society; it is thus the true "essence" of man, as Fromm said. As we saw, the leading modern psychologists have themselves made it the cornerstone of their understanding. But Kierkegaard had already counseled them: "Further than this psychology cannot go . . . and moreover it can verify this point again and again in its observation of human life."[4]

The fall into self-consciousness, the emergence from comfortable ignorance in nature, had one great penalty for man: it gave him *dread,* or anxiety. One does not find dread in the beast, says Kierkegaard, "precisely for the reason that by nature the beast is not qualified by spirit."[5] For "spirit" read "self" or symbolic inner identity. The beast has none. It is ignorant, says Kierkegaard, therefore innocent; but man is a "synthesis of the soulish and bodily"[6] and so experiences anxiety. Again, for "soulish" we must read "self-conscious."

If a man were a beast or an angel, he would not be able to be in dread. [That is, if he were utterly unself-conscious or totally un-animal.] Since he is a synthesis he can be in dread . . . man himself produces dread.[7]

Man's anxiety is a function of his sheer ambiguity and of his complete powerlessness to overcome that ambiguity, to be straightforwardly an animal or an angel. He cannot live heedless of his fate, nor can he take sure control over that fate and triumph over it by being outside the human condition:

The spirit cannot do away with itself [i.e., self-consciousness cannot disappear]. . . . Neither can man sink down into the vegetative life [i.e., be wholly an animal]. . . . He cannot flee from dread.[8]

But the real focus of dread is not the ambiguity itself, it is the result of *the judgment* on man: that if Adam eats of the fruit of the tree of knowledge God tells him "Thou shalt surely die." In other words, the final terror of self-consciousness is the knowledge of one's own death, which is the peculiar sentence on man alone in the animal kingdom. This is the meaning of the Garden of Eden myth and the rediscovery of modern psychology: that death is man's peculiar and greatest anxiety.*

Kierkegaard's Characterology

Kierkegaard's whole understanding of man's character is that it is a structure built up to avoid perception of the "terror, perdition [and] annihilation [that] dwell next door to every man."⁹ He understood psychology the way a contemporary psychoanalyst does: that its task is to discover the strategies that a person uses to avoid anxiety. What style does he use to function automatically and uncritically in the world, and how does this style cripple his true growth and freedom of action and choice? Or, in words that are almost Kierkegaard's: how is a person being enslaved by his characterological lie about himself?

Kierkegaard described these styles with a brilliance that today seems uncanny and with a vocabulary that sums up much of the psychoanalytic theory of character defenses. Whereas today we talk about the "mechanisms of defense" such as repression and denial, Kierkegaard talked about the same things with different terms: he referred to the fact that most men live in a "half-obscurity" about their own condition,¹⁰ they are in a state of "shut-upness" wherein they block off their own perceptions of reality.¹¹ He understood the compulsive character, the rigidity of the person who has had to build extra-thick defenses against anxiety, a heavy character armor, and he described him in the following terms:

---

* Two of the most brilliant uses and analyses of the idea of the duality and ambiguity of man in modern Christian thought are by Reinhold Niebuhr, *The Nature and Destiny of Man*, Volume One (New York: Scribner's Sons, 1941), and Paul Tillich, *Systematic Theology*, Volume Three (Chicago: University of Chicago Press, 1963), Chapter 1. These studies prove beyond a doubt the truth of Kierkegaard's work, that psychological and religious analyses of the human condition are inextricable, *if* they get down to basics.

A partisan of the most rigid orthodoxy . . . knows it all, he bows before the holy, truth is for him an ensemble of ceremonies, he talks about presenting himself before the throne of God, of how many times one must bow, he knows everything the same way as does the pupil who is able to demonstrate a mathematical proposition with the letters ABC, but not when they are changed to DEF. He is therefore in dread whenever he hears something not arranged in the same order.[12]

There is no doubt that by "shut-upness" Kierkegaard means what we today refer to by repression; it is the closed personality, the one who has fenced himself around in childhood, not tested his own powers in action, not been free to discover himself and his world in a relaxed way. If the child is not burdened by too much parental blocking of his action, too much infection with the parents' anxieties, he can develop his defenses in a less monopolizing way, can remain somewhat fluid and open in character. He is prepared to test reality more in terms of his own action and experimentation and less on the basis of delegated authority and prejudgment or preperception. Kierkegaard understood this difference by making a distinction between "lofty" shut-upness and "mistaken" shut-upness. He went on to give a Rousseau-like enjoinder for raising children with the right kind of character orientation:

It is of infinite importance that a child be brought up with a conception of the lofty shut-upness [reserve], and be saved from the mistaken kind. In an external respect it is easy to perceive when the moment has arrived that one ought to let the child walk alone; . . . the art is to be constantly present and yet not be present, to let the child be allowed to develop itself, while nevertheless one has constantly a survey clearly before one. The art is to leave the child to itself in the very highest measure and on the greatest possible scale, and to express this apparent abandonment in such a way that, unobserved, one at the same time knows everything. . . . And the father who educates or does everything for the child entrusted to him, but has not prevented him from becoming shut-up, has incurred a great accountability.[13]

Just as Rousseau and Dewey, Kierkegaard is warning the parent to let the child do his own exploration of the world and develop his own sure experimental powers. He knows that the child has to be protected against dangers and that watchfulness by the parent is of vital importance, but he doesn't want the parent to obtrude his own anxieties into the picture, to cut off the child's action before it is absolutely necessary. Today we know that such an upbringing alone gives the child a self-confidence in the face of experience that he would not have if he were overly blocked: it gives him an "inner sustainment." And it is precisely this inner sustainment that allows the child to develop a "lofty" shut-upness, or reserve: that is, an ego-controlled and self-confident appraisal of the world by a personality that can open up more easily to experience. "Mistaken" shut-upness, on the other hand, is the result of too much blockage, too much anxiety, too much effort to face up to experience by an organism that has been overburdened and weakened in its own controls: it means, therefore, more automatic repression by an essentially *closed* personality. And so, for Kierkegaard, the "good" is the opening toward new possibility and choice, the ability to face into anxiety; the closed is the evil, that which turns one away from newness and broader perceptions and experiences; the closed shuts out revelation, obtrudes a veil between the person and his own situation in the world.[14] Ideally these should be transparent, but for the closed person they are opaque.

It is easy to see that shut-upness is precisely what we have called "the lie of character," and Kierkegaard calls it the same thing:

It is easy to see that shut-upness *eo ipso* signifies a lie, or, if you prefer, untruth. But untruth is precisely unfreedom . . . the elasticity of freedom is consumed in the service of close reserve. . . . Close reserve was the effect of the negating retrenchment of the ego in the individuality.[15]

This is a perfectly contemporary psychoanalytic description of the costs of repression on the total personality. I am omitting Kierkegaard's more detailed and penetrating analysis of how the person becomes fragmented within himself by the repression, how the real perception of reality dwells under the surface, close at hand, ready to break through the repression, how the repression leaves the personality seemingly intact, seemingly functioning as a whole, in continuity—but how that continuity is broken, how the personality is really at the mercy of the discontinuity expressed by the repression.[16] To a modern, clinically-trained mind such an analysis must be truly marvelous.

Kierkegaard understood that the lie of character is built up because the child needs to adjust to the world, to the parents, and to his own existential dilemmas. It is built up before the child has a chance to learn about himself in an open or free way, and thus character defenses are automatic and unconscious. The problem is that the child becomes dependent on them and comes to be encased in his own character armor, unable to see freely beyond his own prison or into himself, into the defenses he is using, the things that are determining his unfreedom.[17] The best that the child can hope is that his shut-upness will not be of the "mistaken" or massive kind, in which his character is too fearful of the world to be able to open itself to the possibilities of experience. But that depends largely on the parents, on accidents of the environment, as Kierkegaard knew. Most people have parents who have "incurred a great accountability," and so they are obliged to shut themselves off from possibility.

Kierkegaard gives us some portrait sketches of the styles of denying possibility, or the lies of character—which is the same thing. He is intent on describing what we today call "inauthentic" men, men who avoid developing their own uniqueness; they follow out the styles of automatic and uncritical living in which they were conditioned as children. They are "inauthentic" in that they do not belong to themselves, are not "their own" person, do not act from their own center, do not see reality on its terms; they are the one-dimensional men totally immersed in the fictional games being played in their society, unable to transcend their social conditioning: the corporation men in the West, the bureaucrats in the East, the tribal men locked up in tradition—man everywhere who doesn't understand what it means to think for himself and who, if he did, would shrink back at the idea of such audacity and exposure. Kierkegaard gives us a description of

the *immediate* man . . . his self or he himself is a something included along with "the other" in the compass of the temporal and the worldly. . . . Thus the self coheres immediately with "the other," wishing, desiring, enjoying, etc., but passively; . . . he manages to imitate the other men, noting how they manage to live, and so he too lives after a sort. In Christendom he too is a Christian, goes to church every Sunday, hears and understands the parson, yea, they understand one another; he dies; the parson introduces him into eternity for the price of $10—but a self he was not, and a self he did not become. . . . For the immediate man does not recognize his self, he recognizes himself only by his dress, . . . he recognizes that he has a self only by externals.[18]

This is a perfect description of the "automatic cultural man"—man as confined by culture, a slave to it, who imagines that he has an identity if he pays his insurance premium, that he has control of his life if he guns his sports car or works his electric toothbrush. Today the inauthentic or immediate men are familiar types, after decades of Marxist and existentialist analysis of man's slavery to his social system. But in Kierkegaard's time it must have been a shock to be a modern European city-dweller and be considered a Philistine at the same time. For Kierkegaard "philistinism" was triviality, man lulled by the daily routines of his society, content with the satisfactions that it offers him: in today's world the car, the shopping center, the two-week summer vacation. Man is protected by the secure and limited alternatives his society offers him, and if he does not look up from his path he can live out his life with a certain dull security:

Devoid of imagination, as the Philistine always is, he lives in a certain trivial province of experience as to how things go, what is possible, what usually occurs. . . . Philistinism tranquilizes itself in the trivial. . . .[19]

Why does man accept to live a trivial life? Because of the danger of a full horizon of experience, of course. This is the deeper motivation of philistinism, that it celebrates the triumph over possibility, over freedom. Philistinism knows its real enemy: freedom is dangerous. If you follow it too willingly it threatens to pull you into the air; if you give it up too wholly, you become a prisoner of necessity. The safest thing is to toe the mark of what is *socially* possible. I think this is the meaning of Kierkegaard's observation:

For philistinism thinks it is in control of possibility, it thinks that when it has decoyed this prodigious elasticity into the field of probability or into the madhouse it holds it a prisoner; it carries possibility around like a prisoner in the cage of the probable, shows it off. . . .[20]

Kierkegaard as Theorist of the Psychoses

But now something new enters our discussion. Kierkegaard talks about decoying the prodigious elasticity of freedom "into the madhouse" where it is held prisoner. What does he mean by such a condensed image? To me he means that one of the great dangers of life is *too much possibility*, and that the place where we find people who have succumbed to this danger is the madhouse. Here Kierkegaard shows that he was a master theorist not only of "normal cultural pathology" but also of abnormal pathology or psychosis. He understands that psychosis is neurosis pushed to its extreme. At least this is how I read many of his observations in the section of his book called "Despair Viewed Under the Aspects of Finitude/ Infinitude."[21] Let us pause on this, because if my reading is correct it will help us understand further how the most extreme forms of mental derangement are clumsy attempts to come to grips with the basic problem of life.

Kierkegaard is painting for us a broad and incredibly rich portrait of types of human failure, ways in which man succumbs to and is beaten by life and the world; beaten because he fails to face up to the existential truth of his situation—the truth that he is an inner symbolic self, which signifies a certain freedom, and that he is bound by a finite body, which limits that freedom. The attempt to ignore either aspect of man's situation, to repress possibility or to deny necessity, means that man will live a lie, fail to realize his true nature, be "the most pitiful of all things." But man is not always so lucky, he cannot always get by with just being pitiful. If the lie that he attempts to live is too flaunting of reality, a man can lose everything during his lifetime—and this is precisely what we mean by psychosis: the complete and utter breakdown of the character structure. If Kierkegaard is to be considered a master analyst of the human situation he must show us that he understands the extremes of man's condition as well as the everyday cultural middle.

This is precisely what he does in his discussion of the extremes of too much and too little possibility. Too much possibility is the attempt by the person to overvalue the powers of the symbolic self. It reflects the attempt to exaggerate one half of the human dualism at the expense of the other. In this sense, what we call schizophrenia is an attempt by the symbolic self to deny the limitations of the finite body; in doing so, the entire person is pulled off balance and destroyed. It is as though the freedom of creativity that stems from within the symbolic self cannot be contained by the body, and the person is torn apart. This is how we understand schizophrenia today, as the split of self and body, a split in which the self is unanchored, unlimited, not bound enough to everyday things, not contained enough in dependable physical behavior.[22] And this is how Kierkegaard understands the problem:

For the self is a synthesis in which the finite is the limiting factor, and the infinite is the expanding factor. Infinitude's despair is therefore the fantastical, the limitless.[23]†

By "infinitude's despair" Kierkegaard means the sickness of the personality, the opposite of health. And so the person becomes sick by plunging into the limitless, the symbolic self becomes "fantastic" —as it does in schizophrenia—when it splits away from the body, from a dependable grounding in real experience in the everyday world. The full-blown schizophrenic is abstract, ethereal, unreal; he billows out of the earthly categories of space and time, floats out of his body, dwells in an eternal now, is not subject to death and destruction. He has vanquished these in his fantasy, or perhaps better, in the actual fact that he has quit his body, renounced its limitations. Kierkegaard's description is not only eloquent, it is also precisely clinical:

Generally the fantastical is that which so carries a man out into the infinite that it merely carries him away from himself and therewith pre-

---

† Kierkegaard's use of "self" may be a bit confusing. He uses it to include the symbolic self and the physical body. It is a synonym really for "total personality" that goes beyond the person to include what we would now call the "soul" or the "ground of being" out of which the created person sprang. But this is not important for us here, except to introduce the idea that the total person is a dualism of finitude and infinitude.

vents him from returning to himself. So when feeling becomes fantastic, the self is simply volatilized more and more. . . . The self thus leads a fantastic existence in abstract endeavor after infinity, or in abstract isolation, constantly lacking itself, from which it merely gets further and further away.

This is pure Ronald Laing's *The Divided Self,* over a century ago. Again:

Now if possibility outruns necessity, the self runs away from itself, so that it has no necessity whereto it is bound to return—then this is the despair [sickness] of possibility. The self becomes an abstract possibility which tries [sic: "tires"?] itself out with floundering in the possible, but does not budge from the spot, not get to any spot, for precisely the necessary is the spot; to become oneself is precisely a movement at the spot.[24]

What Kierkegaard means here is that the development of the person is a development in depth from a fixed center in the personality, a center that unites both aspects of the existential dualism —the self and the body. But this kind of development needs precisely an acknowledgment of reality, the reality of one's limits:

What the self now lacks is surely reality—so one would commonly say, as one says of a man that he has become unreal. But upon closer inspection it is really necessity that man lacks. . . . What really is lacking is the power to . . . submit to the necessary in oneself, to what may be called one's limit. Therefore the misfortune does not consist in the fact that such a self did not amount to anything in the world; no, the misfortune is that the man did not become aware of himself, aware that the self he is, is a perfectly definite something, and so is the necessary. On the contrary, he lost himself, owing to the fact that this self was seen fantastically reflected in the possible.[25]

Of course, this description touches everyday man as well at the extreme of schizophrenia, and it is just the cogency of Kierkegaard's analysis that the two can be placed on the same continuum:

Instead of summoning back possibility into necessity, the man pursues the possibility—and at last cannot find his way back to himself.[26]

The same generality holds true with the following, which could describe the average man who lives in a simple world of billowing inner energy and fantasy, like Walter Mitty or what we today call "ambulatory schizophrenics"—those whose self and body are in a very tenuous relationship but manage nevertheless to carry on without being submerged by inner energies and emotions, by fantastic images, sounds, fears, and hopes they cannot contain:

But in spite of the fact that a man has become fantastic in this fashion, he may nevertheless . . . be perfectly well able to live on, to be a man, as it seems, to occupy himself with temporal things, get married, beget children, win honor and esteem—and perhaps no one notices that in a deeper sense he lacks a self.[27]

That is, he lacks a securely unified self and body, centered on his own controlling ego energies, and facing realistically up to his situation and to the nature of his limits and possibilities in the world. But this, as we shall see, is Kierkegaard's idea of consummate health, not easy to attain.

If schizophrenic psychosis is on a continuum of a kind of normal inflation of inner fantasy, of symbolic possibility, then something similar should be true of depressive psychosis. And so it is in the portrait that Kierkegaard paints. Depressive psychosis is the extreme on the continuum of *too much necessity*, that is, too much finitude, too much limitation by the body and the behaviors of the person in the real world, and not enough freedom of the inner self, of inner symbolic possibility. This is how we understand depressive psychosis today: as a bogging down in the demands of others—family, job, the narrow horizon of daily duties. In such a bogging down the individual does not feel or see that he has alternatives, cannot imagine any choices or alternate ways of life, cannot release himself from the network of obligations even though these obligations no longer give him a sense of self-esteem, of primary value, of being a heroic contributor to world life even by doing his daily family and job duties. As I once speculated,[28] the schizophrenic is not enough built into his world—what Kierkegaard has called the sickness of infinitude; the depressive, on the other hand, is built into his world too solidly, too overwhelmingly. Kierkegaard put it this way:

But while one sort of despair plunges wildly into the infinite and loses itself, a second sort permits itself as it were to be defrauded by "the others." By seeing the multitude of men about it, by getting engaged in all sorts of wordly affairs, by becoming wise about how things go in this world, such a man forgets himself . . . does not dare to believe in himself, finds it too venturesome a thing to be himself, far easier and safer to be like the others, to become an imitation, a number, a cipher in the crowd.[29]

This is a superb characterization of the "culturally normal" man, the one who dares not stand up for his own meanings because this means too much danger, too much exposure. Better not to be oneself, better to live tucked into others, embedded in a safe framework of social and cultural obligations and duties.

Again, too, this kind of characterization must be understood as being on a continuum, at the extreme end of which we find depressive psychosis. The depressed person is so afraid of being himself, so fearful of exerting his own individuality, of insisting on what might be his own meanings, his own conditions for living, that he seems literally *stupid*. He cannot seem to understand the situation he is in, cannot see beyond his own fears, cannot grasp why he has bogged down. Kierkegaard phrases it beautifully:

If one will compare the tendency to run wild in possibility with the efforts of a child to enunciate words, the lack of possibility is like being dumb . . . for without possibility a man cannot, as it were, draw breath.[30]

This is precisely the condition of depression, that one can hardly breathe or move. One of the unconscious tactics that the depressed person resorts to, to try to make sense out of his situation, is to see himself as immensely worthless and guilty. This is a marvelous "invention" really, because it allows him to move out of his condition of dumbness, and make some kind of conceptualization of his situation, some kind of sense out of it—even if he has to take full blame as the culprit who is causing so much needless misery to others. Could Kierkegaard have been referring to just such an imaginative tactic when he casually observed:

Sometimes the inventiveness of the human imagination suffices to procure possibility. . . .[31]

In any event, the condition of depression might permit an inventiveness that creates the illusion of possibility, of meaning, of action, but it does not offer any real possibility. As Kierkegaard sums it up:

The loss of possibility signifies: either that everything has become necessary to man or that everything has become trivial.[32]

Actually, in the extreme of depressive psychosis we seem to see the merger of these two: everything becomes necessary *and* trivial at the same time—which leads to complete despair. Necessity with the illusion of meaning would be the highest achievement for man; but when it becomes trivial there is no sense to one's life.

Why would a person prefer the accusations of guilt, unworthiness, ineptitude—even dishonor and betrayal—to real possibility? This may not seem to be the choice, but it is: complete self-effacement, surrender to the "others," disavowal of any personal dignity or freedom—on the one hand; and freedom and independence, movement away from the others, extrication of oneself from the binding links of family and social duties—on the other hand. This is the choice that the depressed person actually faces and that he avoids partly by his guilty self-accusation. The answer is not far to seek: the depressed person avoids the possibility of independence and more life precisely because these are what threaten him with destruction and death. He holds on to the people who have enslaved him in a network of crushing obligations, belittling interaction, precisely because these people *are his shelter,* his strength, his protection against the world. Like most everyone else the depressed person is a coward who will not stand alone on his own center, who cannot draw from within himself the necessary strength to face up to life. So he embeds himself in others; he is sheltered by the necessary and willingly accepts it. But now his tragedy is plain to see: his *necessity* has become *trivial,* and so his slavish, dependent, depersonalized life has lost its meaning. It is frightening to be in such a bind. One chooses slavery because it is safe and meaningful; then one loses the meaning of it, but fears to move out of it. One has literally died to life but must remain physically in this world. And thus the torture of depressive psychosis: to remain steeped in one's failure and yet to justify it, to continue to draw a sense of worth-whileness out of it.‡

Normal Neurosis

Most people, of course, avoid the psychotic dead ends out of the existential dilemma. They are fortunate enough to be able to stay on the middle ground of "philistinism." Breakdown occurs either because of too much possibility or too little; philistinism, as we observed earlier, knows its real enemy and tries to play it safe with freedom. Here is how Kierkegaard sums up the three alternatives available to men; the first two correspond to the psychotic syndromes of schizophrenia and depression:

For with the audacity of despair that man soared aloft who ran wild in possibility; but crushed down by despair that man strains himself against existence to whom everything has become necessary. But philistinism spiritlessly celebrates its triumph . . . imagines itself to be the master, does not take note that precisely thereby it has taken itself captive to be the slave of spiritlessness and to be the most pitiful of all things.[33]

In other words, philistinism is what we would call "normal neurosis." Most men figure out how to live safely within the probabilities of a given set of social rules. The Philistine trusts that by keeping himself at a low level of personal intensity he can avoid being pulled off balance by experience; philistinism works, as Kierkegaard said, by "tranquilizing itself with the trivial." His analysis was written almost a century before Freud spoke of the possibility of "social neuroses," the "pathology of whole cultural communities."[34]

‡ I am going to be talking about these things in Chapter Ten, but I am lingering on them here in order to show how organic a part of Kierkegaard's own understanding they are and how they can be phrased in his own concepts and language.

Other Urges to Freedom

Kierkegaard's threefold typology does not exhaust the character of man. He knows that all men are not so "immediate" or shallow, so automatically built into their culture, so securely embedded in things and in others, so trustingly a reflex of their world. Also, comparatively few people end up on the psychotic extremes of the continuum of human defeat; some win a degree of self-realization without surrender to complete spiritlessness or slavery. And here Kierkegaard's analysis becomes the most telling: he is attempting to ferret people out of the lie of their lives whose lives do not look like a lie, who seem to succeed in being true, complete and authentic persons.

There is the type of man who has great contempt for "immediacy," who tries to cultivate his interiority, base his pride on something deeper and inner, create a distance between himself and the average man. Kierkegaard calls this type of man the "introvert." He is a little more concerned with what it means to be a person, with individuality and uniqueness. He enjoys solitude and withdraws periodically to reflect, perhaps to nurse ideas about his secret self, what it might be. This, after all is said and done, is the only real problem of life, the only worthwhile preoccupation of man: What is one's true talent, his secret gift, his authentic vocation? In what way is one truly unique, and how can he express this uniqueness, give it form, dedicate it to something beyond himself? How can the person take his private inner being, the great mystery that he feels at the heart of himself, his emotions, his yearnings and use them to live more distinctively, to enrich both himself and mankind with the peculiar quality of his talent? In adolescence, most of us throb with this dilemma, expressing it either with words and thoughts or with simple numb pain and longing. But usually life suck us up into standardized activities. The social hero-system into which we are born marks out paths for our heroism, paths to which we conform, to which we shape ourselves so that we can please others, become what they expect us to be. And instead of working our inner secret we gradually cover it over and forget it, while we become purely external men, playing successfully the standardized hero-game into which we happen to fall by accident, by family connection, by reflex patriotism, or by the simple need to eat and the urge to procreate.

I am not saying that Kierkegaard's "introvert" keeps this inner quest fully alive or conscious, only that it represents somewhat more of a dimly aware problem than it does with the swallowed-up immediate man. Kierkegaard's introvert feels that he is something different from the world, has something in himself that the world cannot reflect, cannot in its immediacy and shallowness appreciate; and so he holds himself somewhat apart from that world. But not too much, not completely. It would be so nice to be the self he wants to be, to realize his vocation, his authentic talent, but it is dangerous, it might upset his world completely. He is after all, basically weak, in a position of compromise: not an immediate man, but not a real man either, even though he gives the appearance of it. Kierkegaard describes him:

. . . outwardly he is completely "a real man." He is a university man, husband and father, an uncommonly competent civil functionary even, a respectable father, very gentle to his wife and carefulness itself with respect to his children. And a Christian? Well, yes, he is that too after a sort; however, he preferably avoids talking on the subject. . . . He very seldom goes to church, because it seems to him that most parsons really don't know what they are talking about. He makes an exception in the case of one particular priest of whom he concedes that he knows what he is talking about, but he doesn't want to hear him for another reason, because he has a fear that this might lead him too far.[35]

"Too far" because he does not really want to push the problem of his uniqueness to any total confrontation:

That which as a husband makes him so gentle and as a father so careful is, apart from his good-nature and his sense of duty, the admission he has made to himself in his most inward reserve concerning his weakness.[36]

And so he lives in a kind of "incognito," content to toy—in his periodic solitudes—with the idea of who he might really be; content to insist on a "little difference," to pride himself on a vaguely-felt superiority.

Introvert.

But this is not an easy position to maintain with equanimity. It is rare, says Kierkegaard, to continue on in it. Once you pose the problem of what it means to be a person, even dumbly, weakly, or with a veneer of pride about your imagined difference from others, you may be in trouble. Introversion is impotence, but an impotence already self-conscious to a degree, and it can become troublesome. It may lead to a chafing at one's dependency on his family and his job, an ulcerous gnawing as a reaction to one's embeddedness, a feeling of slavery in one's safety. For a strong person it may become intolerable, and he may try to break out of it, sometimes by suicide, sometimes by drowning himself desperately in the world and in the rush of experience.

And this brings us to our final type of man: the one who asserts himself out of defiance of his own weakness, who tries to be a god unto himself, the master of his fate, a self-created man. He will not be merely the pawn of others, of society; he will not be a passive sufferer and secret dreamer, nursing his own inner flame in oblivion. He will plunge into life,

into the distractions of great undertakings, he will become a restless spirit . . . which wants to forget . . . Or he will seek forgetfulness in sensuality, perhaps in debauchery. . . .[37]

At its extreme, defiant self-creation can become demonic, a passion which Kierkegaard calls "demoniac rage," an attack on all of life for what it has dared to do to one, a revolt against existence itself.

In our time we would have no trouble recognizing these forms of defiant self-creation. We can see their effects so clearly on both personal and social levels. We are witness to the new cult of sensuality that seems to be repeating the sexual naturalism of the ancient Roman world. It is a living for the day alone, with a defiance of tomorrow; an immersion in the body and its immediate experiences and sensations, in the intensity of touch, swelling flesh, taste and smell. Its aim is to deny one's lack of control over events, his powerlessness, his vagueness as a person in a mechanical world spinning into decay and death. I am not saying that this is bad, this rediscovery and reassertion of one's basic vitality as an animal. The modern world, after all, has wanted to deny the person even his own body, even his emanation from his animal center; it has wanted to make him completely a depersonalized abstraction. But man kept his apelike body and found he could use it as a base for fleshy and hairy self-assertion—and damn the bureaucrats. The only thing that might be undignified about it is its desperate reflexivity, a defiance that is not reflective and so not completely self-possessed.

Socially, too, we have seen a defiant Promethianism that is basically innocuous: the confident power than can catapult man to the moon and free him somewhat of his complete dependence and confinement on earth—at least in his imagination. The ugly side of this Promethianism is that it, too, is thoughtless, an empty-headed immersion in the delights of technics with no thought to goals or meaning; so man performs on the moon by hitting golf balls that do not swerve in the lack of atmosphere. The technical triumph of a versatile ape, as the makers of the film *2001* so chillingly conveyed to us. On more ominous levels, as we shall develop later on, modern man's defiance of accident, evil, and death takes the form of sky-rocketing production of consumer and military goods. Carried to its demonic extreme this defiance gave us Hitler and Vietnam: a rage against our impotence, a defiance of our animal condition, our pathetic creature limitations. If we don't have the omnipotence of gods, we at least can destroy like gods.

The Meaning of Manhood

Kierkegaard did not need to live in our time to understand these things. Like Burckhardt he already saw them prefigured in his own day because he understood what it costs to lie about oneself. All the characters he has so far sketched represent degrees of lying about oneself in relation to the reality of the human condition. Kierkegaard has engaged in this extremely difficult and unbelievably subtle exercise for one reason and for one reason alone: to be able finally to conclude with authority what a person would be like *if he did not lie*. Kierkegaard wanted to show the many ways in which life bogs down and fails when man closes himself off against the reality of his condition. Or at best, what an undignified and pathetic creature man can be when he imagines that by living unto himself alone he is fulfilling his nature. And now Kierkegaard offers us the golden fruit of all his tortuous labors: instead of the dead-ends of human impotence, self-centeredness, and self-destruction, he now shows us *what true possibility* would be like for man.

After all, Kierkegaard was hardly a disinterested scientist. He gave his psychological description because he had a glimpse of freedom for man. He was a theorist of the open personality, of human possibility. In this pursuit, present-day psychiatry lags far behind him. Kierkegaard had no easy idea of what "health" is. But he knew what it was not: it was not normal adjustment—anything but that, as he has taken such excruciating analytical pains to show us. To be a "normal cultural man" is, for Kierkegaard, to be sick—whether one knows it or not: "there is such a thing as fictitious health."[38] Nietzsche later put the same thought: "Are there perhaps —a question for psychiatrists—neuroses of health?" But Kierkegaard not only posed the question, he also answered it. If health is not "cultural normality," then it must refer to something else, must point beyond man's usual situation, his habitual ideas. Mental health, in a word, is not typical, but ideal-typical. It is something far beyond man, something to be achieved, striven for, something that leads man beyond himself. The "healthy" person, the true individual, the self-realized soul, the "real" man, is the one who has *transcended* himself.[39]

How does one transcend himself; how does he open himself to new possibility? By realizing the truth of his situation, by dispelling the lie of his character, by breaking his spirit out of its conditioned prison. The enemy, for Kierkegaard as for Freud, is the Oedipus complex. The child has built up strategies and techniques for keeping his self-esteem in the face of the terror of his situation. These techniques become an armor that hold the person prisoner. The very defenses that he needs in order to move about with self-confidence and self-esteem become his life-long trap. In order to transcend himself he must break down that which he needs in order to live. Like Lear he must throw off all his "cultural lendings" and stand naked in the storm of life. Kierkegaard had no illusions about man's urge to freedom. He knew how comfortable people were inside the prison of their character defenses. Like many prisoners they are comfortable in their limited and protected routines, and the idea of a parole into the wide world of chance, accident, and choice terrifies them. We have only to glance back at Kierkegaard's confession in the epigraph to this chapter to see why. In the prison of one's character one can pretend and feel that he *is somebody*, that the world is manageable, that there is a reason for one's life, a ready justification for one's action. To live automatically and uncritically is to be assured of at least a minimum share of the programmed cultural heroics—what we might call "prison heroics": the smugness of the insiders who "know."

Kierkegaard's torment was the direct result of seeing the world as it really is in relation to his situation as a creature. The prison of one's character is painstakingly built to deny one thing and one thing alone: one's creatureliness. The creatureliness is the terror. Once admit that you are a defecating creature and you invite the primeval ocean of creature anxiety to flood over you. But it is more than creature anxiety, it is also man's anxiety, the anxiety that results from the human paradox that man is an animal who is conscious of his animal limitation. Anxiety is the result of the perception of the truth of one's condition. What does it mean to be a *self-conscious animal*? The idea is ludicrous, if it is not monstrous. It means to know that one is food for worms. This is the terror: to have emerged from nothing, to have a name, consciousness of self, deep inner feelings, an excruciating inner yearning for life and self-expression—and with all this yet to die. It seems like a hoax, which is why one type of cultural man rebels openly against the idea of God. What kind of deity would create such complex and fancy worm food? Cynical deities, said the Greeks, who use man's torments for their own amusement.

But now Kierkegaard seems to have led us into an impasse, an impossible situation. He has told us that by realizing the truth of our condition we can transcend ourselves. And on the other hand he tells us that the truth of our condition is our complete and abject creatureliness, which seems to push us down still further on the scale of self-realization, further away from any possibility of self-transcendence. But this is only an apparent contradiction. The flood of anxiety is not the end for man. It is, rather, a "school" that provides man with the ultimate education, the final maturity. It is a better teacher than reality, says Kierkegaard,[40] because reality can be lied about, twisted, and tamed by the tricks of cultural perception and repression. But anxiety cannot be lied about. Once you face up to it, it reveals the truth of your situation; and only by seeing that truth can you open a new possibility for yourself.

He who is educated by dread [anxiety] is educated by possibility. . . . When such a person, therefore, goes out from the school of possibility, and knows more thoroughly than a child knows the alphabet that he demands of life absolutely nothing, and that terror, perdition, annihilation, dwell next door to every man, and has learned the profitable lesson that every dread which alarms may the next instant become a fact, he will then interpret reality differently. . . .[41]

No mistake about it: the curriculum in the "school" of anxiety is the unlearning of repression, of everything that the child taught himself to deny so that he could move about with a minimal animal equanimity. Kierkegaard is thus placed directly in the Augustinian-Lutheran tradition. Education for man means facing up to his natural impotence and death.[42] As Luther urged us: "I say die, i.e., taste death as though it were present." It is only if you "taste" death with the lips of your living body that you can know emotionally that you are a creature who will die.

What Kierkegaard is saying, in other words, is that the school of anxiety leads to possibility *only by destroying* the vital lie of character. It seems like the ultimate self-defeat, the one thing that one should not do, because then one will have truly nothing left. But rest assured, says Kierkegaard, "the direction is quite normal . . . the self must be broken in order to become a self. . . ."[43] William James summed up beautifully this Lutheran tradition, in the following words:

This is the salvation through self-despair, the dying to be truly born, of Lutheran theology, the passage into *nothing* of which Jacob Behmen [Boehme] writes. To get to it, a critical point must usually be passed, a corner turned within one. Something must give way, a native hardness must break down and liquefy. . . .[44]

Again—as we saw in the last chapter—this is the destruction of the emotional character armor of Lear, of the Zen Buddhists, of modern psychotherapy, and in fact of self-realized men in any epoch. That great spirit, Ortega, has given us a particularly powerful phrasing of it. His statement reads almost exactly like Kierkegaard:

The man with the clear head is the man who frees himself from those fantastic "ideas" [the characterological lie about reality] and looks life in the face, realizes that everything in it is problematic, and feels himself lost. And this is the simple truth—that to live is to feel oneself lost —he who accepts it has already begun to find himself, to be on firm ground. Instinctively, as do the shipwrecked, he will look round for something to which to cling, and that tragic, ruthless glance, absolutely sincere, because it is a question of his salvation, will cause him to bring order into the chaos of his life. These are the only genuine ideas; the ideas of the shipwrecked. All the rest is rhetoric, posturing, farce. He who does not really feel himself lost, is without remission; that is to say, he never finds himself, never comes up against his own reality.[45]

And so the arrival at new possibility, at new reality, by the destruction of the self through facing up to the anxiety of the terror of existence. The self must be destroyed, brought down to nothing, in order for self-transcendence to begin. Then the self can begin to relate itself to powers beyond itself. It has to thrash around in its finitude, it has to "die," in order to question that finitude, in order to see beyond it. To what? Kierkegaard answers: to infinitude, to absolute transcendence, to the Ultimate Power of Creation which made finite creatures. Our modern understanding of psychodynamics confirms that this progression is very logical: if you admit that you are a creature, you accomplish one basic thing: you demolish all your unconscious power linkages or supports. As we saw in the last chapter—and it is worth repeating here—each child grounds himself in some power that transcends him. Usually it is a combination of his parents, his social group, and the symbols of his society and nation. This is the unthinking web of support which allows him to believe in himself, as he functions on the automatic security of delegated powers. He doesn't of course admit to himself that he lives on borrowed powers, as that would lead him to question his own secure action, the very confidence that he needs. He has denied his creatureliness precisely by imagining that he has secure power, and this secure power has been tapped by unconsciously leaning on the persons and things of his society. Once you expose the basic weakness and emptiness of the person, his help- lessness, then you are forced to re-examine the whole problem of power linkages. You have to think about reforging them to a real source of creative and generative power. It is at this point that one can begin to posit creatureliness *vis-à-vis* a Creator who is the First Cause of all created things, not merely the second-hand, inter- mediate creators of society, the parents and the panoply of cultural heroes. These are the social and cultural progenitors who them- selves have been caused, who themselves are embedded in a web of someone else's powers.

Once the person begins to look to his relationship to the Ultimate Power, to infinitude, and to refashion his links from those around him to that Ultimate Power, he opens up to himself the horizon of unlimited possibility, of real freedom. This is Kierkegaard's mes- sage, the culmination of his whole argument about the dead-ends of character, the ideal of health, the school of anxiety, the nature of real possibility and freedom. One goes through it all to arrive at faith, the faith that one's very creatureliness has some meaning to a Creator; that despite one's true insignificance, weakness, death, one's existence has meaning in some ultimate sense because it exists within an eternal and infinite scheme of things brought about and maintained to some kind of design by some creative force. Again and again throughout his writings Kierkegaard repeats the basic formula of faith: one is a creature who can do nothing, but one exists over against a living God for whom "everything is possible."

His whole argument now becomes crystal clear, as the keystone of faith crowns the structure. We can understand why anxiety "is the possibility of freedom," because anxiety demolishes "all finite aims," and so the "man who is educated by possibility is educated in accordance with his infinity."[46] Possibility leads nowhere if it does not lead to faith. It is an intermediate stage between cultural conditioning, the lie of character, and the opening out of infinitude to which one can be related by faith. But without the leap into faith the new helplessness of shedding one's character armor holds one in sheer terror. It means that one lives unprotected by armor, exposed to his aloneness and helplessness, to constant anxiety. In Kierkegaard's words:

Now the dread of possibility holds him as its prey, until it can deliver him saved into the hands of faith. In no other place does he find repose . . . he who went through the curriculum of misfortune offered by possibility lost everything, absolutely everything, in a way that no one has lost it in reality. If in this situation he did not behave falsely towards possibility, if he did not attempt to talk around the dread which would save him, then he received everything back again, as in reality no one ever did even if he received everything tenfold, for the pupil of possibility received infinity. . . .[47]

If we put this whole progression in terms of our discussion of the possibilities of heroism, it goes like this: Man breaks through the bounds of merely cultural heroism; he destroys the character lie that had him perform as a hero in the everyday social scheme of things; and by doing so he opens himself up to infinity, to the possibility of cosmic heroism, to the very service of God. His life thereby acquires ultimate value in place of merely social and cultural, historical value. He links his secret inner self, his authentic talent, his deepest feelings of uniqueness, his inner yearning for absolute significance, to the very ground of creation. Out of the ruins of the broken cultural self there remains the mystery of the private, invisible, inner self which yearned for ultimate significance, for cosmic heroism. This invisible mystery at the heart of every creature now attains cosmic significance by affirming its connection with the invisible mystery at the heart of creation. This is the meaning of faith. At the same time it is the meaning of the merger of psychology and religion in Kierkegaard's thought. The truly open person, the one who has shed his character armor, the vital lie of his cultural conditioning, is beyond the help of any mere "science," of any merely social standard of health. He is absolutely alone and trembling on the brink of oblivion—which is at the same time the brink of infinity. To give him the new support that he needs, the "courage to renounce dread without any dread . . . only faith is capable of," says Kierkegaard. Not that this is an easy out for man, or a cure-all for the human condition—Kierkegaard is never facile. He gives a strikingly beautiful idea:

not that [faith] annihilates dread, but remaining ever young, it is continually developing itself out of the death throe of dread.[48]

In other words, as long as man is an ambiguous creature he can never banish anxiety; what he can do instead is to use anxiety as an eternal spring for growth into new dimensions of thought and trust. Faith poses a new life task, the adventure in openness to a multi-dimensional reality.

We can understand why Kierkegaard had only to conclude his great study of anxiety with the following words which have the weight of an apodictic argument:

The true autodidact [i.e., the one who by himself goes through the school of anxiety to faith] is precisely in the same degree a theodidact . . . So soon as psychology has finished with dread, it has nothing to do but to deliver it over to dogmatics.[49]

In Kierkegaard, psychology and religion, philosophy and science, poetry and truth merge indistinguishably together in the yearning of the creature.[50]

Let us now turn to the other towering figure in the history of psychology who had the same yearning, but for whom these things did not consciously merge. Why is it that probably the two greatest students of human nature could hold such diametrically opposed opinions of the reality of faith?

CHAPTER SIX

The Problem of Freud's Character, Noch Einmal

> *The whole of sexuality and not merely anal*
> *erotism is threatened with falling a victim to the*
> *organic repression consequent upon man's*
> *adoption of the erect posture and the lowering in*
> *value of the sense of smell. . . . All neurotics, and*
> *many others too, take exception to the fact that*
> *"inter urinas et faeces nascimur". . . . Thus we*
> *should find, as the deepest root of the sexual*
> *repression that marches with culture, the organic*
> *defense of the new form of life that*
> *began with the erect posture.*
> —SIGMUND FREUD[1]

I have tried in a few pages to show that Kierkegaard understood the problem of human character and growth with an acuity that showed the uncanny mark of genius, coming as it did so long before clinical psychology. He anticipated some of the fundamentals of psychoanalytic theory and pushed beyond that theory to the problem of faith and so to the deepest understanding of man. This statement has to be defended, which is one of the tasks of this book. Inevitably, part of that defense must be some kind of sketch of the problem of Freud's character as I see it. Freud also pushed psychoanalytic theory to its limits but did not come out at faith; his character should tell us at least some of the reason.

Psychoanalysis as a Doctrine about Man's Creatureliness

One of the striking things about the Freudian revolution in thought is that we still haven't been able to digest it, nor have we been able to ignore it. Freudianism stands over and against contemporary man like an accusing specter. In this sense, as many have remarked, Freud is like a Biblical prophet, a religious iconoclast who spoke a truth that no one wants to hear and no one may ever want to hear. And that truth is, as Norman O. Brown reminded us, that Freud had no illusions about man's *basic creatureliness;* he even quoted St. Augustine.[2] On the problem of man's basic creatureliness Freud evidently felt an affinity with a religion that he otherwise had no high opinion of—to put it mildly. He had no high opinion of any religion and yet, in a matter as fundamental as the basic nature of man, we could stand him shoulder to shoulder with the Augustinian Kierkegaard.

This is a crucial matter; it explains why Freud's very pessimism and cynicism is still the most contemporary thing about his thought: it is a pessimism grounded in reality, in scientific truth. But it explains much more. Freud's dogged insistence on man's creatureliness explains almost all by itself why he insisted on an instinctual view of man, that is, it explains what is *wrong* with psychoanalytic theory. At the same time, with a slight twist to that theory, such as was given first by Rank and now by Brown, the psychoanalytic emphasis on creatureliness emerges as the lasting insight on human character.

On the first point, Freud's insistence on creatureliness as instinctive behavior, there has been no better revelation than in Jung's autobiography. Jung recalls the two occasions, in 1907 and 1910, when he discovered that he could never be friends with Freud because he could never follow the bias of his sexual theory. Let me use Jung's own words at some length to report on this critical encounter in the history of thought at the 1910 meeting in Vienna:

I can still recall vividly how Freud said to me, "My dear Jung, promise me never to abandon the sexual theory. That is the most essential thing of all. You see, we must make a dogma of it, an unshakable bulwark."

He said that to me with great emotion, in the tone of a father saying, "And promise me this one thing, my dear son: that you will go to church every Sunday." In some astonishment I asked him, "A bulwark—against what?" To which he replied, "Against the black tide of mud"—and he hesitated for a moment, then added—"of occultism." . . . What Freud seemed to mean by "occultism" was virtually everything that philosophy and religion, including the rising contemporary science of parapsychology, had learned about the psyche.

And about the earlier 1907 meeting, Jung reveals:

Above all, Freud's attitude toward the spirit seemed to me highly questionable. Wherever, in a person or in a work of art, an expression of spirituality (in the intellectual, not the supernatural sense) came to light, he suspected it, and insinuated that it was repressed sexuality. Anything that could not be directly interpreted as sexuality he referred to as "psychosexuality." I protested that this hypothesis, carried to its logical conclusion, would lead to an annihilating judgment upon culture. Culture would then appear as a mere farce, the morbid consequence of repressed sexuality. "Yes," he assented, "so it is, and that is just a curse of fate against which we are powerless to contend." . . . There was no mistaking the fact that Freud was emotionally involved in his sexual theory to an extraordinary degree. When he spoke of it, his tone became urgent, almost anxious. . . . A strange, deeply moved expression came over his face. . . .[3]

For Jung, such an attitude was unacceptable because it was not scientific. Freud seemed to him to have abandoned his normally critical and skeptical manner:

To me the sexual theory was just as occult, that is to say, just as unproven an hypothesis, as many other speculative views. As I saw it, a scientific truth was a hypothesis which might be adequate for the moment but was not to be preserved as an article of faith for all time.[4]

Jung was confused and put off by this aspect of Freud, but today it is very clear to us what was at stake. Freud evidently had the most intense belief that his authentic talent, his most private and cherished self-image and his mission for that talent, was that of a truth-teller on the unspeakables of the human condition. He saw these unspeakables as instinctive sexuality and instinctive aggression in the service of that sexuality. "Won't they get a surprise when they hear what we have to say to them!" he exclaimed to Jung as they sighted the New York skyline in 1909.[5] The "occult" was anything that lied about man's basic creatureliness, anything that tried to make out of a man a lofty, spiritual creator, qualitatively different from the animal kingdom. This kind of self-deluding and self-inflating "occultism" was ingrained in the human spirit, a matter of smug social agreement; it had been preached in all climates and from all pulpits, both religious and secular, for too long, had obscured man's real motive. It was now up to psychoanalysis all alone to attack this age-old mask, smash at it with a counter-dogma securely placed on an unshakable bulwark. Nothing weaker would do; nothing less could attack so ancient and formidable an enemy as human self-deception. And so we have the emotion of Freud's earliest entreaties to Jung, as well as the serious and measured scientific debunking of his very last writings, as in the epigraph of this chapter. His life identity was single and unbroken.

It is clear to us today, too, that Freud was wrong about the dogma, just as Jung and Adler knew right at the beginning. Man has no innate instincts of sexuality and aggression. Now we are seeing something more, the new Freud emerging in our time, that he was right in his dogged dedication to revealing man's creatureliness. His emotional involvement was correct. It reflected the true intuitions of genius, even though the particular intellectual counterpart of that emotion—the sexual theory—proved to be wrong. Man's body *was* "a curse of fate," and culture was built upon repression—not because man was a seeker only of sexuality, of pleasure, of life and expansiveness, as Freud thought, but because man was also primarily an avoider of death. *Consciousness of death* is the primary repression, not sexuality. As Rank unfolded in book after book, and as Brown has recently again argued, the new perspective on psychoanalysis is that its crucial concept is the repression of death.[6] *This* is what is creaturely about man, *this* is the repression on which culture is built, a repression unique to the self-conscious animal. Freud saw the curse and dedicated his life to revealing it with all the power at his command. But he ironically missed the precise scientific reason for the curse.

This is one of the reasons that his life until the very end was a dialogue with himself on the mainsprings of human motives. Freud tugged at his work, tried to get the truth to emerge more clearly and starkly, and yet always it seemed to become more shaded, more complex, more elusive. We admire Freud for his serious dedication, his willingness to retract, the stylistic tentativeness of some of his assertions, his lifelong review of his pet notions.* We admire him for his very deviousness, his hedgings, and his misgivings, because they seem to make of him more of an honest scientist, reflecting truthfully the infinite manifold of reality. But this is to admire him for the wrong reason. A basic cause for his own lifelong twistings was that he would never cleanly leave the sexual dogma, never clearly see or admit that the terror of death was the basic repression.

The First Great Reluctance of Freud:
the Idea of Death

It would take us into too much complexity to try to trace this problem using the writings of Freud as evidence. We mentioned earlier that in his later work he moved away from narrow sexual formulations of the Oedipus complex and turned more to the nature of life itself, to the general problems of human existence. We might say that he moved from a father-fear theory of culture to a nature-terror one.[7] But, as always, he hedged. He never became frankly an existentialist but remained bound to his instinct theory.

There seems to have been a certain reluctance in Freud, and without attempting to probe minutely into his writings, I think that this reluctance can be revealed by one key idea. This is the most important idea that emerged in his later writings, the "death instinct." After reading his introduction of this idea in *Beyond the Pleasure Principle* the conclusion seems to me inescapable that the idea of a "death instinct" was an attempt to patch up the instinct

---

* But see Paul Roazen's insight into how confident Freud was behind his use of style. See *Brother Animal: The Story of Freud and Tausk* (London: Allen Lane the Penguin Press, 1970), pp. 92–93.

theory or libido theory that he did not want to abandon but that was becoming very cumbersome and questionable in explaining human motivation. It was becoming difficult to maintain the casuistry of the dream theory that all dreams, even anxiety dreams, are fulfillments of wishes.[8] It was becoming difficult to maintain the fundamental assertion of psychoanalysis that man is purely a pleasure-seeking animal.[9] Also, man's terrors, his struggles with and against himself and others, were not easily explainable as an instinctual conflict between sexuality and aggression—especially when the individual was thought to be animated by Eros, by the libido, by the raw life force that seeks its own satisfaction and expansion.[10] Freud's new idea of the "death instinct" was a device that enabled him to keep intact the earlier instinct theory, now by attributing human evil to a deeper organic substratum than merely ego conflict with sexuality. He now held that there was a built-in urge toward death as well as toward life; and thereby he could explain violent human aggression, hate, and evil in a new—yet still biological—way: Human aggressiveness comes about through a fusion of the life instinct and the death instinct. The death instinct represents the organism's desire to die, but the organism can save itself from its own impulsion toward death by redirecting it outward. The desire to die, then, is replaced by the desire to kill, and man defeats his own death instinct by killing others. Here then was a simple new dualism that tidied up the libido theory, that allowed Freud to keep it as the bulwark of his main prophetic task: to proclaim man firmly embedded in the animal kingdom. Freud could still keep his basic allegiance to physiology, chemistry, and biology and his hopes for a total and simple reductionist science of psychology.[11]

Admittedly, by talking about defusing the instinct to die by killing others, Freud did get at the connection between one's own death and the butchery practiced by mankind. But he got at it at the price of continually intruding instincts into explanations of human behavior. Again, we see how the fusion of truthful insight with fallacious explanation has made it so difficult to untangle Freud. He seems to have been unable to reach for the really direct existentialist level of explanation, to establish both man's continuity and his difference from the lower animals on the basis of his *protest* against death rather than his built-in instinctive urge toward it. The fearfulness of human aggression, the ease with which the animal governed by Eros slaughters other living things, would be explained by such a theory even more simply and directly.[12] Killing is a symbolic solution of a biological limitation; it results from the fusion of the biological level (animal anxiety) with the symbolic one (death fear) in the human animal. As we will see in the next section, no one explained this dynamic more elegantly than Rank: "the death fear of the ego is lessened by the killing, the sacrifice, of the other; through the death of the other, one buys oneself free from the penalty of dying, of being killed."[13]

Freud's tortuous formulations on the death instinct can now securely be relegated to the dust bin of history. They are of interest only as the ingenious efforts of a dedicated prophet to maintain intellectually intact his basic dogma. But the second conclusion that we draw from Freud's labors on that problem is much more important. Despite all his leanings toward the idea of death, the hopeless situation of the child, the real terror of the external world, and the like, Freud did not need to give them a central place in his thought. He did not need to rework his vision of man from that of primarily a pleasure-seeker of sex to that of the terrified, death-avoiding animal. All he had to do was to say that man carried death within him unconsciously as part of his biology. The fiction of death as an "instinct" allowed Freud to keep the terror of death outside his formulations as a primary human problem of ego mastery. He did not have to say that death was *repressed* if the organism carried it naturally in its processes.[14] In this formulation, it is not a general human problem, much less *the* primary human problem, but is magically transformed, as Rank so succinctly put it, "from an un-wished-for necessity to a desired instinctual goal." He adds that "the comfort-giving nature of this ideology could stand neither logic nor experience for long."[15] In this way, as Rank says, Freud disposed of the "death problem" and made it into a "death instinct":

. . . even when he finally stumbled upon the inescapable death problem, he sought to give a new meaning to that also in harmony with the wish, since he spoke of death instinct instead of death fear. The fear itself he had meantime disposed of elsewhere, where it was not so threatening.... [He] made the general fear into a special sexual fear (castration fear) ... [and then sought] to cure *this* fear through the freeing of sexuality.[16]

This is a superb critique of psychoanalysis still today. As Rank lamented,

If one had held to the phenomena, it would be impossible to understand how a discussion of the death impulse could neglect the universal and fundamental death fear to such an extent as is the case in psychoanalytic literature.[17]

The psychoanalytic literature remained almost silent on the fear of death until the late 1930's and World War II. And the reason was as Rank revealed: how could psychoanalytic therapy *scientifically cure* the terror of life and death? But it could cure the problems of sex, which *it itself posited*.[18]

But more to the point of our discussion is whether the fiction of the death instinct revealed anything in Freud's personal attitude toward reality. Rank intimates that it did, by mentioning the "threatening" nature of the death fear—threatening, one must assume, not only to Freud's systematic theory. Another writer also says that it is highly probable that the idea of death as a natural goal of life brought some peace to Freud.[19] And so we are back to Freud's personal character and whatever edification we can get from it, specifically in relation to the most fundamental and terrifying problem of a human life.

Fortunately, thanks largely to Ernest Jones's biographical labor of love, we have a well-documented picture of Freud the man. We know about his lifelong migraines, his sinus, his prostate trouble, his lengthy constipations, his compulsive smoking of cigars. We have a picture of how suspicious he was of people around him, how he wanted loyalty and recognition of his seniority and priority as a thinker; how ungenerous he was toward dissenters like Adler, Jung, and Rank. His famous comment on Adler's death is absolutely cynical:

For a Jew-boy out of a Viennese suburb a death in Aberdeen is an unheard-of career in itself, and a proof how far he had got on. The world really rewarded him richly for his service of contradicting psychoanalysis.[†]

In his early years especially, Freud worked like a frenzy. This kind of frenzy requires a certain kind of work atmosphere—and Freud didn't hesitate to structure his family relations around his work in a truly patriarchal way. At the noonday meal after his psychoanalytic interviews he observed a strict silence but required everyone to be there; if there were an empty chair he would gesticulate questioningly with his fork to Martha about the absence. The completely rapt and slavish attitude of his daughter Anna alarmed even him, and he sent her to be analyzed; it is as though he was unaware of how his own staging of his greatness in the family could not fail to mesmerize those around him. We know he took his long vacation trips with his brother but never with his wife and in dozens of ways arranged his life to reflect his own sense of mission and historical destiny.

None of this is unusual: it is just interesting gossip about a great man. I mention it merely to show that Freud was neither better nor worse than other men. He seems to have had more narcissism than most, but his mother had raised him that way, as the special focus of attention and of her high hopes; she called him "my golden Sigi" until her death. His whole life style was of a dramatistic piece with the way he had always been treated. Certainly his mother's attitude had given him some added strength, as he remarked; and he carried his incurable cancer, with its horrible and painful effects, with an admirable dignity and patience. But is this, too, so truly

[†] Jones's biography, for all the wealth of candid detail it reveals about Freud, is tailored to give an heroic image of him; it is now generally agreed that it is hardly the last word in objectivity about Freud the man. Erich Fromm has shown this very pointedly in his *Sigmund Freud's Mission: An Analysis of His Personality and Influence* (New York: Grove Press, 1959). Recently, Paul Roazen has re-examined the Jones archives, along with much other digging, to present a more roundedly "human" picture of Freud. See his important book *Brother Animal*, and compare especially Freud's comments on Tausk (p. 140) to the quotation on Adler. We will introduce later more of Roazen's perspective on Freud's character. Another excellent human portrait of Freud is Helen Walker Puner's brilliant critical biography: *Freud, His Life and His Mind* (London: The Grey Walls Press, 1949).

out of the ordinary? Someone once lauded to him Franz Rosenzweig's courageous tolerance of his total paralysis, and Freud responded "What else can he do?" The same remark can be turned on Freud, as it can on all of us who suffer from illness. As for his dedication to his work, writing to the end with as little use of drugs as possible despite his pain—didn't Georg Simmel also continue to the end with his cancer, also refusing medication because it dulled his thought? Yet no one thinks of Simmel as a particularly strong character. This kind of courage is not unusual in men who see themselves as historical figures; the self-image marshals the necessary dedication to the work that will give them immortality; what is pain next to that? I think we can fairly conclude that in all this there was hardly anything about Freud that would mark him off from other men. Freud in his self-centeredness; Freud at home ruling the roost and revolving family life around his own work and ambitions; Freud in his interpersonal life, trying to influence and coerce others, wanting special esteem and loyalty, mistrusting others, lashing out at them with cutting and denigrating epithets; in all these things Freud is everyman, at least everyman who has the talent and style to be able to pull off the scenario that he would like.

But Freud was hardly the "immediate" man, dashing headlong into life without reflection. In the ways we just sketched he was ordinary; in one great way he was extraordinary—and it was this that fed directly into his genius: He was extremely self-analytic, lifted the veil from his own repressions, and tried to decipher his deepest motivations to the very end of his life. We remarked previously on what the death instinct might have meant to Freud personally, and this subject is out in the open. Unlike most men, Freud was conscious of death as a very personal and intimate problem. He was haunted by death anxiety all his life and admitted that not a day went by that he did not think about it. This is clearly unusual for the run of mankind; and it is here, I think, that we can justifiably fish around for some hints about Freud's special orientation to reality and about a "problem" unique to him. If we get hints of such a problem, I think we can use it to throw light on the overall structure of his work and its possible limits.

Freud's experiences seem to show two different approaches to the problem of death. The first is what we might call a fairly routine compulsiveness, a magic toying with the idea. For example, he seems to have played with the date of his death all his life. His friend Fliess played mystically with numbers, and Freud believed in his ideas. When Fliess predicted Freud's death at 51, according to his calculations, Freud "thought it more likely he would die in the forties from rupture of the heart."[20] When the age of 51 passed uneventfully, "Freud adopted another superstitious belief—that he had to die in February, 1918."[21] Freud often wrote and spoke to his disciples about his growing old, that he had not long to live. He especially feared dying before his mother because he was terrified at the thought that she might have to hear of his death, which would cause her grief. He had similar fears about dying before his father. Even as a young man he was in the habit of taking leave of friends by saying "Goodbye, you may never see me again."

What are we to make of all this? I think it is a fairly routine and superficial way of handling the problem of death. All these examples seem to boil down to "magical control games." Freud's concern for his mother seems like transparent displacement and rationalization: "My death does not terrify me, what terrifies me is the thought of the grief it would cause her." One is frightened by the emptiness, the gap that would be left by one's disappearance. One can't cope easily with it, but one can cope with someone else's grief over one's disappearance. Instead of experiencing the stark terror of losing oneself as a disappearing object, one clings to the image of someone else. There is nothing complicated in Freud's use of these intellectual devices.

But there is another side to Freud's response to the problem of death that is very confused. According to his biographer Jones, Freud was subject to periodic anxiety attacks in which the anxiety was localized as a real dread of dying and of traveling by rail.[22] In his attacks of dread of dying he had images of himself dying and of farewell scenes.[23] Now this is quite a different matter than compulsive, magical games with the idea of death. Here Freud seems to have unrepressed the thought of his own fading away and to have responded to it with full emotional anxiety. The train anxiety is of course a slight displacement, but not as uncontrolled as a phobia would be, as Jones agrees.[24]

Now, right away we see problems with this line of speculation. It is impossible to be clear about these things when you are dealing with them at such a distance, with printed words and not the living man. We don't know exactly how the mind works in relation to emotion, how deeply words go when dealing with reality or with repressions. Sometimes just to admit an idea to consciousness is to experience that idea vitally. At other times to admit even a deep anxiety may not mean the actual experience of that anxiety, at least not the deep experience of it, as something else may be troubling the person. Psychoanalysts talk about anxiety without affect. Can one admit the terror of death and still not experience it on deeper levels? Are images of dying and farewell as deep as the real feeling that one has absolutely no power to oppose death? To what extent can there be a partial rationalization of even the deepest anxiety? Or do these relationships change according to the period in one's life, the stress one is under?

There is no way to be clear about these subjects in the case of Freud. Jones himself is quite puzzled by Freud's different ways of reacting to the problem of death—on the one hand, anxiety attacks, on the other, heroic resignation. And in his attempt to understand them he says:

Freud always faced with complete courage any real danger to his life, which proves that the neurotic dread of dying must have had some other meaning than the literal one.[25]

Not necessarily: one can face up to the real danger of a known disease, as Freud did, because it gives one an *object*, an adversary, something against which to marshal one's courage; disease and dying are still *living* processes in which one is engaged. But to fade away, leave a gap in the world, disappear into oblivion—that is quite another matter.

Yet Jones's statement offers us a real clue about Freud because, it seems to me, he is saying that there is a difference between the fact of death and the justification of it. As one's whole life is a style or a scenario with which one tries to deny oblivion and to extend oneself beyond death in symbolic ways, one is often untouched by the fact of his death because he has been able to surround it by larger meanings. On the basis of this distinction we can say some intelligible things about Freud's death anxiety. We can try to get at what bothered him by clues from the larger style of his life, instead of by the fruitless method of trying to speculate about how deeply his thoughts made contact with his emotions.

The Second Great Reluctance of Freud

The first thing that seems to emerge clearly about Freud's stance toward reality is that, like many men, he had great trouble yielding. He could submit neither to the world nor to other men. He tried to keep a center of gravity within himself and not to let go of himself and place that center elsewhere, as is clear from his relationship to his disciples, to dissenters, and to external threats of all kinds. When at the time of the Nazi invasion his daughter wondered why they did not all just kill themselves, Freud characteristically remarked, "Because that is exactly what they want us to do."

But Freud was ambivalent about yielding. There is a lot to suggest that he toyed with the idea. A very telling anecdote is his remark when the superstitious date he had set for his death, February of 1918, passed uneventfully. He remarked: "That shows what little trust one can place in the supernatural."[26] This is a marvelous example of how one can toy with the idea of submission to larger laws and powers, but only in one's mind, dishonestly, while remaining emotionally aloof and unyielding. But there are other reports that suggest that Freud not only played with yielding but actually longed to be able to shift his center elsewhere. Once while discussing psychic phenomena, Jones made the remark: "If one could believe in mental processes floating in the air, one could go on to a belief in angels." At which point Freud closed the discussion with the comment: "Quite so, even *der liebe Gott*." Jones goes on to say that the words of Freud were said in a jocular, slightly quizzical tone. But Jones was clearly put off by the master's broaching the problem of a belief in God without a firmly negative stance. He reports: ". . . there was something searching also in the glance, and

I went away not entirely happy lest there be some more serious undertone as well."[27]

On another occasion Freud met a sister of a former patient who had died some time earlier. The sister bore a resemblance to her dead brother, and a spontaneous thought passed through Freud's mind: "So after all, it is true that the dead may return." Zilboorg, in his important discussion of Freud and religion, makes the following comment on this episode, as well as on Freud's whole ambivalent stance toward supernaturalism:

Even though Freud related that this thought was followed at once by a sense of shame, the fact remains undeniable that there was a strong emotional "streak" in Freud which bordered now on superstition, then on belief in the physical immortality of man here on earth.

It becomes also clear that Freud fought deliberately against certain spiritual trends within himself. . . . [He] seems to have been in a state of searching and painful conflict in which the positivist scholar (conscious) and the potential believer (unconscious) fought an open battle.[28]

Zilboorg then makes the following conclusion about these spiritual trends, a conclusion that supports our view that Freud was toying ambivalently with yielding to transcendent powers, being very tempted in that direction:

These trends tried to assert themselves by way of the well-known mechanism of distortion and secondary elaboration, described by Freud as characteristic of the unconscious and dreams. The trend took the form of anxious little superstitions, of involuntary and unreasonable beliefs in what the common jargon calls spiritualism.[29]

In other words, Freud gave as much vent to his spiritual trends as his character allowed him to, without his having to remake the basic foundations of that character. The most he could do was to give way to common superstitions. I think this conclusion is beyond dispute on the basis of Jones's reports alone; but we also have Freud's telling personal admission that "my own superstition has its roots in suppressed ambition (immortality). . . ."[30] That is, it has its roots in the strictly spiritual problem of transcending death, a problem that for Freud was characteristically one of *ambition*, of striving, and not of trust or yielding.

The very next logical and vital question is this: what makes the matter of yielding an ambivalent one, so difficult for Freud? The same reason that makes it so for everyman. To *yield* is to disperse one's shored-up center, let down one's guard, one's character armor, admit one's lack of *self-sufficiency*. And this shored-up center, this guard, this armor, this supposed self-sufficiency are the very things that the entire project of coming-of-age from childhood to manhood is all about. Here we have to recall our discussion in Chapter Three where we saw that the basic task that the person cuts out for himself is the attempt to father himself—what Brown so well calls the "Oedipal project." The *causa-sui* passion is an energetic fantasy that covers over the rumbling of man's fundamental creatureliness, or what we can now more pointedly call his *hopeless lack of genuine centering on his own energies to assure the victory of his life*. No creature can assure this, and man can only attempt to do so in his *fantasy*. The ambivalence of the *causa-sui* project is based on the ever-present threat of reality that peeks through. One suspects at all times that one is fundamentally helpless and impotent, but one must protest against it. The fathers and mothers always cast their shadow. What, then, is the problem of yielding? It represents nothing less than the abandonment of the *causa-sui* project, the deepest, completest, total emotional admission that there is no strength within oneself, no power to bear the superfluity of experience. To yield is to admit that support has to come from outside oneself and that justification for one's life has to come *totally* from some self-transcending web in which one consents to be suspended —as a child in its hammock-cradle, glaze-eyed in helpless, dependent admiration of the cooing mother.

If the *causa-sui* project is a lie that is too hard to admit because it plunges one back to the cradle, it is a lie that must take its toll as one tries to avoid reality. This brings us to the very heart of our discussion of Freud's character. Now we can talk pointedly about his engineering of his *causa-sui* project, and we can connect it with his absolute denial of threatening reality. I am referring, of course, to the two occasions on which Freud fainted. Fainting represents, in these cases, the ultimate denial—the refusal or inability to remain conscious in the face of a threat. The two occasions on which a great man loses complete control of himself must contain some vital intelligence about the very heart of his life-problem. Fortunately we have Jung's first-hand reports of both incidents, and I would like to quote him in full.

The first fainting took place in Bremen in 1909, while Freud and Jung were on their way to the United States to lecture about their work. Jung says that this incident was provoked—indirectly—by his interest in the "peat-bog corpses":

I knew that in certain districts of Northern Germany these so-called bog corpses were to be found. They are the bodies of prehistoric men who either drowned in the marshes or were buried there. The bog water in which the bodies lie contains humic acid, which consumes the bones and simultaneously tans the skin, so that it and the hair are perfectly preserved. . . .

Having read about these peat-bog corpses, I recalled them when we were in Bremen, but, being a bit muddled, confused them with the mummies in the lead cellars of the city. This interest of mine got on Freud's nerves. "Why are you so concerned with these corpses?" he asked me several times. He was inordinately vexed by the whole thing and during one such conversation, while we were having dinner together, he suddenly fainted. Afterward he said to me that he was convinced that all this chatter about corpses meant that I had death-wishes toward him.[31]

The second fainting incident occurred in 1912 at the time of a special strategy meeting that brought Freud and some of his followers together in Munich. Here is Jung's intimate report of the incident:

Someone had turned the conversation to Amenophis IV (Ikhnaton). The point was made that as a result of his negative attitude toward his father he had destroyed his father's cartouches on the steles, and that at the back of his great creation of a monotheistic religion there lurked a father complex. This sort of thing irritated me, and I attempted to argue that Amenophis had been a creative and profoundly religious person whose acts could not be explained by personal resistances toward his father. On the contrary, I said, he had held the memory of his father in honor, and his zeal for destruction had been directed only against the name of the god Amon, which he had everywhere annihilated; it was also chiseled out of the cartouches of his father Amon-hotep. Moreover, other pharaohs had replaced the names of their actual or divine forefathers on monuments and statues by their own, feeling that they had a right to do so since they were incarnations of the same god. Yet they, I pointed out, had inaugurated neither a new style nor a new religion.

At that moment Freud slid off his chair in a faint.[32]

The Faintings in Relation to Freud's General Life-Problem

There has been a lot of interpretation of the meaning of these fainting episodes by many sensitive students of Freud's life; Freud and Jung both gave their own interpretations. I am lingering on this subject not only because it may unlock the problem of Freud's character, but because it confirms better than anything, I think, the whole post-Freudian understanding of man that we have sketched in the first five chapters. We get the clearest understanding when we can reflect abstractions in the living mirror of a great man's life.

It was Paul Roazen who, in his recent brilliant interpretation, revealed the central meaning of these fainting spells.[33] Like Rank, Roazen understood that the psychoanalytic movement as a whole was Freud's distinctive *causa-sui* project; it was his personal vehicle for heroism, for transcendence of his vulnerability and human limitations. As we will see in the following chapters, Rank was the one who showed that the true genius has an immense problem that other men do not. He has to earn his value as a person from his work, which means that his work has to carry the burden of justifying him. What does "justifying" mean for man? It means transcending death by qualifying for immortality. The genius repeats the narcissistic inflation of the child; he lives the fantasy of the control of life and death, of destiny, in the "body" of his work. The uniqueness of the genius also cuts off his roots. He is a phenomenon that was not foreshadowed; he doesn't seem to have any traceable debts to the qualities of others; he seems to have sprung self-generated out of nature. We might say that he has the "purest" *causa-sui* project: He is truly without a family, the father of himself. As

Roazen points out, Freud had soared so far beyond his natural family that it is no surprise that he should indulge in fantasies of self-creation: "Freud came back again and again to the fantasy of being raised father-less."[34] Now, you cannot become your own father until you can have your own sons, as Roazen so well says; and natural-born sons would not do, because they do not have "the qualities of immortality associated with genius."[35] This formulation is perfect. Ergo, Freud had to create a whole new family—the psychoanalytic movement—that would be his distinctive immortality-vehicle. When he died the genius of the movement would assure his eternal remembrance and hence an eternal identity in the minds of men and in the effects of his work on earth.

But now the problem of the *causa-sui* project of the genius. In the normal Oedipal project the person internalizes the parents and the superego they embody, that is, the culture at large. But the genius cannot do this because his project is unique; it cannot be filled up by the parents or the culture. It is created specifically by a renunciation of the parents, a renunciation of what they represent and even of their own concrete persons—at least in fantasy— as there doesn't seem to be anything in them that has caused the genius. Here we see whence the genius gets his extra burden of guilt: he has renounced the father both spiritually and physically. This act gives him extra anxiety because now he is vulnerable in his turn, as he has no one to stand on. He is alone in his freedom. Guilt is a function of fear, as Rank said.

It is no surprise, then, that Freud would be particularly sensitive to the idea of father-murder. We can imagine that father-murder would be a complex symbol for him, comprising the heavy guilt of standing alone in his vulnerability, an attack on his identity as a father, on the psychoanalytic movement as his *causa-sui* vehicle, and thus on his immortality. In a word, father-murder would mean his own insignificance as a creature. It is just such an interpretation that the fainting episodes point to. The years around 1912 were the time when the future of the psychoanalytic movement crystallized as a problem. Freud was looking for an heir, and it was Jung who was to be the "son" whom he had proudly chosen as his spiritual successor and who would assure the success and continuation of psychoanalysis. Freud literally burdened Jung with his hopes and expectations, so prominent was his place in Freud's life-plan.[36] Thus we can understand how completely logical it is that Jung's defection from the movement would—all by itself—invoke the complex symbol of father-murder and stand for the death of Freud.[37]

No wonder that on the occasion of the first fainting Freud accused Jung of "death-wishes" toward him and that Jung felt himself entirely innocent of any such wishes. He says that he "was more than surprised by this interpretation."[38] To him these were fantasies of Freud's, but fantasies of great intensity, "so strong that, obviously, they could cause him to faint." Of the second occasion Jung says that the whole atmosphere was very tense; whatever other causes may have contributed to Freud's fainting, the fantasy of father-murder was evidently again involved. In fact, the atmosphere of rivalry hovered over the whole luncheon meeting. It was a strategy meeting loaded with possibilities of dissention in the psychoanalytic ranks. Jones communicated this in his version of the 1912 faintings:

. . . as we were finishing luncheon . . . [Freud] began reproaching the two Swiss, Jung, and Riklin, for writing articles expounding psychoanalysis in the Swiss periodicals without mentioning his name. Jung replied that they had thought it unnecessary to do so, it being so well known, but Freud had sensed already the first signs of the dissension that was to follow a year later. He persisted, and I remember thinking he was taking the matter rather personally. Suddenly, to our consternation, he fell on the floor in a dead faint.[39]

Jung is hardly convincing in his graceful denials of rivalry with Freud, in his disingenuous explanations for why the Swiss were omitting to mention Freud's name. Even in his denial of harboring death-wishes toward Freud, he makes plain his competitiveness.

Why should I want him to die? I had come to learn. He was not standing in my way; he was in Vienna, I was in Zurich.[40]

On the one hand he admits that he is in a learning relationship to Freud the master; on the other he attempts to establish that he stands on his own, on equal footing. Freud could surely sense the threat to his priority, which would actually be an act of filial treason to him.[41] Jung was drifting away from the fold, threatening a rivalry with the Swiss branch of psychoanalysis. What would happen to the "father" then, and all he stood for? The fact is that Freud fainted at the precise moment that Jung made light of the matter of priorities in the founding of a new Egyptian religion by Amenophis IV. This threatened Freud's whole life's missionary work. Freud had a picture of the Sphinx and the pyramids prominently displayed in his consulting room, his innermost sanctum. This was for him no romantic image or archaeological hobby. Egypt stood for the whole mysterious and dark past of mankind that psychoanalysis was chosen to decipher.[42] There is, Roazen says, a direct association between twentieth-century psychoanalysis and ancient Egyptology, between Amenophis' scratching out his father's name on the steles and Jung's doing the same from Zurich. Jung was attacking Freud's immortality.

But this attack was in Freud's eyes and not necessarily in Jung's. That he talked on about the peat-bog corpses at the time of the first fainting could well reflect existential anxieties, pure and simple. Jung was fascinated by the idea of death. We can well imagine the younger Jung, also anxious about the voyage to America, lingering on the problem of bodies in the presence of a man he looked up to because he wanted to broach something that fascinated him to a thinker who might ruminate with him, perhaps add his own insight into the mystery of bodies, death, and destiny. On the other hand, Erich Fromm (who is hardly a fan of Jung's) has diagnosed him as a necrophilous character. On the basis of one of Jung's dreams at the time of his break with Freud, Fromm believes that Jung did have unconscious death-wishes toward Freud.[43]

Yet all this speculation is beside the point, because we are talking about Freud's own perceptions and problems. From this point of view the significant thing about the occasion of the first fainting is that the talk of mummies came up because of Jung's confusion about the corpses. Freud's anxieties on *both* occasions are thereby tied to the same subjects of Egypt and the effacing of the father. Also, it is important to note that on this historic voyage Jung had been invited for his own work and not necessarily because of his connection with Freud; he was literally and openly a competitor.

The Interpretations of Jones and Freud

We get even further "inside" the problem of Freud's perceptions when we look at his own attempts to understand what had happened to him. Jones tells a somewhat different story of the occasion of the first fainting than did Jung. Jones says that what characterized the 1909 meeting was that Freud, after some argument, persuaded Jung to drink wine during the luncheon party and so broke Jung's fanatical abstinence. It was "just after that" that Freud fell down in a faint.[44] At the later 1912 meeting, a similar thing happened. There had been some strain between Jung and Freud, and after a "good fatherly lecture" Jung became "extremely contrite, accepted all the criticisms" of Freud, and "promised to reform." Freud was in very high spirits, having won Jung round again. Jones concludes that what characterized both meetings was that Freud had won a victory over Jung.[45]

What relationship does victory have to fainting? Only with the genius of Freud's own theory can such a relationship be meaningfully explained. As we saw in Chapter Four, it was Freud who discovered the idea of being "wrecked by success": that when a person achieves the truly superlative, it is often felt as an intolerable burden because it means that he has won out in competition with the father, having excelled him. No wonder, then, that when Freud himself later analyzed the fainting attacks, he could lean on his own discovery with a probing and ruthless honesty. He explained that as a child he had often wished the death of his baby brother Julius, and when Julius did die when Freud was a year and seven months old, it left Freud with a terrible sense of guilt. Jones comments:

It would therefore seem that Freud was himself a mild case of the type he described as "those who are wrecked by success," in this case the success of defeating an opponent [Jung]—the earliest example of which was his successful death-wish against his little brother Julius. One thinks in this connection of the curious attack of obfuscation Freud suffered on the Acropolis in 1904, one which, when he was eighty-one years old, he analyzed and traced to his having gratified the forbidden wish to excel his father. In fact Freud himself mentioned the resemblance between that experience and the type of reaction we are considering.[46]

In other words, all victories over a rival, including his own father, reawaken the guilt of victory and trigger the reaction of being unable to bear it. We have to understand what "victory" means in Freud's cosmology in order to get the impact of the anxiety and understand why one would faint. It is explained by the dynamics of the classic Oedipus complex. The victory "prize" is of course the mother whom the boy covets, and to win out against the father means to do away with him. If the child loses, the vengeance will be terrible; and if he wins, the guilt is naturally overwhelming.

Now the classic Oedipus complex does undoubtedly explain some cases of fear of victory; but Freud himself later abandoned the strictly sexual dynamics of the problem, at least in his own case. He frankly admitted toward the end of his life that his reluctance to surpass his father was based on a feeling of "piety" for him.[47] This was the meaning of the attack on the Acropolis that Jones mentions. Today, as some writers are arguing, we would guess that the word "piety" might be a euphemism for other feelings that Freud had toward his father: that he was really troubled by the weakness of his father, which cast a shadow on his own strength, and that for that reason he felt exposed and anxious when he thought about his own success.

We are thus already on a broader and more existential ground in explaining the overwhelmingness of victory. Already two generations of students have raised their eyebrows over how a 19-month-old Freud could be so acutely analytic about his experience that he could reproach himself that his jealousy and evil wishes resulted in his brother Julius's death. Even Freud himself discounted this level of awareness in his own theoretical work: he said that it was almost impossible for a child that young to be jealous of a newcomer. Jones, who recorded all this, evidently cannot make sense out of it.[48]

Jones says that Freud's own "wrecked-by-success" analysis of his fainting is confirmed by the fact that on the occasion of each fainting there was an argumentative discussion on the topic of death-wishes. This is perfectly true, but not in the precise way that Freud wanted to show it, as tied to the strength of victory. Very likely Freud is making a mistake that he often makes, of trying to peg down too precisely what is actually part of a complex symbol and a much larger problem. I mean of course the sense of the overwhelmingness of experience, of being carried too far off one's home base, of not having the power to support the superlative. That sense is what characterizes both fainting incidents, in addition to the specific presence of Jung. It is reasonable to broaden the burden placed on Freud beyond that of a reaction to Jung alone. After all, he supported on his shoulders one of the great iconoclastic movements of human thought, against all competition, all hostility, all denigration, all the other more "spiritual" ("occult") meanings that mankind held so sacred, all the other minds who thought such sublime thoughts, insisted on such widely-held truths, enjoyed so much support and acclaim throughout the ages. His organism in its deepest layers is well entitled to feel impossibly burdened by such a weight and to sink beneath it in pleasureful oblivion. Would we dare to imagine that one can support all this superordinacy easily, without superhuman powers on which to lean? How to take a stance toward all this impersonal and historical, as well as personal, concrete, and physical transcendence: the pyramids, the peat-bog corpses, one's own new religion? It is as though one's whole organism were to declare: "I can't bear it, I haven't the strength to stand up to it." Admittedly, the strong and large figure of Jung, an original thinker, standing independently and even arguing and opposing Freud, adds to all this; but Jung's concrete presence is only one aspect of a general power problem. In this sense, even to finally win out against Jung was for Freud to put the whole weight of the psychoanalytic movement squarely on his own shoulders. We can see how apt the "wrecked-by-success" insight is, though not according to the specific dynamics that Freud had in mind.

The Emotional Ambivalence of Causa Sui

The crux of our whole discussion is contained in one confession of Freud's to Karl Abraham: that helplessness was one of the two things that he always hated most.[49] (The other was poverty—because it means helplessness.) Freud hated helplessness and fought against it, and the emotional feeling of utter helplessness in the face of experience was too much for him to stand. It gave full play to the underside of dependency that he tried to control. This kind of continued self-shaping by a man thrust into Freud's leadership position must have consumed enormous amounts of energy. No wonder that, as Freud was coming to after his second fainting, he was heard to say: "How sweet it must be to die."[50] And there is no reason to doubt Jung's report of the occasion, which is all of a piece:

As I was carrying him, he half came to, and I shall never forget the look he cast at me as if I were his father.[31]

How sweet it must be to let go of the colossal burden of a self-dominating, self-forming life, to relax one's grip on one's own center, and to yield passively to a superordinate power and authority—and what joy in such yielding: the comfort, the trust, the relief in one's chest and shoulders, the lightness in one's heart, the sense of being sustained by something larger, less fallible. With his own distinctive problems, man is the only animal who can often willingly embrace the deep sleep of death, even while knowing that it means oblivion.

But there is the ambivalence that Freud—like all of us—was caught in. To melt oneself trustingly into the father, or the father-substitute, or even the Great Father in the sky, is to abandon the *causa-sui* project, the attempt to be father of oneself. And if you abandon that you are diminished, your destiny is no longer your own; you are the eternal child making your way in the world of the elders. And what kind of world is that, if you are trying to bring into it something of your own, something distinctively new, world-historical, and revolutionary? That is why Freud had to fight against yielding—he risked effacing his whole identity. He was spinning his own web; how could he suspend himself in someone else's? It was Rank more than anyone who understood the problem of mere mortals who are saddled with the works of genius: Where are they to get the support for their own daring and overshadowing creations? We will see Rank's views in the next chapter; here it is already obvious that Freud chose to pursue his *causa-sui* project by using his own work and his own organization—the psychoanalytic movement—as a mirror *to reflect power back upon himself*. We said earlier that the *causa-sui* project is a lie that must take its toll; now we can understand that this toll is an emotional one that must always carry both the temptation to admit helpless dependence and the fight against that admission. One lives with a certain amount of tight-lipped determination.‡

There is further support for this view in Freud's fifteen-year relationship with Fliess. Brome is of the opinion that this relationship was an emotional one more powerful than any previous biographer has acknowledged; and he cites Freud's own admissions of his very profound and "obscure" feelings in relation to Fliess. It is more than a coincidence, then, that years earlier Freud had suffered symptoms in relationship to Fliess similar to those he suffered toward Jung— and in the very same room of the same hotel as at the 1912 meeting. At that earlier time the symptoms were not so intense, and they were directed not toward a strong opposing figure but toward an ailing Fliess. When Freud analyzed this he said that "there is some piece of unruly homosexual feeling at the root of the matter." Jones reports that Freud several times remarked on the "feminine side of his nature."[52]

Even though Freud's self-analytic honesty was unusual, we still have to be skeptical about it. It is possible for any man to have specific homosexual urges, and Freud need be no exception. Still, knowing Freud's lifelong tendency to reduce vaguely anxious feelings to specific sexual motivations, we are entitled to assume that his "unruly" urges could just as well have represented the ambivalence of dependency needs. Jones himself has honestly averaged the problem of homosexuality into his appraisal of Freud's character, and I think gave it its proper weight. Jones says that this was part of the underside of dependency in Freud, a dependency that led him astray in some ways, for example, in his tendency to overestimate certain people—Breuer, especially Fliess, and also Jung. Jones goes so far as to say that this side of Freud stemmed from "some impairment of self-confidence."[53] Certainly Freud loathed

‡ Erich Fromm, in his important discussion of Freud's character, also fixes on helplessness and dependency as the underside of Freud and so also confirms Jones. But Fromm seems to me to accent it too much as an ambivalent reflex of Freud's childhood relationship to his mother, whereas I am seeing it more as a universal phenomenon reacting to Freud's distinctive heroic ambition and burdens. See Fromm, *Sigmund Freud's Mission,* Chapter 5.

this side of his nature and welcomed the self-dependence he earned when a part of his "homosexual" dependency was revealed for the weakness that it was. He wrote to Ferenczi on October 6, 1910, that he had overcome the passivity he experienced toward Fliess and that he no longer had any need to uncover his personality completely:

Since Fliess's case . . . that need has been extinguished. A part of homosexual cathexis has been withdrawn and made use of to enlarge my ego.[54]

The ego is the thing; it alone gives self-governance, the ability to have a certain freedom of action and choice, to shape one's own destiny as much as possible. Today we generally see homosexuality as a broad problem of ineptness, vague identity, passivity, helplessness—all in all, an inability to take a powerful stance toward life. In this sense, Jones would be right to talk about an impairment of self-confidence in Freud, as he showed it both toward the strong figure of Jung and the ailing one of Fliess. In both cases it is one's own strength that is threatened with an added burden.

On the other hand, our modern understanding of homosexuality goes to an even deeper level of the problem—to the level of immortality and heroism that we have already discussed in relation to Freud and to genius in general. Rank wrote about this subject brilliantly. We will want to talk about his work in Chapter Ten, but we need to linger on it here in specific relation to Freud. We said that the truly gifted and free spirit attempts to bypass the family as the instrument of distinctive procreation. It is only logical, then, that if the genius is going to follow to the letter the *causa-sui* project, he comes up against one large temptation: to bypass the woman and the species role of his own body. It is as though he reasons: "I do not exist to be used as an instrument of physical procreation in the interests of the race; my individuality is so total and integral that I include my body in my *causa-sui* project." And so, the genius can try to procreate himself spiritually through a linkage with gifted young men, to create them in his own image, and to pass the spirit of his genius on to them. It is as though he were to try to duplicate himself exactly, spirit and body. After all, anything that detracts from the free flight of one's spiritual talent must seem debasing. The woman is already a threat to the man in his physical-ness; it is only a small step to bypass sexual intercourse with her; in that way one keeps one's carefully girded center from dispersing and being undermined by ambiguous meanings. Most men are con-tent to keep their meanings firmly in hand by refraining from extra-marital infidelity; but one can narcissistically harbor his meanings even more by refraining from "heterosexual infidelity," so to speak.

From this point of view, when Freud talked about "the feminine side of his nature" he could just as well have been speaking from the strength of his ego rather than its weakness, from his own single-minded determination to engineer his own immortality. It is common knowledge that sexual relations between Freud and his wife came to an end around the age of forty-one and that he was strictly monogamous so far as we know. This behavior would be all of a piece with his *causa-sui* project: the narcissistic self-inflation that denies dependency on the female body and on one's species-given role and the control and harboring of the power and meaning of one's individuality. As Roazen points out, in Freud's own words he saw his hero as:

. . . a man whose sexual need and activity were exceptionally reduced, as if a higher aspiration had raised him above the common animal need of mankind.[55]

Evidently Freud poured his whole passion into the psychoanalytic movement and his own immortality. They were his "higher aspira-tion," which could also reasonably include a spiritual homosexuality that offered no threat as an "animal need."

The Conceptual Ambivalence of Causa Sui

So far we have been talking about emotional ambivalence, but there is also a conceptual side to the matter. It is one thing to face up to and admit an emotional reaction to the experience of fading away; it is still another thing to justify that fading. Freud could admit dependency and helplessness, but how give his own death any meaning? He either had to justify it from within his *causa-sui* project, the psychoanalytic movement, or from somewhere outside that project. Here is the ambivalence of *causa sui* on a conceptual level: how can one trust any meanings that are not man-made? These are the only meanings that we securely know; nature seems unconcerned, even viciously antagonistic to human meanings; and we fight by trying to bring our own dependable meanings into the world. But human meanings are fragile, ephemeral: they are constantly being discredited by historical events and natural calamities. One Hitler can efface centuries of scientific and religious meanings; one earthquake can negate a million times the meaning of a personal life. Mankind has reacted by trying to secure human meanings from beyond. Man's best efforts seem utterly fallible without appeal to something higher for justification, some conceptual support for the meaning of one's life from a transcendental dimension of some kind. As this belief has to absorb man's basic terror, it cannot be merely abstract but must be rooted in the emotions, in an inner feeling that one is secure in something stronger, larger, more important than one's own strength and life. It is as though one were to say: "My life pulse ebbs, I fade away into oblivion, but "God" (or "It") remains, even grows more glorious with and through my living sacrifice." At least, this feeling is belief at its most effective for the individual.

The problem of how far a life has to reach to earn secure heroic meaning obviously bothered Freud very much. According to psychoanalytic theory, the child meets the terror of life and aloneness first by asserting his own omnipotence and then by using the cultural morality as the vehicle for his immortality. By the time we grow up, this confident, delegated immortality becomes a major defense in the service of the equanimity of our organism in the face of danger. One of the main reasons that it is so easy to march men off to war is that deep down each of them feels sorry for the man next to him who will die. Each protects himself in his fantasy until the shock that he is bleeding. It is logical that if you are one of the few who admits the anxiety of death, then you must question the fantasy of immortality, which is exactly the experience of Freud. Zilboorg affirms that the problem troubled Freud all his life. He yearned for fame, anticipated it, hoped that through it he could create his own immortality: "Immortality means being loved by many anonymous people." This definition is the Enlightenment view of immortality: living in the esteem of men yet unborn, for the works that you have contributed to their life and betterment.

But it is an entirely "this-worldly" immortality—there's the rub. It must have rubbed Freud very gratingly. His views on immortality were charged with a "severe ambivalence, even multivalence."[56] Even early in life he told his fiancée that he had destroyed all the letters he had received, adding ironically and triumphantly that his future biographers would be hard put to find data about him after he had gone from this earth. Later in life he said a similar thing about his letters to Fliess: if he had gotten hold of them instead of one of his disciples, he would have destroyed them rather than letting "so-called posterity" have them. Zilboorg seems to think that this oscillation between desire for immortality and scorn for it reflects Freud's unfortunate habit of forming polarities in his thought; but to me it seems like more magical toying with reality: As you fear that life in this dimension may not count, may not have any real meaning, you relieve your anxiety by being especially scornful of the very thing that you wish for most, while underneath your writing desk you have your fingers crossed.

On the one hand you make psychoanalysis your private religion, your own royal road to immortality; on the other you are unique and isolated enough to question the whole career of man on this planet. At the same time you cannot abandon the project of your own creation of immortality, because the religious promise of immortality is a pure illusion, fit for children and for the credulous man in the street. Freud was in this terrible bind; as he confessed to the Reverend Oskar Pfister:

I can imagine that several million years ago in the Triassic age all the great -odons and -therias were very proud of the development of the Saurian race and looked forward to heaven knows what magnificent future for themselves. And then, with the exception of the wretched crocodile, they all died out. You will object that . . . man is equipped with mind, which gives him the right to think about and believe in his future. Now there is certainly something special about mind, so little is known about it and its relation to nature. I personally have a vast respect for mind, but has nature? Mind is only a little bit of nature, the rest of which seems to be able to get along very well without it. Will it really allow itself to be influenced to any great extent by regard for mind?

Enviable he who can feel more confident about that than I.[57]

It is hard for a man to work steadfastly when his work can mean no more than the digestive noises, wind-breakings, and cries of dinosaurs—noises now silenced forever. Or perhaps one works all the harder to defy the callous unconcern of nature; in that way one might even compel her to defer to the products of mysterious mind, by making words and thoughts an unshakable monument to man's honesty about his condition. This is what makes man strong and true—that he defies the illusory comforts of religion. Human illusions prove that men do not deserve any better than oblivion. So Freud must have reasoned as he made psychoanalysis the competitor of religion. Psychoanalytic science would establish the true facts of the moral world and would reform it—if anything could. We see why psychoanalysis itself was a religion for Freud, as so many authoritative thinkers from Jung and Rank to Zilboorg and Rieff have remarked.

All this can be put another way: that Freud set out to defy nature by redoubling efforts to make true the lie of *causa sui*. Zilboorg, in his penetrating assessment of Freud and religion, closed on these remarks:

Ever since man started his so-called "conquest of nature," he has tried to fancy himself the conqueror of the universe. In order to assure himself of the mastery of a conqueror, he grabbed the trophy (nature, universe). He had to feel that the Maker of the trophy was annihilated, or his own fantasied sovereignty over the universe would be endangered. It is this trend that is reflected in Freud's unwillingness to accept religious faith in its true meaning. . . . It is no surprise, therefore, to find that in the field of human psychology a man, no matter how great—a man like Freud—had constantly before him the vision of a man who is always unhappy, helpless, anxious, bitter, looking into nothingness with fright, and turning away from "so-called posterity" in anticipatory . . . disgust.[58]

Zilboorg says that Freud was driven into a rigid, almost solipsistic intellectual attitude by "his need to rid himself of any suspicion of intellectual dependence on others or spiritual dependence on a personal God."[59] The lie of *causa sui* becomes especially driven because of what one will not or cannot acknowledge; then the very truth with which one seeks to defy nature suffers.

Jung, who would agree with Zilboorg, offers what to me seems the briefest and most apt summary of Freud's characterological life-problem:

Freud never asked himself why he was compelled to talk continually of sex, why this idea had taken such possession of him. He remained unaware that his "monotony of interpretation" expressed a flight from himself, or from that other side of him which might perhaps be called mystical. So long as he refused to acknowledge that side, he could never be reconciled with himself. . . .

There was nothing to be done about this one-sidedness of Freud's. Perhaps some inner experience of his own might have opened his eyes. . . . He remained the victim of the one aspect he could recognize, and for that reason I see him as a tragic figure; for he was a great man, and what is more, a man in the grip of his daimon.[60]

What, actually, does it mean to be a tragic figure firmly in the grip of one's daimon? It means to possess great talent, to relentlessly pursue the expression of that talent through the unswerving affirmation of the *causa-sui* project that alone gives it birth and form. One is consumed by what he must do to express his gift. The passion of his character becomes inseparable from his dogma. Jung says the same thing beautifully when he concludes that Freud "must himself be so profoundly affected by the power of Eros that he actually wished to elevate it into a dogma . . . like a religious numen."[61] Eros is precisely the natural energy of the child's organism that will not let him rest, that keeps propelling him forward in a driven way while he fashions the lie of his character—which ironically *permits* that very drivenness to continue, but now under the illusion of self-control.

Conclusion

Now as we draw the circle on the very beginning of our discussion of Freud, we can see that his two great reluctances, as we have called them, are related, and in fact merge into one. On the one hand he refused to move away cleanly from his instinct theory to the more blanket idea of a death fear. In the second place he refused to move into a yielding posture toward external nature; he was unable to give large expression to the mystical, dependent side of himself. It seems to me that the two reluctances are related in his refusal to abandon the *causa-sui* project, which would have led to a larger problematic view of human creatureliness. But such a view is the seeding-ground of faith, or at least brings the person right up to faith as an experiential reality and not an illusion. Freud never allowed himself to step upon this ground. Eros is a narrowing down, in Freud, of a broader experiential horizon. Or, put another way, in order to move from *scientific* creatureliness to *religious* creatureliness, the terror of *death* would have to replace *sex*, and inner *passivity* would have to replace obsessive Eros, the drive of the creature. And it was just this twofold yielding—inner emotional and conceptual—that Freud could not quite manage. For to do so, as Jung judged with understanding, would mean to abandon his own diamon, his whole unique passion as a genius, the very gift that he had fashioned for mankind.

PART II

THE FAILURES
OF HEROISM

Neurosis and psychosis are modes of expression for human beings who have lost courage. Anyone who has acquired this much insight . . . will thenceforth refrain from undertaking with persons in this state of discouragement tedious excursions into mysterious regions of the psyche.
—ALFRED ADLER

CHAPTER SEVEN

The Spell Cast by Persons—
The Nexus of Unfreedom

*Ah, mon cher, for anyone who is alone, without
God and without a master, the weight of days
is dreadful. Hence one must choose a master, God
being out of style.*
—ALBERT CAMUS[1]

*. . . men, incapable of liberty—who cannot stand
the terror of the sacred that manifests itself
before their open eyes—must turn to mystery,
must hide . . . the . . . truth.*
—CARLO LEVI[2]

For ages men have reproached themselves for their folly—that they gave their loyalty to this one or that, that they believed so blindly and obeyed so willingly. When men snap out of a spell that has very nearly destroyed them and muse on it, it doesn't seem to make sense. How can a mature man be so fascinated, and why? We know that all through history masses have followed leaders because of the magic aura they projected, because they seemed larger than life. On the surface this explanation seems enough because it is reasonable and true to fact: men worship and fear power and so give their loyalty to those who dispense it.

But this touches only the surface and is besides too practical. Men don't become slaves out of mere calculating self-interest; the slavishness is in the soul, as Gorky complained. The thing that has to be explained in human relations is precisely the *fascination of the person* who holds or symbolizes power. There is something about him that seems to radiate out to others and to melt them into his aura, a "fascinating effect," as Christine Olden called it, of "the narcissistic personality"[3] or, as Jung preferred to call him, the "mana-personality."[4] But people don't actually radiate blue or golden auras. The mana-personality may try to work up a gleam in his eye or a special mystification of painted signs on his forehead, a costume, and a way of holding himself, but he is still *Homo sapiens*, standard vintage, practically indistinguishable from others unless one is especially interested in him. The mana of the mana-personality is in the eyes of the beholder; the fascination is in the one who experiences it. This is the very thing that has to be explained: if all people are more or less alike, why do we burn with such all-consuming passions for some of them? What are we to make of the following report by a winner of the Miss Maryland contest who describes her first meeting with Frank Sinatra (a crooner and film star who gained wealth and notoriety in the middle decades of the 20th century in the United States):

He was my date. I got a massage, and I must have taken five aspirins to calm myself down. In the restaurant, I saw him from across the room, and I got such butterflies in my stomach and such a thing that went from head to toe. He had like a halo around his head of stars to me. He projected something I have never seen in my life. . . . when I'm with him I'm in awe, and I don't know why I can't snap out of it. . . . I can't think. He's so fascinating. . . .[5]

Imagine a scientific theory that could explain human slavishness by getting at its nexus; imagine that after ages of laments about human folly men would at last understand exactly why they were so fatally fascinated; imagine being able to detail the precise causes of personal thralldom as coldly and as objectively as a chemist separates elements. When you imagine all these things you will realize better than ever the world-historical importance of psychoanalysis, which alone revealed this mystery. Freud saw that a patient in analysis developed a peculiarly intense attachment to the person of the analyst. The analyst became literally the center of his world and his life; he devoured him with his eyes, his heart swelled with joy at the sight of him; the analyst filled his thoughts even in his dreams. The whole fascination has the elements of an intense love affair, but it is not limited to women. Men show the "same attachment to the physician, the same overestimation of his qualities, the same adoption of his interest, the same jealousy against all those connected with him."[6] Freud saw that this was an uncanny phenomenon, and in order to explain it he called it "transference." The patient transfers the feelings he had towards his parents as a child to the person of the physician. He blows the physician up larger than life just as the child sees the parents. He becomes as dependent on him, draws protection and power from him just as the child merges his destiny with the parents, and so on. In the transference we see the grown person as a child at heart, a child who distorts the world to relieve his helplessness and fears, who sees things as he wishes them to be for his own safety, who acts automatically and uncritically, just as he did in the pre-Oedipal period.[7]

Freud saw that transference was just another form of the basic human suggestibility that makes hypnosis possible. It was the same passive surrender to superior power,[8] and in this lay its real uncanniness. What, after all, is more "mysterious" than hypnosis, the sight of adults falling into instant stupors and obeying like automatons the commands of a stranger? It seems like some truly supernatural power at work, as if some person really did possess a mana that could enmesh others in a spell. However, it seemed that way only because man ignored the slavishness in his own soul. He wanted to believe that if he lost his will it was because of someone else. He wouldn't admit that this loss of will was something that he himself carried around as a secret yearning, a readiness to respond to someone's voice and the snap of his fingers. Hypnosis was a mystery only as long as man did not admit his own unconscious motives. It baffled us because we denied what was basic in our nature. Perhaps we could even say that men were all too willingly mystified by hypnosis because they had to deny the big lie upon which their whole conscious lives were based: the lie of self-sufficiency, of free self-determination, of independent judgment and choice. The continuing vogue of vampire movies may be a clue to how close to the surface our repressed fears are: the anxiety of losing control, of coming completely under someone's spell, of not really being in command of ourselves. One intense look, one mysterious song, and our lives may be lost forever.

All this was brought out beautifully by Ferenczi in 1909, in a
basic essay that has not been much improved upon in a half-century
of psychoanalytic work.[9]* Ferenczi pointed out how important it
was for the hypnotist to be an imposing person, of high social rank,
with a self-confident manner. When he gave his commands the
patient would sometimes go under as if struck by *"coup de foudre."*
There was nothing to do but obey, as by his imposing, authoritarian
figure the hypnotist took the place of the parents. He knew "just
those ways of frightening and being tender, the efficacy of which
has been proved for thousands of years in the relations of parent
to child."[10] We see the same technique used by revivalists as they
alternatingly harangue their audiences with a shrieking voice and
then immediately soothe them with a soft one. With a heart-rending
scream of agony and ecstasy one throws himself at the revivalist's
feet to be saved.

As the highest ambition of the child is to obey the all-powerful
parent, to believe in him, and to imitate him, what is more natural
than an instant, imaginary return to childhood via the hypnotic
trance? The explanation of the ease of hypnosis, said Ferenczi, is
that "In our innermost soul we are still children, and we remain
so throughout life."[11] And so, in one theoretical sweep Ferenczi

---

* I am aware of the enormous literature on transference and the extensions,
modifications, and debates raging around it; but it would go far beyond my
purposes to attempt to reflect the technical literature here. We will see further
on some of the crucial ways in which our understanding of transference goes
beyond Freud and Ferenczi. But I am not sure that the technical arguments
among psychoanalysts, on the precise nature of transference, hypnosis, and the
like add much to their basic understanding of the phenomenon. Trigant Burrow's early attempt to make transference entirely a problem of social learning
seems to me a clear fallacy, as we will see further on. (Trigant Burrow, "The
Problem of the Transference," *British Journal of Medical Psychology,* 1927,
vol. 7, pp. 193–202) Freud seems to me still correct to discount physiological
theories of induction into the hypnotic trance, in spite of Kubie and Margolin's
later argument (cf. Freud, *Group Psychology and the Analysis of the Ego,*
1922 (New York: Bantam Books edition, 1960), p. 74; and L. S. Kubie and
Sydney Margolin, "The Process of Hypnotism and the Nature of the Hypnotic
State," *American Journal of Psychiatry,* 1944, vol. 180, pp. 611–622); cf. also
Merton M. Gill and Margaret Brenman, *Hypnosis and Related States: Psychoanalytic Studies in Regression* (New York: Science Editions, 1959), pp. 143,
196–7. The area where the most meaningful revision of the theory of the
transference has been made is, of course, its use and interpretation in therapy;
and this is clearly outside my discussion.

could destroy the mystery of hypnosis by showing that the subject carries in himself the predisposition to it:

> . . . there is no such thing as a "hypnotising," a "giving of ideas" in the sense of psychical incorporating of something quite foreign from without, but only procedures that are able to set going unconscious, preexisting, auto-suggestive mechanisms. . . . According to this conception, the application of suggestion and hypnosis consists in the deliberate establishment of conditions under which the tendency to blind belief and uncritical obedience present in everyone, but usually kept repressed . . . may unconsciously be transferred to the person hypnotising or suggesting.[12]

I am lingering on Ferenczi's unlocking of the secret of hypnosis for a very important reason. By discovering a universal predisposition at the heart of man, Freudian psychology itself gained the key to a universal underlying historical psychology. As not everyone undergoes formal hypnosis, most people can hide and disguise their inner urge to merge themselves with power figures. But the predisposition to hypnosis is the same one that gives rise to transference, and no one is immune to that, no one can argue away the manifestations of transference in everyday human affairs. It is not visible on the surface: adults walk around looking quite independent; they play the role of parent themselves and seem quite grown up—and so they are. They couldn't function if they still carried with them the childhood feeling of awe for their parents, the tendency to obey them automatically and uncritically. But, says Ferenczi, although these things normally disappear, "the need to be subject to someone remains; only the part of the father is transferred to teachers, superiors, impressive personalities; the submissive loyalty to rulers that is so wide-spread is also a transference of this sort."[13]

Freud's Great Work on Group Psychology

With a theoretical background that unlocked the problem of hypnosis and that discovered the universal mechanism of the transference, Freud was almost obliged to provide the best insights ever into the psychology of leadership; and so he wrote his great work *Group Psychology and the Analysis of the Ego,* a book of fewer than 100 pages that in my opinion is probably the single most potentially liberating tract that has ever been fashioned by man. In his later years Freud wrote a few books that reflected personal and ideological preferences; but *Group Psychology* was a serious scientific work that consciously placed itself in a long tradition. Early theorists of group psychology had tried to explain why men were so sheeplike when they functioned in groups. They developed ideas like "mental contagion" and "herd instinct," which became very popular. But as Freud was quick to see, these ideas never really did explain what men did with their judgment and common sense when they got caught up in groups. Freud saw right away what they did with it: they simply became dependent children again, blindly following the inner voice of their parents, which now came to them under the hypnotic spell of the leader. They abandoned their egos to his, identified with his power, tried to function with him as an ideal.

It is not so much that man is a herd animal, said Freud, but that he is a horde animal led by a chief.[14] It is this alone that can explain the "uncanny and coercive characteristics of group formations." The chief is a "dangerous personality, toward whom only a passive-masochistic attitude is possible, to whom one's will has to be surrendered,—while to be alone with him, 'to look him in the face,' appears a hazardous enterprise." This alone, says Freud, explains the "paralysis" that exists in the link between a person with inferior power to one of superior power. Man has "an extreme passion for authority" and "wishes to be governed by unrestricted force."[15] It is this trait that the leader hypnotically embodies in his own masterful person. Or as Fenichel later put it, people have a "longing for being hypnotized" precisely because they want to get back to the magical protection, the participation in omnipotence, the "oceanic feeling" that they enjoyed when they were loved and protected by their parents.[16] And so, as Freud argues, it is not that groups bring out anything new in people; it is just that they satisfy the deep-seated erotic longings that people constantly carry around unconsciously. For Freud, this was the life force that held groups together. It functioned as a kind of psychic cement that locked people into mutual and mindless interdependence: the magnetic powers of the leader, reciprocated by the guilty delegation of everyone's will to him.

No one who honestly remembers how hazardous it could be to look certain people in the face or how blissful to bask trustingly in the glow of another's power can accuse Freud of psychoanalytic rhetoric. By explaining the precise power that held groups together Freud could also show why groups did not fear danger. The members do not feel that they are alone with their own smallness and helplessness, as they have the powers of the hero-leader with whom they are identified. Natural narcissism—the feeling that the person *next to* you will die, but not you—is reinforced by trusting dependence on the leader's power. No wonder that hundreds of thousands of men marched up from trenches in the face of blistering gunfire in World War I. They were partially self-hypnotised, so to speak. No wonder men imagine victories against impossible odds: don't they have the omnipotent powers of the parental figure? Why are groups so blind and stupid?—men have always asked. Because they demand illusions, answered Freud, they "constantly give what is unreal precedence over what is real."[17] And we know why. The real world is simply too terrible to admit; it tells man that he is a small, trembling animal who will decay and die. Illusion changes all this, makes man seem important, vital to the universe, immortal in some way. Who transmits this illusion, if not the parents by imparting the macro-lie of the cultural *causa sui?* The masses look to the leaders to give them just the untruth that they need; the leader continues the illusions that triumph over the castration complex and magnifies them into a truly heroic victory. Furthermore, he makes possible a new experience, the expression of forbidden impulses, secret wishes, and fantasies. In group behavior anything goes because the leader okays it.[18] It is like being an omnipotent infant again, encouraged by the parent to indulge oneself plentifully, or like being in psychoanalytic therapy where the analyst doesn't censure you for anything you feel or think. In the group each man seems an omnipotent hero who can give full vent to his appetites under the approving eye of the father. And so we understand the terrifying sadism of group activity.

Thus Freud's great work on group psychology, on the dynamics of blind obedience, illusion, communal sadism. In recent writings Erich Fromm especially has seen the durable value of Freud's insights, as part of a developing and continuing critique of human viciousness and blindness. From his early work *Escape from Freedom* to his recent *The Heart of Man*, Fromm has developed Freud's views on the need for a magic helper. He has kept alive Freud's basic insight into narcissism as the primary characteristic of man: how it inflates one with the importance of his own life and makes for the devaluation of others' lives; how it helps to draw sharp lines between "those who are like me or belong to me" and those who are "outsiders and aliens." Fromm has insisted, too, on the importance of what he calls "incestuous symbiosis": the fear of emerging out of the family and into the world on one's own responsibility and powers; the desire to keep oneself tucked into a larger source of power. It is these things that make for the mystique of "group," "nation," "blood," "mother- or fatherland," and the like. These feelings are embedded in one's earliest experiences of comfortable merger with the mother. As Fromm put it, they keep one "in the prison of the motherly racial-national-religious fixation."[19] Fromm is exciting reading, and there is no point in my repeating or developing what he has already so well said. One has to go directly to him and study how compelling are these insights, how well they continue what is essential in Freud and apply it to present-day problems of slavishness, viciousness, and continuing political madness. This, it seems to me, is the authentic line of cumulative critical thought on the human condition. The astonishing thing is that this central line of work on the problem of freedom since the Enlightenment occupies so little of the concern and ongoing activity of scientists. It should form the largest body of theoretical and empirical work in the human sciences, if these sciences are to have any human meaning.

Developments Beyond Freud

Today we do not accept uncritically all of Freud's arguments on group dynamics or consider them necessarily complete. One of the weaknesses of Freud's theory was that he was too fond of his own phylogenetic myth of the "primal horde," Freud's attempt to reconstruct the earliest beginnings of society, when proto-men—like baboons—lived under the tyrannical rule of a dominant male. For Freud this craving of people for the strong personality, their awe and fear of him, remained the model for the basic functioning of all groups. It was Redl, in his important essay, who showed that Freud's attempt to explain everything by the "strong personality" was not true to fact. Redl, who studied many different kinds of groups, found that domination by a strong personality occurred in some of them, but not all.[20] But he did find that in all groups there was what he called a "central person" who held the group together due to certain of his qualities. This shift of emphasis is slight and leaves Freud basically intact, but it allows us to make more subtle analyses of the real dynamics of groups.

For example, Freud found that the <u>leader allows us to express forbidden impulses and secret wishes</u>. Redl saw that in some groups there is indeed what he perfectly calls the "infectiousness of the unconflicted person." There are leaders who seduce us because they do not have the conflicts that we have; we admire their equanimity where we feel shame and humiliation. Freud saw that the <u>leader wipes out fear and permits everyone to feel omnipotent</u>. Redl refined this somewhat by showing how important the leader often was by the simple fact that it was he who performed the "initiatory act" when no one else had the daring to do it. Redl calls this beautifully the "magic of the initiatory act." This initiatory act can be anything from swearing to sex or murder. As Redl points out, according to <u>its logic only the one who first commits murder is the murderer; all others are followers</u>. Freud has said in *Totem and Taboo* that acts that are illegal for the individual can be justified if the whole group shares responsibility for them. But they can be justified in another way: <u>the one who initiates the act takes upon himself both the risk and the guilt</u>. The result is truly magic: <u>each member of the group can repeat the act without guilt</u>. They are <u>not responsible, only</u> the leader is. Redl calls this, aptly, "priority magic." But it does something even more than relieve guilt: it actually *transforms the fact* of murder. This crucial point initiates us directly into the phenomenology of group transformation of the everyday world. If one murders without guilt, and in imitation of the hero who runs the risk, why then it is no longer murder: it is "holy aggression. For the first one it was not."[21] In other words, participation in the group redistills everyday reality and gives it the aura of the sacred—just as, in childhood, play created a heightened reality.

This penetrating vocabulary of "initiatory acts," "the infectiousness of the unconflicted person," "priority magic," and so on allows us to understand more subtly the dynamics of group sadism, the utter equanimity with which groups kill. It is not just that "father permits it" or "orders it." It is more: *the magical heroic transformation* of the world and of oneself. This is the illusion that man craves, as Freud said, and that makes the central person so effective a vehicle for group emotion.

I am not going to try to repeat or sum up the subtleties of Redl's essay here. Let us just underline the brunt of his argument which is that the "spell cast by persons"—as we have called it—is a very complex one, which includes many more things than meet the eye. In fact, it may include everything but a spell. Redl showed that groups use leaders for several types of exculpation or relief of conflict, for love, or for even just the opposite—targets of aggressions and hate that pull the group together in a common bond. (As one recent popular film advertisement put it: "They follow him bravely into hell only for the pleasure of killing him and revenging themselves.") Redl was not out to replace Freud's basic insights but only to extend and add nuances to them. The instructive thing about his examples is that most of the "central person's" functions do have to do with guilt, expiation, and unambiguous heroics. The important conclusion for us is that the groups "use" the leader sometimes with little regard for him personally, but always with regard to fulfilling their own needs and urges. W. R. Bion, in an important recent paper[22] extended this line of thought even further from Freud, arguing that the leader is as much a creature of the group as they of him and that he loses his "individual distinctiveness" by being a leader, as they do by being followers. He has no more freedom to be himself than any other member of the group, precisely because he has to be a reflex of their assumptions in order to qualify for leadership in the first place.[23]

All of which leads us to muse wistfully on how unheroic is the average man, even when he follows heroes. He simply loads them up with his own baggage; he follows them with reservations, with a dishonest heart. The noted psychoanalyst Paul Schilder had already observed that man goes into the hypnotic trance itself with reservations. He said penetratingly that it was this fact that deprived hypnosis of the "profound seriousness which distinguishes every truly great passion." And so he called it "timid" because it lacked "the great, free, unconditional surrender."[24] I think this characterization is beautifully apt to describe the timid "heroisms" of group behavior. There is nothing free or manly about them. Even when one merges his ego with the authoritarian father, the "spell" is in his own narrow interests. People use their leaders almost as an excuse. When they give in to the leader's commands they can always reserve the feeling that these commands are alien to them, that they are the leader's responsibility, that the terrible acts they are committing are in his name and not theirs. This, then, is another thing that makes people feel so guiltless, as Canetti points out: they can imagine themselves as temporary victims of the leader.[25] The more they give in to his spell, and the more terrible the crimes they commit, the more they can feel that the wrongs are not natural to them. It is all so neat, this usage of the leader; it reminds us of James Frazer's discovery that in the remote past tribes often used their kings as scapegoats who, when they no longer served the people's needs, were put to death. These are the many ways in which men can play the hero, all the while that they are avoiding responsibility for their own acts in a cowardly way.

Very few people, for example, have been impressed with the recent "heroics" of the Manson "family." When we look at them in the light of the group dynamics we have been discussing, we can understand better why we are shocked—not only by the gratuitous murders they committed, but by something more. When people try for heroics from the position of willing slavishness there is nothing to admire; it is all so automatic, predictable, pathetic. Here was a group of young men and women who had identified with Charles Manson and who lived in masochistic submission to him. They gave him their total devotion and looked upon him as a human god of some kind. In fact he filled the description of Freud's "primal father": he was authoritarian, very demanding of his followers, and a great believer in discipline. His eyes were intense, and for those who came under his spell there is no doubt that he projected a hypnotic aura. He was a very self-assured figure. He even had his own "truth," his megalomanic vision for taking over the world. To his followers his vision seemed like a heroic mission in which they were privileged to participate. He had convinced them that only by following out his plan could they be saved. The "family" was very close, sexual inhibitions were nonexistent, and members had free access to each other. They even used sex freely for the purpose of attracting outsiders into the family. It seems obvious from all this that Manson combined the "fascinating effect of the narcissistic personality" with the "infectiousness of the unconflicted personality." Everyone could freely drop his repressions under Manson's example and command, not only in sex but in murder. The members of the "family" didn't seem to show any remorse, guilt, or shame for their crimes.

People were astonished by this ostensible "lack of human feeling." But from the dynamics that we have been surveying, we are faced with the even more astonishing conclusion that homicidal communities like the Manson "family" are not really devoid of basic humanness. What makes them so terrible is that they exaggerate the dispositions present in us all. Why should they feel guilt or remorse? The leader takes responsibility for the destructive act, and those who destroy on his command are no longer murderers, but "holy heroes." They crave to serve in the powerful aura that he projects and to carry out the illusion that he provides them, an illusion that allows them to heroically transform the world. Under his hypnotic spell and with the full force of their own urges for heroic self-expansion, they need have no fear; they can kill with equanimity. In fact they seemed to feel that they were doing their victims "a favor," which seems to mean that they sanctified them by including them in their own "holy mission." As we have learned from the anthropological literature, the victim who is sacrificed becomes a holy offering to the gods, to nature, or to fate. The community gets more life by means of the victim's death, and so the victim has the privilege of serving the world in the highest possible way by means of his own sacrificial death.

One direct way, then, of understanding homicidal communities like the Manson family is to view them as magical transformations, wherein passive and empty people, torn with conflicts and guilt, earn their cheap heroism, really feeling that they can control fate and influence life and death. "Cheap" because not in their command, not with their own daring, and not in the grip of their own fears: everything is done with the leader's image stamped on their psyche.

The Larger View of Transference

From this discussion of transference we can see one great cause of the large-scale ravages that man makes on the world. He is not just a naturally and lustily destructive animal who lays waste around him because he feels omnipotent and impregnable. Rather, he is a trembling animal who pulls the world down around his shoulders as he clutches for protection and support and tries to affirm in a cowardly way his feeble powers. The qualities of the leader, then, and the problems of people fit together in a natural symbiosis. I have lingered on a few refinements of group psychology to show that the powers of the leader stem from what he can do for people, beyond the magic that he himself possesses. People project their problems onto him, which gives him his role and stature. Leaders need followers as much as they are needed by them: the leader projects onto his followers his own inability to stand alone, his own fear of isolation. We must say that if there were no natural leaders possessing the magic of charisma, men would have to invent them, just as leaders must create followers if there are none available. If we accent this natural symbiotic side of the problem of transference we come into the broadest understanding of it, which forms the main part of the discussion I now want to dwell on.†

† Now that we have sketched some of the highlights of the easy symbiosis of groups and leaders, we have to be careful not to leave a one-sided picture; there is another side to show, a very different one. The guilt of all the followers does not vanish so easily under the spell of a leader, no matter how much he takes upon himself or how godlike he seems. Not everyone can be equally caught up in identification with him, and not everyone's guilt is so easily overcome. Many people may feel deeply guilty if they violate long-

standing and deep-felt moral codes on his behalf. Yet, ironically, it is just this that puts them even more in the leader's power, makes them even more willing putty in his hands.

If, as we have seen, the group comes ready-made to the leader with the thirst for servitude, he tries to deepen that servitude even further. If they seek to be free of guilt in his cause, he tries to load them up with an extra burden of guilt and fear to draw the mesh of his immorality around them. He gets a really coercive hold on the members of the group precisely because they follow his lead in committing outrageous acts. He can then use their guilt against them, binding them closer to himself. He uses their anxiety for his purposes, even arousing it as he needs to; and he can use their fear of being found out and revenged by their victims as a kind of blackmail that keeps them docile and obedient for further atrocities. We saw a classic example of this technique on the part of the Nazi leaders. It was the same psychology that criminal gangs and gangsters have always used: to be bound closer together through the crime itself. The Nazis called it blood cement (*Blutkitt*), and the SS used it freely. For the lower echelons, service in the concentration camps accomplished this loyalty; but the technique was also used on the highest levels, especially with reluctant persons of prominence and talent whom they wanted to recruit. These they induced to commit extra atrocities that indelibly identified them with the SS and gave them a new, criminal identity. (See Leo Alexander's excellent paper: "Sociopsychologic Structure of the SS," *Archives of Neurology and Psychiatry*, 1948, 59: 622–634.) And, as the Nazi epoch wore on and the toll of victims mounted, the leaders played upon the fears of reprisal by those who would revenge the victims the Nazis had made. It was the old gangster trick, this time used to cement together a whole nation. Thus, what may begin as the heroic mission of a Hitler or a Manson comes to be sustained by bullying and threats, by added fear and guilt. The followers find that they have to continue on with the megalomanic plan because it becomes their only chance of survival in a hostile world. The followers must do what the leader wants, which becomes what they themselves must want in order to survive. If the leader loses, they too perish; they cannot quit, nor does he allow them to. And so the German nation fought on until the final destruction of Berlin; the Manson family held together under persecution and his threats, to flee to the desert and await the end of the world. This gives an added dimension, too, to our understanding of why people stick with their leaders even in defeat, as the Egyptians did with Nasser. Without him they may feel just too exposed to reprisal, to total annihilation. Having been baptized in his fire they can no longer stand alone. (On all this see Ernst Kris, "The Covenant of the Gangsters," *Journal of Criminal Psychopathology*, 1942–3, 4:441–454; Paul Roazen, *Freud*, pp. 238–242; T. W. Adorno, "Freudian Theory and the Pattern of Fascist Propaganda," in *Psychoanalysis and the Social Sciences*, 1951, pp. 298–300; and Ed Sanders, *The Family: The Story of Charles Manson's Dune Buggy Attack Battalion*, (New York: Dutton, 1971). Cf. esp. pp. 145, 199, 257.)

Freud had already revealed as much about the problems of followers as about the magnetism of the leader, when he taught us
about the longing for transference and what it accomplished. But
just here, trouble lies. As always, he showed us where to look but
focussed down too narrowly. He had a conception, as Wolstein
succinctly put it, "of why man got into trouble,"[26] and his explanations of trouble almost always came to rest on the sexual motive.
The fact that people were so prone to suggestibility in hypnosis
was for him proof that it depended on sexuality. The transference
attraction that we feel for people is merely a manifestation of the
earliest attractions that the child felt for those around him, but now
this purely sexual attraction is so buried in the unconscious that we
don't realize what really motivates our fascinations. In Freud's unmistakable words:

. . . we have to conclude that all the feelings of sympathy, friendship,
trust and so forth which we expend in life are genetically connected with
sexuality and have developed out of purely sexual desires by an enfee-
bling of their sexual aim, however pure and non-sensual they may appear
in the forms they take on to our conscious self-perception. To begin with
we knew none but sexual objects; psycho-analysis shows us that those
persons whom in real life we merely respect or are fond of may be sexual
objects to us in our unconscious minds still.[27]

We have already seen how this kind of reductionism to the sexual
motive got psychoanalysis itself into trouble very early and how it
has taken a succession of thinkers of great stature to extricate psychoanalysis from this obsession of Freud's. But in his later work
Freud himself was not too troubled by his obsession when it came
to explaining some things more broadly; the same holds true for his
narrow sexual emphasis on transference surrender. In 1912 he said
that the fact that transference could lead to complete subjection was
for him "unmistakable" proof of its "erotic character."[28] But in his
later work, when he accented more and more the terror of the
human condition, he talked of the child's longing for a powerful
father as a "protection against strange superior powers," as a consequence of "human weakness" and "childish helplessness."[29] Yet,
this phrasing doesn't represent an absolute abandonment of his
earlier explanations. For Freud, "eros" covered not only specific

sexual drives but also the child's longing for omnipotence, for the oceanic feeling that comes with a merger with the parental powers. With this kind of generalization Freud could have both his broader and narrower views at the same time. This complicated mixture of specific error and correct generalization has made it a difficult and lengthy task for us to separate out what is true from what is false in psychoanalytic theory. But as we said earlier with Rank, it seems fairly conclusive that if you accent the terrors of external nature—as Freud did in his later work—then you are talking about the general human condition and no longer about specific erotic drives. We might say that the child would then seek merger with the parental omnipotence not out of *desire* but out of *cowardice*. And now we are on a wholly new terrain. The fact that transference could lead to complete subjection proves not its "erotic character" but something quite different: its "truthful" character, we might say. As Adler saw with complete clarity long before Freud's later work: transference is fundamentally a problem of *courage*.[30] As we have learned conclusively from Rank and Brown, it is the immortality motive and not the sexual one that must bear the larger burden of our explanation of human passion. What does this crucial shift of emphasis mean for our understanding of transference? A truly fascinating and comprehensive view of the human condition

Transference as Fetish Control

If transference relates to cowardice we can understand why it goes all the way back to childhood; it reflects the whole of the child's attempts to create an environment that will give him safety and satisfaction; he learns to act and to perceive his environment in such a way that he banishes anxiety from it. But now the fatality of transference: when you set up your perception-action world to eliminate what is basic to it (anxiety), then you fundamentally falsify it. This is why psychoanalysts have always understood transference as a regressive phenomenon, uncritical, wishful, a matter of *automatic control* of one's world. Silverberg gives a classic psycho-analytic definition: Transference indicates a need to exert complete control over external circumstances. . . . In all its variety and multiplicity of manifestation . . . transference may be regarded as the enduring monument of man's profound rebellion against reality and his stubborn persistence in the ways of immaturity.[31]

For Erich Fromm transference reflects man's alienation:

In order to overcome his sense of inner emptiness and impotence, [man] . . . chooses an object onto whom he projects all his own human qualities: his love, intelligence, courage, etc. By submitting to this object, he feels in touch with his own qualities; he feels strong, wise, courageous, and secure. To lose the object means the danger of losing himself. This mechanism, idolatric worship of an object, based on the fact of the individual's alienation, is the central dynamism of transference, that which gives transference its strength and intensity.[32]

Jung's view was similar: fascination with someone is basically a matter of

. . . always trying to deliver us into the power of a partner who seems compounded of all the qualities we have failed to realize in ourselves.[33]

And so was the Adlerian view:

[transference] . . . is basically a maneuver or tactic by which the patient seeks to perpetuate his familiar mode of existence that depends on a continuing attempt to divest himself of power and place it in the hands of the "Other."[34]

I am citing these several authorities at length for two reasons: to show the general truth of their insights and also to be able, later on, to bring up the immense problems that these truths raise. Already we can see that transference is not a matter of unusual cowardice but rather of the basic problems of an organismic life, problems of power and control: the strength to oppose reality and keep it ordered for our own organismic expansion and fulfillment.

What is more natural than choosing a person with whom to establish this dialogue with nature? Fromm uses the word "idol" which is another way of talking about what is nearest at hand. This is how we understand the function of even the "negative" or "hate" transference: it helps us to fix ourselves in the world, to create a target for our own feelings even though those feelings are destructive. We can establish our basic organismic footing with hate as well as by submission. In fact, hate enlivens us more, which is why we see more intense hate in the weaker ego states. The only thing is that hate, too, blows the other person up larger than he deserves. As Jung put it, the "negative form of transference in the guise of resistance, dislike, or hate endows the other person with great importance from the start. . . ."[35] We need a concrete object for our control, and we get one in whatever way we can. In the absence of persons for our dialogue of control we can even use our own body as a transference object, as Szasz has shown.[36] The pains we feel, the illnesses that are real or imaginary give us something to relate to, keep us from slipping out of the world, from bogging down in the desperation of complete loneliness and emptiness. In a word, illness is an object. We transfer to our own body as if it were a friend on whom we can lean for strength or an enemy who threatens us with danger. At least it makes us feel real and gives us a little purchase on our fate.

From all this we can already draw one important conclusion: that transference is a form of fetishism, a form of narrow control that anchors our own problems. We take our helplessness, our guilt, our conflicts, and we fix them to a spot in the environment. *We* can create *any locus* at all for projecting our cares onto the world, even the locus of our own arms and legs. Our own cares are the thing; and if we look at the basic problems of human slavishness it is always them that we see. As Jung put it in some beautiful words: ". . . unless we prefer to be made fools of by our illusions, we shall, by carefully analysing every fascination, extract from it a portion of our own personality, like a quintessence, and slowly come to recognize that we meet ourselves time and again in a thousand disguises on the path of life."[37]

Transference as Fear of Life

But this discussion has led us even further away from a simple, clinical approach to the phenomenon of transference. The fact is that fascination is a reflex of the fatality of the human condition;

and as we saw in Part I of this book, the human condition is just too much for an animal to take; it is overwhelming. It is on this aspect of the problem of transference that I now want to dwell. Of all the thinkers who have understood it, none has written with greater breadth and depth on the meanings of the transference than Rank.

We have seen in several different contexts how Rank's system of thought rests on the fact of human fear, the fear of life and death. Here I want to accent how global or total this fear is. As William James said, with his unfailing directness, fear is "fear of the universe." It is the fear of childhood, the fear of emerging into the universe, of realizing one's own independent individuality, one's own living and experiencing. As Rank said, "The adult may have fear of death or fear of sex, the child has a fear of life itself."[38] This idea has been given wide currency by Fromm in several books, as the "fear of freedom." Schachtel put it well in speaking of the fear of emerging out of "embeddedness." This is how we understand the "incestuousness" of the symbiosis with the mother and the family: the person remains "tucked into" a protective womb, so to speak. It is what Rank meant when he talked about the "trauma of birth" as being the paradigm for all other traumas of emergence. It is logical: if the universe is fundamentally and globally terrifying to the natural perceptions of the young human animal, how can he dare to emerge into it with confidence? Only by relieving it of its terror.

This is how we can understand the essence of transference: as a *taming of terror*. Realistically the universe contains overwhelming power. Beyond ourselves we sense chaos. We can't really do much about this unbelievable power, except for one thing: we can endow certain persons with it. The child takes natural awe and terror and focusses them on individual beings, which allows him to find the power and the horror all in one place instead of diffused throughout a chaotic universe. *Mirabile!* The transference object, being endowed with the transcendent powers of the universe, now has in himself the power to control, order, and combat them.[39] In Rank's words the transference object comes to represent for the individual "the great biological forces of nature, to which the ego binds itself emotionally and which then form the essence of the human and his fate."[40] By this means, the child can control his fate. As ultimately power means power over life and death, the child can now safely emerge in relation to the transference object. The object becomes his locus of safe operation. All he has to do is conform to it in the ways that he learns; conciliate it if it becomes terrible; use it serenely for automatic daily activities. For this reason Angyal could well say that transference is not an "emotional mistake" but the experience of the other as one's *whole world*—just as the home actually is, for the child, his whole world.[41]

This totality of the transference object also helps explain its ambivalence. In some complex ways the child has to fight against the power of the parents in their awesome miraculousness. They are just as overwhelming as the background of nature from which they emerge. The child learns to naturalize them by techniques of accommodation and manipulation. At the same time, however, he has to focus on them the whole problem of terror and power, making them the center of it in order to cut down and naturalize the world around them. Now we see why the transference object poses so many problems. The child does partly control his larger fate by it, but it becomes his new fate. He binds himself to one person to automatically control terror, to mediate wonder, and to defeat death by that person's strength. But then he experiences "transference terror"; the terror of losing the object, of displeasing it, of not being able to live without it. The terror of his own finitude and impotence still haunts him, but now in the precise form of the transference object. How implacably ironic is human life. The transference object always looms larger than life size because it represents all of life and hence all of one's fate. The transference object becomes the focus of the problem of one's freedom because one is compulsively dependent on it; it sums up all other natural dependencies and emotions.[42] This quality is true of either positive or negative transference objects. In the negative transference the object becomes the focalization of terror, but now experienced as evil and constraint. It is the source, too, of much of the bitter memories of childhood and of our accusations of our parents. We try to make them the sole repositories of our own unhappiness in a fundamentally demonic world. We seem to be pretending that the world does not contain terror and evil but only our parents. In the negative transference, too, then, we see an attempt to control our fate in an automatic way.

No wonder Freud could say that transference was a "universal phenomenon of the human mind" that "dominates the whole of each person's relation to his human environment."[43] Or that Ferenczi could talk about the "neurotic passion for transference," the "stimulus-hungry affects of neurotics."[44] We don't have to talk only about neurotics but about the hunger and passion of everyone for a *localized stimulus* that takes the place of the whole world. We might better say that transference proves that everyone is neurotic, as it is a universal distortion of reality by the artificial fixation of it. It follows, of course, that the less ego power one has and the more fear, the stronger the transference. This explains the peculiar intensity of schizophrenic transference: the total and desperate focalization of horror and wonder in one person, and the abject surrender to him and complete worship of him in a kind of dazed, hypnotic way. Only to hear his voice or touch a piece of his clothing or be granted the privilege of kissing and licking his feet—that would be heaven itself. This is a logical fate for the utterly helpless person: the more you fear death and the emptier you are, the more you people your world with omnipotent father-figures, extra-magical helpers.[45] The schizophrenic transference helps us to understand how naturally we remain glued to the object even in "normal" transference: all the power to cure the diseases of life, the ills of the world, are present in the transference object. How can we not be under its spell?

Remember we said the transference did not prove "eroticism," as Freud earlier thought, but actually a certain "truthfulness" about the terror of man's condition. The schizophrenic's extreme transference helps us to understand this statement too. After all, one of the reasons that his world is so terrifying is that he sees it in many ways unblurred by repression. And so he sees, too, the human transference object in all of its awe and splendor—something we talked about in an early chapter. The human face is really an awesome primary miracle; it naturally paralyzes you by its splendor if you give in to it as the fantastic thing it is. But mostly we repress this miraculousness so that we can function with equanimity and can use faces and bodies for our own routine purposes. We may remember that as children there were those we did not dare talk to, or even look at—hardly something that we could carry over into our adult lives without seriously crippling ourselves. But now we can point out, too, that this fear of looking the transference object full in the face is not necessarily what Freud said it was: the fear of the terrifying primal father. It is, rather, the fear of the reality of the intense focalization of natural wonder and power; the fear of being overwhelmed by the truth of the universe as it exists, as that truth is focussed in one human face. But Freud is right about tyrannical fathers: the more terrifying the object, the stronger the transference; the more that the powerful object embodies in itself the natural power of the world, the more terrifying it can be, in reality, without any imagination on our part.

Transference as Fear of Death

If fear of life is one aspect of transference, its companion fear is right at hand. As the growing child becomes aware of death, he has a twofold reason for taking shelter in the powers of the transference object. The castration complex makes the body an object of horror, and it is now the transference object who carries the weight of the abandoned *causa-sui* project. The child uses him to assure his immortality. What is more natural? I can't resist quoting from another writing, Gorki's famous sentiment on Tolstoi, because it sums up so well this aspect of transference: "I am not bereft on this earth, so long as this old man is living on it."[46] This comes from the depth of Gorki's emotion; it is not a simple wish or a comforting thought: it is more like a driving belief that the mystery and solidity of the transference object will give one shelter as long as he lives.

This use of the transference object explains the urge to deification of the other, the constant placing of certain select persons on pedestals, the reading into them of extra powers: the more they have, the more rubs off on us. We participate in their immortality, and so we create immortals.[47] As Harrington put it graphically: "I am making a deeper impression on the cosmos because I know this famous person. When the ark sails I will be on it."[48] Man is always hungry, as Rank so well put it, for material for his own immortalization. Groups need it too, which explains the constant hunger for heroes:

Every group, however small or great, has, as such, an "individual" impulse for eternalization, which manifests itself in the creation of and care for national, religious, and artistic heroes . . . the individual paves the way for this collective eternity impulse. . . .[49]

This aspect of group psychology explains something that otherwise staggers our imagination: have we been astonished by fantastic displays of grief on the part of whole peoples when one of their leaders dies? The uncontrolled emotional outpouring, the dazed masses standing huddled in the city squares sometimes for days on end, grown people groveling hysterically and tearing at themselves, being trampled in the surge toward the coffin or funeral pyre—how to make sense out of such a massive, neurotic "vaudeville of despair"?[50] In one way only: it shows a profound state of shock at losing one's bulwark against death. The people apprehend, at some dumb level of their personality: "Our locus of power to control life and death can *himself* die; therefore our own immortality is in doubt." All the tears and all the tearing is after all for oneself, not for the passing of a great soul but for one's own imminent passing. Immediately men begin to rename city streets, squares, airports with the name of the dead man: it is as though to declare that he will be immortalized physically in the society, in spite of his own physical death. Compare the recent mournings of the Americans for the Kennedys, the French for De Gaulle, and especially the Egyptians for Nasser, which was a more primitive and elemental outpouring: immediately the cry was raised to renew the war with Israel. As we have learned, only scapegoats can relieve one of his own stark death fear: "*I* am threatened with death—let us kill plentifully." On the demise of an immortality-figure the urge to scapegoating must be especially intense. So, too, is the susceptibility to sheer panic, as Freud showed.[51] When the leader dies the device that one has used to deny the terror of the world instantly breaks down; what is more natural, then, than to experience the very panic that has always threatened in the background?

The void of immortality-substance that would be left by the absolute abandonment of the leader is evidently too painful to support, especially if the leader has possessed striking mana or has summed up in himself some great heroic project that carried the people on. One can't help musing about how one of the most advanced scientific societies of the 20th century resorted to improvements on ancient Egyptian mummification techniques to embalm the leader of their revolution. It seems as though the Russians could not let go of Lenin even in death and so have entombed him as a permanent immortality-symbol. Here is a supposedly "secular" society that holds pilgrimages to a tomb and that buries heroic figures in the "sacred wall" of the Kremlin, a "hallowed" place. No matter how many churches are closed or how humanistic a leader or a movement may claim to be, there will never be anything wholly secular about human fear. Man's terror is always "holy terror"—which is a strikingly apt popular phrase. Terror always refers to the ultimates of life and death.[52]

The Twin Ontological Motives

Much of what we have said so far about transference puts mankind in an unflattering light; it is now time to shift the tone. True, transference is a reflex of cowardice in the face of both life and death, but it is also a reflex of the urge to heroism and self-unfolding. This puts our discussion of transference on still a different level, and on this new perspective I now want to linger.

One thing that has always amazed man is his own inner yearning to be good, an inner sensitivity about the "way things ought to be," and an excruciatingly warm and melting attraction toward the "rightness" of beauty, goodness, and perfection. We call this inner sensitivity "conscience." For the great philosopher Immanuel Kant it was one of the two sublime mysteries of creation, this "moral law within" man, and there was no way to explain it—it was just given. Nature carries feeling right in her own "heart," in the interiors of striving organisms. This self-feeling in nature is more fantastic than any science-fiction fact. Any philosophy or any science that is going to speak intelligently about the meaning of life has to take it into account and treat it with the highest reverence—as 19th-century thinkers like Vincenzo Gioberti and Antonio Rosmini understood.[53]

Curiously, this vital ontology of organismic self-feeling—which was central for thinkers like Thomas Davidson and Henri Bergson—hardly made a rustle in modern science until the appearance of the new "humanistic psychology." This fact alone seems to me to explain the unbelievable sterility of the human sciences in our time and, more especially, their willingness to manipulate and negate man. I think that the true greatness of Freud's contribution emerges when we see it as directly related to this tradition of ontological thought. Freud showed how the particular rules for goodness or conscience were built into the child in a given society, how he learns the *rules for feeling* good. By showing the artificiality of these social rules for feeling good, Freud mapped out the dream of freedom of the Enlightenment: to expose artificial moral constraints on the expansive self-feeling of the life force.

But the recognition of such social constraints still leaves unexplained the inner urge of the human being to feel good and right —the very thing that awed Kant seems to exist independent of any rules: as far as we can tell—as I put it elsewhere—"all organisms like to 'feel good' about themselves."[54] They push themselves to maximize this feeling. As philosophers have long noted, it is as though the heart of nature is pulsating in its own joyful self-expansion. When we get to the level of man, of course, this process acquires its greatest interest. It is most intense in man and in him relatively undetermined—he can pulsate and expand both organismically and symbolically. This expansion takes the form of man's tremendous urge for a feeling of total "rightness" about himself and his world. This perhaps clumsy way to talk seems to me to sum up what man is really trying to do and why conscience is his fate. Man is the only organism in nature fated to puzzle out what it actually means to feel "right."

But on top of this special burden nature has arranged that it is impossible for man to feel "right" in any straightforward way. Here we have to introduce a paradox that seems to go right to the heart of organismic life and that is especially sharpened in man. The paradox takes the form of two motives or urges that seem to be part of creature consciousness and that point in two opposite directions. On the one hand the creature is impelled by a powerful desire to identify with the cosmic process, to merge himself with the rest of nature. On the other hand he wants to be unique, to stand out as something different and apart. The first motive—to merge and lose oneself in something larger—comes from man's horror of isolation, of being thrust back upon his own feeble energies alone; he feels tremblingly small and impotent in the face of transcendent nature. If he gives in to his natural feeling of cosmic dependence, the desire to be part of something bigger, it puts him at peace and at oneness, gives him a sense of self-expansion in a larger beyond, and so heightens his being, giving him truly a feeling of transcendent value. This is the Christian motive of Agape—the natural melding of created life in the "Creation-in-love" which transcends it. As Rank put it, man yearns for a "feeling of kinship with the All." He wants to be "delivered from his isolation" and become "part of a greater and higher whole." The person reaches out naturally for a self beyond his own self in order to know who he is at all, in order to feel that he belongs in the universe. Long before Camus penned the words of the epigraph to this chapter, Rank said: "For only by living in close union with a god-ideal that has been erected outside one's own ego is one able to live at all."[55]

The strength of Rank's work, which enabled him to draw such an unfailing psychological portrait of man in the round, was that he connected psychoanalytic clinical insight with the basic ontological motives of the human creature. In this way he got as deep into human motives as he could and produced a group psychology that was really a psychology of the human condition. For one thing, we could see that what the psychoanalysts call "identification" is a natural urge to join in the overwhelming powers that transcend one.[56] Childhood identification is then merely a special case of this urge: the child merges himself with the representatives of the cosmic process—what we have called the "transference focalization" of terror, majesty, and power. When one merges with the self-transcending parents or social group he is, in some real sense, trying to live in some larger expansiveness of meaning. We miss the complexity of heroism if we fail to understand this point; we miss its complete grasp of the person—a grasp not only in the support of power that self-transcendence gives *to* him but a grasp *of* his whole being in joy and love. The urge to immortality is not a simple reflex of the death-anxiety but a reaching out by one's whole being toward life. Perhaps this natural expansion of the creature alone can explain why transference is such a universal passion.

From this point of view too we understand the idea of God as a logical fulfillment of the Agape side of man's nature. Freud seems to have scorned Agape as he scorned the religion that preached it. He thought that man's hunger for a God in heaven represented everything that was immature and selfish in man: his helplessness, his fear, his greed for the fullest possible protection and satisfaction. But Rank understood that the idea of God has never been a simple reflex of superstitious and selfish fear, as cynics and "realists" have claimed. Instead it is an outgrowth of genuine life-longing, a reaching-out for a plenitude of meaning—as James taught us.[57] It seems that the yielding element in heroic belongingness is inherent in the life force itself, one of the truly sublime mysteries of created life. It seems that the life force reaches naturally even beyond the earth itself, which is one reason why man has always placed God in the heavens.

We said it is impossible for man to feel "right" in any straightforward way, and now we can see why. He can expand his self-feeling not only by Agape merger but also by the other ontological motive Eros, the urge for more life, for exciting experience, for the development of the self-powers, for developing the uniqueness of the individual creature, the impulsion to stick out of nature and shine. Life is, after all, a challenge to the creature, a fascinating opportunity to expand. Psychologically it is the urge for individuation: how do I realize my distinctive gifts, make my own contribution to the world through my own self-expansion?

Now we see what we might call the ontological or creature tragedy that is so peculiar to man: If he gives in to Agape he risks failing to develop himself, his active contribution to the rest of life. If he expands Eros too much he risks cutting himself off from natural dependency, from duty to a larger creation; he pulls away from the healing power of gratitude and humility that he must naturally feel for having been created, for having been given the opportunity of life experience.

Man thus has the absolute tension of the dualism. Individuation means that the human creature has to oppose itself to the rest of nature. It creates precisely the isolation that one can't stand—and yet needs in order to develop distinctively. It creates the difference that becomes such a burden; it accents the smallness of oneself and the sticking-outness at the same time. This is *natural* guilt. The person experiences this as "unworthiness" or "badness" and dumb inner dissatisfaction.[58] And the reason is realistic. Compared to the rest of nature man is not a very satisfactory creation. He is riddled with fear and powerlessness.

The problem becomes how to get rid of badness, of natural guilt, which is really a matter of reversing one's position *vis-à-vis* the universe. It is a matter of achieving size, importance, durability: how to be bigger and better than one really is. The whole basis of the urge to goodness is to be something that has value, that endures.[59] We seem to know it intuitively when we console our children after their nightmares and other frights. We tell them not to worry, that they are "good" and nothing can hurt them, and so on: goodness = safety and special immunity. You might say that the urge to morality is based entirely on the physical situation of the creature. Man is moral because he senses his true situation and what lies in store for him, whereas other animals don't. He uses morality to try to get a place of special belongingness and perpetuation in the universe, in two ways. First, he overcomes badness (smallness, un-importance, finitude) by conforming to the rules made by the representatives of natural power (the transference-objects); in this way his safe belongingness is assured. This too is natural: we tell the child when he is good so that he doesn't have to be afraid. Second, he attempts to overcome badness by developing a really valuable heroic gift, becoming extra-special.

Do we wonder why one of man's chief characteristics is his tortured dissatisfaction with himself, his constant self-criticism? It is the only way he has to overcome the sense of hopeless limitation inherent in his real situation. Dictators, revivalists, and sadists know that people like to be lashed with accusations of their own basic unworthiness because it reflects how they truly feel about them-selves. The sadist doesn't create a masochist; he finds him ready-made. Thus people are offered one way of overcoming unworth-iness: the chance to idealize the self, to lift it onto truly heroic levels. In this way man sets up the complementary dialogue with himself that is natural to his condition. He criticizes himself because he falls short of the heroic ideals he needs to meet in order to be a really imposing creation.

You can see that man wants the impossible: He wants to lose his isolation and keep it at the same time. He can't stand the sense of separateness, and yet he can't allow the complete suffocating of his vitality. He wants to expand by merging with the powerful beyond that transcends him, yet he wants while merging with it to remain individual and aloof, working out his own private and smaller-scale self-expansion. But this feat is impossible because it belies the real tension of the dualism. One obviously can't have merger in the power of another thing and the development of one's own personal power at the same time, at any rate not without ambivalence and a degree of self-deception. But one can get around the problem in one way: one can, we might say, "control the glaringness of the contradiction." You can try to choose the fitting kind of beyond, the one in which you find it most natural to practice self-criticism and self-idealization.[60] In other words, you try to keep your beyond safe. The fundamental use of transference, of what we could better call "transference heroics," is the practice of a safe heroism. In it we see the reach of the ontological dualism of motives right into the problem of transference and heroism, and we are now in a position to sum up this matter.

Transference as the Urge to Higher Heroism

The point of our brief discursus on ontological motives is to make compellingly clear how transference is connected to the foundations of organismic life. We can now understand fully how wrong it would be to look at transference in a totally derogatory way when it fulfills such vital drives toward human wholeness. Man needs to infuse his life with value so that he can pronounce it "good." The transference-object is then a natural fetishization for man's highest yearnings and strivings. Again we see what a marvelous "talent" transference is. It is a form of creative fetishism, the establishment of a locus from which our lives can draw the powers they need and want. What is more wanted than immortality-power? How wonderful and how facile to be able to take our whole immortality-striving and make it part of a dialogue with a single human being. We don't know, on this planet, what the universe wants from us or is prepared to give us. We don't have an answer to the question that troubled Kant of what our duty is, what we should be doing on earth. We live in utter darkness about who we are and why we are here, yet we know it must have some meaning. What is more natural, then, than to take this unspeakable mystery and dispel it straightaway by addressing our performance of heroics to another human being, knowing thus daily whether this performance is good enough to earn us eternity. If it is bad, we know that it is bad by his reactions and so are able instantly to change it. Rank sums up this vital matter in a particularly rich, synthetic paragraph:

Here we come upon the age-old problem of good and evil, originally designating eligibility for immortality, in its emotional significance of being liked or disliked by the other person. On this plane . . . personality is shaped and formed according to the vital need to please the other person whom we make our "God," and not incur his or her displeasure. All the twistings of the . . . self, with its artificial striving for perfection and the unavoidable "relapses" into badness, are the result of these attempts to humanize the spiritual need for goodness.[61]

As we will see in the next chapters, one can nourish and expand his identity of all kinds of "gods," on heavens as well as hells. How a person solves his natural yearnings for self-expansion and significance determines the quality of his life. Transference heroics gives man precisely what he needs: a certain degree of sharply defined individuality, a definite point of reference for his practice of goodness, and all within a certain secure level of safety and control.

If transference heroics were safe heroism we might think it demeaning. Heroism is by definition defiance of safety. But the point that we are making is that all the strivings for perfection, the twistings and turnings to please the other, are not necessarily cowardly or unnatural. What makes transference heroics demeaning is that the process is unconscious and reflexive, not fully in one's control. Psychoanalytic therapy directly addresses itself to this problem. Beyond that, the other person is man's fate and a natural one. He is forced to address his performance to qualify for goodness to his fellow creatures, as they form his most compelling and immediate environment, not in the physical or evolutionary sense in which like creatures huddle unto like, but more in the spiritual sense. Human beings are the only things that mediate meaning, which is to say that they give the only human meaning we can know. Jung has written some particularly brilliant and penetrating pages on transference, and he has seen that the urge is so strong and natural that he has even called it an "instinct"—a "kinship libido." This instinct, he says, cannot be satisfied in any abstract way:

It wants the *human* connection. That is the core of the whole transference phenomenon, and it is impossible to argue it away, because relationship to the self is at once relationship to our fellow man. . . .[62]

A century earlier Hermann Melville had put the same thought into the mouth of Ahab:

Close! stand close to me, Starbuck; let me look into a human eye; it is better than to gaze into sea or sky; better than to gaze upon God. By the green land; by the bright hearthstone! this is the magic glass, man; I see my wife and my child in thine eye.[63]

The meaning of this need for other men to affirm oneself was seen beautifully by the theologian Martin Buber. He called it "imagining the real": seeing in the other person the self-transcending life process that gives to one's self the larger nourishment it needs.[64] In terms of our earlier discussion we could say that the transference object contains its own natural awesomeness, its own miraculousness, which infects us with the significance of *our* own lives if we give in to it. Paradoxically, then, transference surrender to the "truth of the other," even if only in his physical being, gives us a feeling of heroic self-validation. No wonder that Jung could say that it is "impossible to argue away."

No wonder too, for a final time, that transference is a universal passion. It represents a natural attempt to be healed and to be whole, through heroic self-expansion in the "other." Transference represents the larger reality that one needs, which is why Freud and Ferenczi could already say that transference represents psychotherapy, the "self-taught attempts on the patient's part to cure himself."[65] People create the reality they need in order to discover themselves. The implications of these remarks are perhaps not immediately evident, but they are immense for a theory of the transference. If transference represents the natural heroic striving for a "beyond" that gives self-validation and if people need this validation in order to live, then the psychoanalytic view of transference as simply unreal projection is destroyed.[66] Projection is necessary and desirable for self-fulfillment. Otherwise man is overwhelmed by his loneliness and separation and negated by the very burden of his own life. As Rank so wisely saw, projection is *a necessary unburdening* of the individual; man cannot live closed upon himself and for himself. He must project the meaning of his life outward, the reason for it, even the blame for it. We did not create ourselves, but we are stuck with ourselves. Technically we say that transference is a distortion of reality. But now we see that this distortion has two dimensions: distortion due to the fear of life and death and distortion due to the heroic attempt to assure self-expansion and the intimate connection of one's inner self to surrounding nature. In other words, transference reflects the whole of the human condition and raises the largest philosophical question about that condition.

How big a piece of "reality" can man bite off without narrowing it down distortingly? If Rank, Camus, and Buber are right, man cannot stand alone but has to reach out for support. If transference is a natural function of heroism, a necessary projection in order to stand life, death, and oneself, the question becomes: What is *creative projection?* What is *life-enhancing* illusion? These are questions that take us way beyond the scope of this chapter, but we shall see the reach of them in our concluding section.

CHAPTER EIGHT

Otto Rank and the Closure of
Psychoanalysis on Kierkegaard

> *It seems to be difficult for the individual to*
> *realize that there exists a division between one's*
> *spiritual and purely human needs, and that the*
> *satisfaction or fulfillment for each has to be*
> *found in different spheres. As a rule, we find the*
> *two aspects hopelessly confused in modern*
> *relationships, where one person is made the god-*
> *like judge over good and bad in the other person.*
> *In the long run, such symbiotic relationship*
> *becomes demoralizing to both parties, for it is*
> *just as unbearable to be God as it is*
> *to remain an utter slave.*
> —OTTO RANK[1]

One of the things we see as we glance over history is that creature consciousness is always absorbed by culture. Culture opposes nature and transcends it. Culture is in its most intimate intent a heroic denial of creatureliness. But this denial is more effective in some epochs than in others. When man lived securely under the canopy of the Judeo-Christian world picture he was part of a great whole; to put it in our terms, his cosmic heroism was completely mapped out, it was unmistakable. He came from the invisible world into the visible one by the act of God, did his duty to God by living out his life with dignity and faith, marrying as a duty, procreating as a duty, offering his whole life—as Christ had—to the Father. In turn he was justified by the Father and rewarded with eternal life in the invisible dimension. Little did it matter that the earth was a vale of tears, of horrid sufferings, of incommensurateness, of torturous and humiliating daily pettiness, of sickness and death, a place where man felt he did not belong, "the wrong place," as Chesterton said,[2] the place where man could expect nothing, achieve nothing for himself. Little did it matter, because it served God and so would serve the servant of God. In a word, man's cosmic heroism was assured, even if he was as nothing. This is the most remarkable achievement of the Christian world picture: that it could take slaves, cripples, imbeciles, the simple and the mighty, and make them all secure heroes, simply by taking a step back from the world into another dimension of things, the dimension called heaven. Or we might better say that Christianity took creature consciousness— the thing man most wanted to deny—and made it the very *condition for* his cosmic heroism.

The Romantic Solution

Once we realize what the religious solution did, we can see how modern man edged himself into an impossible situation. He still needed to feel heroic, to know that his life mattered in the scheme of things; he still had to be specially "good" for something truly special. Also, he still had to merge himself with some higher, self-absorbing meaning, in trust and in gratitude—what we saw as the universal motive of the Agape-merger. If he no longer had God, how was he to do this? One of the first ways that occurred to him, as Rank saw, was the "romantic solution": he fixed his urge to cosmic heroism onto *another person* in the form of a love object.[3] The self-glorification that he needed in his innermost nature he now looked for in the love partner. The love partner becomes the divine ideal within which to fulfill one's life. All spiritual and moral needs now become focussed in one individual. Spirituality, which once referred to another dimension of things, is now brought down to this earth and given form in another individual human being. Salvation itself is no longer referred to an abstraction like God but can be sought "in the beatification of the other." We could call this "transference beatification." Man now lives in a "cosmology of two."[4] To be sure, all through history there has been some competition between human objects of love and divine ones—we think of Héloïse and Abelard, Alcibiades and Socrates, or even the Song of Solomon. But the main difference is that in traditional society the human partner would not absorb into himself the whole dimension of the divine; in modern society he does.

In case we are inclined to forget how deified the romantic love object is, the popular songs continually remind us. They tell us that the lover is the "springtime," the "angel-glow," with eyes "like stars," that the experience of love will be "divine," "like heaven" itself, and so on and on; popular love songs have surely had this content from ancient times and will likely continue to have it as long as man remains a mammal and a cousin of the primates. These songs reflect the hunger for real experience, a serious emotional yearning on the part of the creature. The point is that if the love object is divine perfection, then one's own self is elevated by joining one's destiny to it. One has the highest measure for one's ideal-striving; all of one's inner conflicts and contradictions, the many aspects of guilt—all these one can try to purge in a perfect consummation with perfection itself. This becomes a true "moral vindication in the other."[5] Modern man fulfills his urge to self-expansion in the love object just as it was once fulfilled in God: "God as . . . representation of our own will does not resist us except when we ourselves want it, and just as little does the lover resist us who, in yielding, subjects himself to our will."[6] In one word, the love object is God. As a Hindu song puts it: "My lover is like God; if he accepts me my existence is utilized." No wonder Rank could conclude that the love relationship of modern man is a *religious* problem.[7]

Understanding this, Rank could take a great step beyond Freud. Freud thought that modern man's moral dependence on another was a result of the Oedipus complex. But Rank could see that it was the result of a continuation of the *causa-sui* project of denying creatureliness. As now there was no religious cosmology into which to fit such a denial, one grabbed onto a partner. Man reached for a "thou" when the world-view of the great religious community overseen by God died. Modern man's dependency on the love partner, then, is a result of the loss of spiritual ideologies, just as is his dependency on his parents or on his psychotherapist. He needs *somebody*, some "individual ideology of justification" to replace the declining "collective ideologies."[8] Sexuality, which Freud thought was at the heart of the Oedipus complex, is now understood for what it really is: another twisting and turning, a groping for the meaning of one's life. If you don't have a God in heaven, an invisible dimension that justifies the visible one, then you take what is nearest at hand and work out your problems on that.

As we know from our own experience this method gives great and real benefits. Is one oppressed by the burden of his life? Then he can lay it at his divine partner's feet. Is self-consciousness too painful, the sense of being a separate individual, trying to make some kind of meaning out of who one is, what life is, and the like? Then one can wipe it away in the emotional yielding to the partner, forget oneself in the delirium of sex, and still be marvellously quickened in the experience. Is one weighed down by the guilt of his body, the drag of his animality that haunts his victory over decay and death? But this is just what the comfortable sex relationship is for: in sex the body and the consciousness of it are no longer separated; the body is no longer something we look at as alien to ourselves. As soon as it is fully accepted *as a body* by the partner, our self-consciousness vanishes; it merges with the body and with the self-consciousness and body of the partner. Four fragments of existence melt into one unity and things are no longer disjointed and grotesque: everything is "natural," functional, expressed as it should be—and so it is stilled and justified. All the more is guilt wiped away when the body finds its natural usage in the production of a child. Nature herself then proclaims one's innocence, how fitting it is that one should have a body, be basically a procreative animal.[9]

But we also know from experience that things don't work so smoothly or unambiguously. The reason is not far to seek: it is right at the heart of the paradox of the creature. Sex is of the body, and the body is of death. As Rank reminds us, this is the meaning of the Biblical account of the ending of paradise, when the discovery of sex brings death into the world. As in Greek mythology too, Eros and Thanatos are inseparable; death is the natural twin brother of sex.[10] Let us linger on this for a moment because it is so central to the failure of romantic love as a solution to human problems and is so much a part of modern man's frustration. When we say that sex and death are twins, we understand it on at least two levels. The first level is philosophical-biological. Animals who procreate, die. Their relatively short life span is somehow connected with their procreation. Nature conquers death not by creating eternal organisms but by making it possible for ephemeral ones to procreate. Evolutionarily this seems to have made it possible for really complex organisms to emerge in the place of simple—and almost literally eternal—self-dividing ones.

But now the rub for man. If sex is a fulfillment of his role as an animal in the species, it reminds him that he is nothing himself but a link in the chain of being, exchangeable with any other and completely expendable in himself. Sex represents, then, species consciousness and, as such, the defeat of individuality, of personality. But it is just this personality that man wants to develop: the idea of himself as a special cosmic hero with special gifts for the universe. He doesn't want to be a mere fornicating animal like any other—this is not a truly human meaning, a truly distinctive contribution to world life. From the very beginning, then, the sexual act represents a double negation: by physical death and of distinctive personal gifts. This point is crucial because it explains why sexual taboos have been at the heart of human society since the very beginning. They affirm the triumph of human personality over animal sameness. With the complex codes for sexual self-denial, man was able to impose the cultural map for personal immortality over the animal body. He brought sexual taboos into being because he needed to triumph over the body, and he sacrificed the pleasures of the body to the highest pleasure of all: self-perpetuation as a spiritual being through all eternity. This is the substitution that Roheim was really describing when he made his penetrating observation on the Australian aborigines: "The repression and sublimation of the primal scene is at the bottom of totemistic ritual and religion,"[11] that is, the denial of the body as the transmitter of peculiarly human life.

This explains why people chafe at sex, why they resent being reduced to the body, why sex to some degree terrifies them: it represents two levels of the negation of oneself. Resistance to sex is a resistance to fatality. Here Rank has written some of his most brilliant lines. He saw that the sexual conflict is thus a universal one because the body is a universal problem to a creature who must die. One feels guilty toward the body because the body is a bind, it overshadows our freedom. Rank saw that this natural guilt began in childhood and led to the anxious questions of the child about sexual matters. He wants to know why he feels guilt; even more, he wants the parents to tell him that his guilt feeling *is justified*. Here we have to remind ourselves of the perspective we used in Part I to introduce the problem of human nature. We saw that the child stands right at the crossroads of the human dualism. He discovers that he has a fallible body, and he is learning that there is a whole cultural world-view that will permit him to triumph over it. The questions about sex that the child asks are thus not— at a fundamental level—about sex at all. They are about the meaning of the body, the terror of living with a body. When the parents give a straightforward biological answer to sexual questions, they do not answer the child's question at all. He wants to know why he has a body, where it came from, and what it means for a self-conscious creature to be limited by it. He is asking about the ultimate mystery of life, not about the mechanics of sex. As Rank says, this explains why the adults suffer as much from the sexual problem as the child: the "biological solution of the problem of humanity is also ungratifying and inadequate for the adult as for the child."[12]

Sex is a "disappointing answer to life's riddle," and if we pretend that it is an adequate one, we are lying both to ourselves and to our children. As Rank beautifully argues, in this sense "sex education" is a kind of wishful thinking, a rationalization, and a pretense: we try to make believe that if we give instruction in the mechanics of sex we are explaining the mystery of life. We might say that modern man tries to replace vital awe and wonder with a "How to do it" manual.[13] We know why: if you cloak the mystery of creation in the easy steps of human manipulations you banish the terror of the death that is reserved ʾor us as species-sexual animals. Rank goes so far as to conclude that the child is sensitive to this kind of lying. He refuses the "correct scientific explanation" of sexuality, and he refuses too the mandate to guilt-free sex enjoyment that it implies.[14]

I think that the reason probably is that if he is to grow into an immortal culture hero he must have a clear antagonist, especially at the beginning of his struggles to incorporate the cultural *causa-sui* project. As the body is the clear problem over which he must triumph in order to build a cultural personality at all, he must resist, at some level, the adult's attempt to deny that the body is an adversary. We might say that the child is still too weak to be able to bear the conflict of trying to be a personality and a species animal at the same time. The adult is, too, but he has been able to develop the necessary mechanisms of defense, repression and denial, that allow him to live with the problem of serving two masters.

After this reminder of the fundamental problems of the child and the adult that we talked about in Part I, I hope that we can better understand the roots of Rank's critique of the "romantic" psychological type that has emerged in modern times. It then becomes perfectly clear what he means when he says that "personality is ultimately destroyed by and through sex."[15] In other words the sexual partner does not and cannot represent a complete and lasting solution to the human dilemma.[16] The partner represents a kind of fulfillment in freedom from self-consciousness and guilt; but at the same time he represents the negation of one's distinctive personality. We might say the more guilt-free sex the better, but only up to a certain point. In Hitlerism, we saw the misery that resulted when man confused two worlds, when he tried to get a clear-cut triumph over evil, a perfection in this world that could only be possible in some more perfect one. Personal relationships carry the same danger of confusing the real facts of the physical world and the ideal images of spiritual realms. The romantic love "cosmology of two" may be an ingenious and creative attempt, but because it is still a continuation of the *causa-sui* project in this world, it is a lie that must fail. If the partner becomes God he can just as easily become the Devil; the reason is not far to seek. For one thing, one becomes *bound* to the object in dependency. One needs it for self-justification. One can be utterly dependent whether one needs the object as a source of strength, in a masochistic way, or whether one needs it to feel one's own self-expansive strength, by manipulating it sadistically. In either case one's self-development is restricted by the object, absorbed by it. It is too narrow a fetishization of meaning, and one comes to resent it and chafe at it. If you find the ideal love and try to make it the sole judge of good and bad in yourself, the measure of your strivings, you become simply the reflex of another person. You lose yourself in the other, just as obedient children lose themselves in the family. No wonder that dependency, whether of the god or the slave in the relationship, carries with it so much underlying resentment. As Rank put it, explaining the historical bankruptcy of romantic love: a "person no longer wanted to be used as another's soul even with its attendant compensations."[17] When you confuse personal love and cosmic heroism you are bound to fail in both spheres. The impossibility of the heroism undermines the love, even if it is real. As Rank so aptly says, this double failure is what produces the sense of utter despair that we see in modern man. It is impossible to get blood from a stone, to get spirituality from a physical being, and so one feels "inferior" that his life has somehow not succeeded, that he has not realized his true gifts, and so on.[18]

No wonder. How can a human being be a god-like "everything" to another? No human relationship can bear the burden of godhood, and the attempt has to take its toll in some way on both parties. The reasons are not far to seek. The thing that makes God the perfect spiritual object is precisely that he is abstract—as Hegel saw.[19] He is not a concrete individuality, and so He does not limit our development by His own personal will and needs. When we look for the "perfect" human object we are looking for someone who allows us to express our will completely, without any frustration or false notes. We want an object that reflects a truly ideal image of ourselves.[20] But no human object can do this; humans have wills and counterwills of their own, in a thousand ways they can move against us, their very appetites offend us.[21] God's greatness and power is something that we can nourish ourselves in, without its being compromised in any way by the happenings of this world. No human partner can offer this assurance because the partner is real. However much we may idealize and idolize him, he inevitably reflects earthly decay and imperfection. And as he is our ideal measure of value, this imperfection falls back upon us. If your partner is your "All" then any shortcoming in him becomes a major threat to *you*.

If a woman loses her beauty, or shows that she doesn't have the strength and dependability that we once thought she did, or loses her intellectual sharpness, or falls short of our own peculiar needs in any of a thousand ways, then all the investment we have made in her is undermined. The shadow of imperfection falls over our lives, and with it—death and the defeat of cosmic heroism. "She lessens" = "I die." This is the reason for so much bitterness, shortness of temper and recrimination in our daily family lives. We get back a reflection from our loved objects that is less than the grandeur and perfection that we need to nourish ourselves. We feel diminished by their human shortcomings. Our interiors feel empty or anguished, our lives valueless, when we see the inevitable pettinesses of the world expressed through the human beings in it. For this reason, too, we often attack loved ones and try to bring them down to size. We see that our gods have clay feet, and so we must hack away at them in order to save ourselves, to deflate the unreal over-investment that we have made in them in order to secure our own apotheosis. In this sense, the deflation of the over-invested partner, parent, or friend is a creative act that is necessary to correct the lie that we have been living, to reaffirm our own inner freedom of growth that transcends the particular object and is not bound to it. But not everybody can do this because many of us need the lie in order to live. We may have no other God and we may prefer to deflate *ourselves* in order to keep the relationship, even though we glimpse the impossibility of it and the slavishness to which it reduces us.[22] This is one direct explanation—as we shall see—of the phenomenon of depression.

After all, what is it that we want when we elevate the love partner to the position of God? We want redemption—nothing less. We want to be rid of our faults, of our feeling of nothingness. We want to be justified, to know that our creation has not been in vain. We turn to the love partner for the experience of the heroic, for perfect validation; we expect them to "make us good" through love.[23] Needless to say, human partners can't do this. The lover does not dispense cosmic heroism; he cannot give absolution in his own name. The reason is that as a finite being he too is doomed, and we read that doom in his own fallibilities, in his very deterioration. Redemption can only come from outside the individual, from beyond, from our conceptualization of the ultimate source of things, the perfection of creation. It can only come, as Rank saw, when we lay down our individuality, give it up, admit our creatureliness and helplessness.[24] What partner would ever permit us to do this, would bear us if we did? The partner needs us to be as God. On the other hand, what partner could ever want to give redemption—unless he was mad? Even the partner who plays God in the relationship cannot stand it for long, as at some level he knows that he does not possess the resources that the other needs and claims. He does not have perfect strength, perfect assurance, secure heroism. He cannot stand the burden of godhood, and so he must resent the slave. Besides, the uncomfortable realization must always be there: how can one be a genuine god if one's slave is so miserable and unworthy?

Rank saw too, with the logic of his thought, that the spiritual burdens of the modern love relationship were so great and impossible on both partners that they reacted by completely despiritualizing or depersonalizing the relationship. The result is the *Playboy* mystique: over-emphasis on the body as a purely sensual object.[25] If I can't have an ideal that fulfills my life, then at least I can have guilt-free sex—so modern man seems to reason. But we can quickly conclude how self-defeating this solution is because it brings us right back to the dreaded equation of sex with inferiority and death, with service to the species and the negation of one's distinctive personality, the real symbolic heroism. No wonder the sexual mystique is such a shallow creed. It has to be practised by those who have despaired of cosmic heroism, who have narrowed their meanings down to the body and to this world alone. No wonder too that the people who practice it become just as confused and despairing as the romantic lovers. To want too little from the love object is as self-defeating as to want too much.

When you narrow your meanings down to this world you are still looking for the absolute, for the supreme self-transcending power, mystery, and majesty. Only now you must find it in the things of this world. The romantic lover seeks it in the deep interiority of the woman, in her natural mystery. He looks for her to be a source of wisdom, of sure intuition, a bottomless well of continually renewed strength. The sensualist seeks the absolute no longer in the woman, who is a mere thing that one works on. He must then find the absolute in himself, in the vitality that the woman arouses and un-leashes. This is why virility becomes such a predominant problem for him—it is his absolute self-justification in this world. Mike Nichols recently contrasted the romantic and the sensualist in his brilliant film *Carnal Knowledge:* the romantic ends up with an 18-year-old hippie who is "wise beyond her years" and who comes out with unexpected things from the deep of her natural femininity; the sensualist ends a 20-year span of sexual conquests stuck with the problem of his own virility. In the marvelous scene at the end we see the well-schooled prostitute giving him an erection by con-vincing him of his own inner powers and natural strength. Both of these types meet, in the film, on the middle ground of utter confu-sion about what one should get out of a world of breasts and but-tocks and of rebellion against what the species demands of them. The sensualist tries to avoid marriage with all his might, to defeat the species role by making sexuality a purely personal affair of con-quests and virility. The romantic rises above marriage and sex by trying to spiritualize his relationship to women. Neither type can understand the other except on the level of elemental physical desire; and the film leaves us with the reflection that both are pitifully immersed in the blind groping of the human condition, the reaching out for an absolute that can be seen and experienced. It is as though Rank himself had helped write the script; but it was that modern artistic "Rankian" of the love relationship, Jules Feiffer, who did.

Sometimes, it is true, Rank seems so intent on calling our atten-tion to problems that transcend the body that one gets the impres-sion that he failed to appreciate the vital place that it has in our relationships to others and to the world. But that is not at all true. The great lesson of Rank's depreciation of sexuality was not that he played down physical love and sensuality, but that he saw—like Augustine and Kierkegaard—that man cannot fashion an absolute from within his condition, that cosmic heroism must transcend human relationships.[26] What is at stake in all this is, of course, the question of freedom, the quality of one's life and one's individuality.

As we saw in the previous chapter, people need a "beyond," but they reach first for the nearest one; this gives them the fulfillment they need but at the same time limits and enslaves them. You can look at the whole problem of a human life in this way. You can ask the question: What kind of beyond does this person try to expand in; and how much individuation does he achieve in it? Most people play it safe: they choose the beyond of standard transference objects like parents, the boss, or the leader; they accept the cultural definition of heroism and try to be a "good provider" or a "solid" citizen. In this way they earn their species immortality as an agent of procreation, or a collective or cultural immortality as part of a social group of some kind. Most people live this way, and I am hardly implying that there is anything false or unheroic about the standard cultural solution to the problems of men. It represents both the truth and the tragedy of man's condition: the problem of the consecration of one's life, the meaning of it, the natural surrender to something larger—these driving needs that inevitably are resolved by what is nearest at hand.

Women are peculiarly caught up in this dilemma, that the now surging "women's liberation movement" has not yet conceptualized. Rank understood it, both in its necessary aspect and in its constrictive one. The woman, as a source of new life, a part of nature, can find it easy to willingly submit herself to the procreative role in marriage, as a natural fulfillment of the Agape motive. At the same time, however, it becomes self-negating or masochistic when she sacrifices her individual personality and gifts by making the man and his achievements into her immortality-symbol. The Agape surrender is natural and represents a liberating self-fulfillment; but the reflexive internalization of the male's life role is a surrender to one's own weakness, a blurring of the necessary Eros motive of one's own identity. The reason that women are having such trouble disentangling the problems of their social and female roles from that of their distinctive individualities is that these things are intricately confused. The line between natural self-surrender, in wanting to be a part of something larger, and masochistic or self-negating surrender is thin indeed, as Rank saw.[27] The problem is further complicated by something that women—like everyone else—are loathe to admit: their own natural inability to stand alone in freedom. This is why almost everyone consents to earn his immortality in the popular ways mapped out by societies everywhere, in the beyonds of others and not their own.

The Creative Solution

The upshot of all this is that personal heroism through individuation is a very daring venture precisely because it separates the person out of comfortable "beyonds." It takes a strength and courage the average man doesn't have and couldn't even understand—as Jung so well points out.[28] The most terrifying burden of the creature is to be isolated, which is what happens in individuation: one separates himself out of the herd. This move exposes the person to the sense of being completely crushed and annihilated because he sticks out so much, has to carry so much in himself. These are the risks when the person begins to fashion consciously and critically his own framework of heroic self-reference.

Here is precisely the definition of the artist type, or the creative type generally. We have crossed a threshold into a new type of response to man's situation. No one has written about this type of human response more penetratingly than Rank; and of all his books, *Art and Artist* is the most secure monument to his genius. I don't want, here, to get into the kind of agonizingly subtle insights on the artist that Rank has produced or to try to present his comprehensive picture; but it will reward us if we take this opportunity to go a bit deeper than we have into the problem of personality dynamics. It will prepare us, too, for a discussion of Rank's views on neurosis, which are unparalleled in the psychoanalytic literature so far as I know.

The key to the creative type is that he is separated out of the common pool of shared meanings. There is something in his life experience that makes him take in the world as a *problem;* as a result he has to make personal sense out of it. This holds true for all creative people to a greater or lesser extent, but it is especially obvious with the artist. Existence becomes a problem that needs an ideal answer; but when you no longer accept the collective solution to the problem of existence, then you must fashion your own. The work of art is, then, the ideal answer of the creative type to the problem of existence as he takes it in—not only the existence of the external world, but especially his own: who he is as a painfully separate person with nothing shared to lean on. He has to answer to the burden of his extreme individuation, his so painful isolation.

He wants to know how to earn immortality as a result of his own unique gifts. His creative work is at the same time the expression of his heroism and the justification of it. It is his "private religion" —as Rank put it.[29] Its uniqueness gives him personal immortality; it is his own "beyond" and not that of others.

No sooner have we said this than we can see the immense problem that it poses. How can one justify his own heroism? He would have to be as God. Now we see even further how guilt is inevitable for man: even as a creator he is a creature overwhelmed by the creative process itself.[30] If you stick out of nature so much that you yourself have to create your own heroic justification, it is too much. This is how we understand something that seems illogical: that the more you develop as a distinctive free and critical human being, the *more guilt* you have. Your very work accuses you; it makes you feel inferior. What right do you have to play God? Especially if your work is great, absolutely new and different. You wonder where to get authority for introducing new meanings into the world, the strength to bear it.[31] It all boils down to this: the work of art is the artist's attempt to justify his heroism objectively, in the concrete creation. It is the testimonial to his absolute uniqueness and heroic transcendence. But the artist is still a creature and he can feel it more intensely than anyone else. In other words, he knows that the work is he, therefore "bad," ephemeral, potentially meaningless— unless justified from outside *himself* and outside *itself*.

In Jung's terms—that we noted previously—the work is the artist's own transference projection, and he knows that consciously and critically. Whatever he does he is stuck with himself, can't get securely outside and beyond himself.[32] He is also stuck with the work of art itself. Like any material achievement it is visible, earthly, impermanent. No matter how great it is, it still pales in some ways next to the transcending majesty of nature; and so it is ambiguous, hardly a solid immortality symbol. In his greatest genius man is still mocked. No wonder that historically art and psychosis have had such an intimate relationship, that the road to creativity passes so close to the madhouse and often detours or ends there. The artist and the madman are trapped by their own fabrications; they wallow in their own anality, in their protest that they really are something special in creation.

The whole thing boils down to this paradox: if you are going to be a hero then you must give a gift. If you are the average man you give your heroic gift to the society in which you live, and you give the gift that society specifies in advance. If you are an artist you fashion a peculiarly personal gift, the justification of your own heroic identity, which means that it is always aimed at least partly over the heads of your fellow men. After all, they can't grant the immortality of your personal soul. As Rank argued in the breathtaking closing chapters of *Art and Artist,* there is no way for the artist to be at peace with his work or with the society that accepts it. The artist's gift is always to creation itself, to the ultimate meaning of life, to God. We should not be surprised that Rank was brought to exactly the same conclusion as Kierkegaard: that the only way out of human conflict is full renunciation, to give one's life as a gift to the highest powers. Absolution has to come from the absolute beyond. As Kierkegaard, Rank showed that this rule applied to the strongest, most heroic types—not to trembling and empty weaklings. To renounce the world and oneself, to lay the meaning of it to the powers of creation, is the hardest thing for man to achieve—and so it is fitting that this task should fall to the strongest personality type, the one with the largest ego. The great scientific world-shaker Newton was the same man who always carried the Bible under his arm.

Even in such cases, the combination of fullest self-expression and renunciation is rare, as we saw in Chapter Six when we speculated about Freud's lifelong problem. From all that we have now covered —the self in history and in personal creativity—we can perhaps draw even closer to the problem of Freud. We know that he was a genius, and we can now see the real problem that genius has: how to develop a creative work with the full force of one's passion, a work that saves one's soul, and at the same time to renounce that very work because it cannot by itself give salvation. In the creative genius we see the need to combine the most intensive Eros of self-expression with the most complete Agape of self-surrender. It is almost too much to ask of men that they contrive to experience fully both these intensities of ontological striving. Perhaps men with lesser gifts have it easier: a small dosage of Eros and a comfortable Agape. Freud lived the *daimon* of his Eros to the hilt and more honestly than most, and it consumed him and others around him, as it always does more or less. Psychoanalysis was his personal heroic bid for immortality. As Rank said: ". . . he himself could so easily confess his agnosticism while he had created for himself a private religion. . . ."[33] But this was precisely Freud's bind; as an agnostic he had no one to offer his gift to—no one, that is, who had any more security of immortality than he did himself. Not even mankind itself was secure. As he confessed, the spectre of the dinosaurs still haunts man and will always haunt him. Freud was anti-religious because he somehow could not personally give the gift of his life to a religious ideal. He saw such a step as weakness, a passivity that would defeat his own creative urge for more life.

Here Rank joins Kierkegaard in the belief that one should not stop and circumscribe his life with beyonds that are near at hand, or a bit further out, or created by oneself. One should reach for the highest beyond of religion: man should cultivate the passivity of renunciation to the highest powers no matter how difficult it is. Anything less is less than full development, even if it seems like weakness and compromise to the best thinkers. Nietzsche railed at the Judeo-Christian renunciatory morality; but as Rank said, he "overlooked the deep need in the human being for just that kind of morality. . . ."[34] Rank goes so far as to say that the "need for a truly religious ideology . . . is inherent in human nature and its fulfillment is basic to any kind of social life."[35] Do Freud and others imagine that surrender to God is masochistic, that to empty oneself is demeaning? Well, answers Rank, it represents on the contrary the furthest reach of the self, the highest idealization man can achieve. It represents the fulfillment of the Agape love-expansion, the achievement of the truly creative type. Only in this way, says Rank, only by surrendering to the bigness of nature on the highest, least-fetishized level, can man conquer death. In other words, the true heroic validation of one's life lies beyond sex, beyond the other, beyond the private religion—all these are makeshifts that pull man down or that hem him in, leaving him torn with ambiguity. Man feels inferior precisely when he lacks "true inner values in the personality," when he is merely a reflex of something next to him and has no steadying inner gyroscope, no centering in himself. And in order to get such centering man has to look beyond the "thou," beyond the consolations of others and of the things of this world.[36]

Man is a "theological being," concludes Rank, and not a biological one. In all this it is as though Tillich[37] were speaking and, behind him, Kierkegaard and Augustine; but what makes it uncanny in the present world of science is that these are the conclusions of the life-work of a psychoanalyst, not a theologian. The net effect of it is overwhelming, and to someone trained narrowly in a field of science the whole thing seems confused. Such a mixture of intensive clinical insight and pure Christian ideology is absolutely heady. One doesn't know what kind of emotional attitude to assume towards it; it seems to pull one in several irreconcilable directions at the same time.

At this point the "tough-minded" scientist (as he likes to call himself) slams shut the covers of the book by Rank and turns away with a shudder. "What a shame that Freud's closest collaborator should turn so soft in the head, should deliver over to the easy consolations of religion the hard-won knowledge of psychoanalysis." So he would think—and he would be wrong. Rank made complete closure of psychoanalysis on Kierkegaard, but he did not do it out of weakness or wishfulness. He did it out of the logic of the his-torical-psychoanalytic understanding of man. There is simply no way for the critic of Rank to get around this. If he thinks Rank is not hard-headed or empirical enough it is because he has not really come to grips with the heart of Rank's whole work—his elaboration of the nature of neurosis. *This* is Rank's answer to those who imagine that he stopped short in his scientific quest or went soft out of personal motives. Rank's understanding of the neurotic is the key to his whole thought. It is of vital importance for a full post-Freudian understanding of man and at the same time represents the locus of the intimate merger of Rank's thought with Kierkegaard's, on terms and in language that Kierkegaard himself would have found comfortable. Let us explore it in more detail in the next chapter.

CHAPTER NINE

The Present Outcome of Psychoanalysis

If man is the more normal, healthy and happy,
the more he can . . . successfully . . . repress,
displace, deny, rationalize, dramatize himself
and deceive others, then it follows that the
suffering of the neurotic comes . . . from painful
truth. . . . Spiritually the neurotic has been long
since where psychoanalysis wants to bring him
without being able to, namely at the point of
seeing through the deception of the world of
sense, the falsity of reality. He suffers, not from
all the pathological mechanisms which are
psychically necessary for living and wholesome
but in the refusal of these mechanisms which is
just what robs him of the illusions important for
living. . . . [He] is much nearer to the actual
truth psychologically than the others and it is just
that from which he suffers.
—OTTO RANK[1]

Rank wrote about neurosis all through his work, a line or a paragraph here, a page or two there; and he gave many different and
even contradictory definitions of it. Sometimes he made it seem
normal and universal, at other times he saw it as unhealthy and
private; sometimes he used the term for small problems of living, at
others he used it to include actual psychosis. This elasticity of
Rank's is not due to confused thinking: the fact is—as we shall
shortly see—that neurosis sums up all the problems of a human

life. But Rank could have helped his own work enormously by putting conceptual order into his insights on mental illness. If a thinker throws off too many unsystematic and rich insights, there is no place to grab onto his thought. The thing he is trying to illuminate seems as elusive as before. It is certain that Freud's prominence is due to no small extent to his ability to make clear, simple, and systematic all of his insights and always to reduce the most complex theory to a few fundamentals. You can do this with Rank too, but the rub is that you must do it yourself by putting your own order into the broadside of Rank's work. Although Rank knew that this requirement wasn't fair either to the reader or to himself, he never did find anyone to rewrite his books; and so we ourselves have to try to go beyond the confusion of insights and penetrate to the heart of the problem.

As a point of departure let us first sum up everything that neurosis covers and then take up one thing at a time to show how they all fit together. Neurosis has three interdependent aspects. In the first place it refers to people who are having trouble living with the truth of existence; it is universal in this sense because everybody has some trouble living with the truth of life and pays some vital ransom to that truth. In the second place, neurosis is private because each person fashions his own peculiar stylistic reaction to life. Finally, beyond both of these is perhaps the unique gift of Rank's work: that neurosis is also historical to a large extent, because all the traditional ideologies that disguised and absorbed it have fallen away and modern ideologies are just too thin to contain it. So we have modern man: increasingly slumping onto analysts' couches, making pilgrimages to psychological guru-centers and joining therapy groups, and filling larger and larger numbers of mental hospital beds. Let us look at each of these three aspects in more detail.

The Neurotic Type

First, as a problem of personal character. When we say neurosis represents the truth of life we again mean that life is an overwhelming problem for an animal free of instinct. The individual has to protect himself against the world, and he can do this only as any other animal would: by narrowing down the world, shutting off experience, developing an obliviousness both to the terrors of the world and to his own anxieties. Otherwise he would be crippled for action. We cannot repeat too often the great lesson of Freudian psychology: that repression is normal self-protection and creative self-restriction—in a real sense, man's natural substitute for instinct. Rank has a perfect, key term for this natural human talent: he calls it "partialization" and very rightly sees that life is impossible without it. What we call the well-adjusted man has just this capacity to partialize the world for comfortable action.[2] I have used the term "fetishization," which is exactly the same idea: the "normal" man bites off what he can chew and digest of life, and no more. In other words, men aren't built to be gods, to take in the whole world; they are built like other creatures, to take in the piece of ground in front of their noses. Gods can take in the whole of creation because they alone can make sense of it, know what it is all about and for. But as soon as a man lifts his nose from the ground and starts sniffing at eternal problems like life and death, the meaning of a rose or a star cluster—then he is in trouble. Most men spare themselves this trouble by keeping their minds on the small problems of their lives just as their society maps these problems out for them. These are what Kierkegaard called the "immediate" men and the "Philistines." They "tranquilize themselves with the trivial"—and so they can lead normal lives.

Right away we can see the immensely fertile horizon that opens up in all of our thinking on mental health and "normal" behavior. In order to function normally, man has to achieve from the beginning a serious constriction of the world and of himself. We can say that the essence of normality is the *refusal of reality*.[3] What we call neurosis enters precisely at this point: Some people have more trouble with their lies than others. The world is too much with them, and the techniques that they have developed for holding it at bay and cutting it down to size finally begin to choke the person himself. This is neurosis in a nutshell: the miscarriage of clumsy lies about reality.

But we can also see at once that there is no line between normal and neurotic, as we all lie and are all bound in some ways by the lies. Neurosis is, then, something we all share; it is universal.[4] Or, putting it another way, normality is neurosis, and vice versa. We call a man "neurotic" when his lie begins to show damaging effects on him or on people around him and he seeks clinical help for it— or others seek it for him. Otherwise, we call the refusal of reality "normal" because it doesn't occasion any visible problems. It is really as simple as that. After all, if someone who lives alone wants to get out of bed a half-dozen times to see if the door is *really* locked, or another washes and dries his hands exactly three times every time or uses a half-roll of toilet tissue each time he relieves himself—there is really no human problem involved. These people are earning their safety in the face of the reality of creatureliness in relatively innocuous and untroublesome ways.

But the whole thing becomes more complex when we see how the lies about reality begin to miscarry. Then we have to begin to apply the label "neurotic." And there are any number of occasions for this, from many ranges of human experience. Generally speaking, we call neurotic any life style that begins to constrict too much, that prevents free forward momentum, new choices, and growth that a person may want and need. For example, a person who is trying to find his salvation only in a love relationship but who is being defeated by this too narrow focus is neurotic. He can become overly passive and dependent, fearful of venturing out on his own, of making his life without his partner, no matter how that partner treats him. The object has become his "All," his whole world; and he is reduced to the status of a simple reflex of another human being.[5] This type frequently looks for clinical help. He feels stuck in his narrow horizon, needs his particular "beyond" but fears moving past it. In terms we used earlier we could say that his "safe" heroics is not working out; it is choking him, poisoning him with the dumb realization that it is so safe that it is not heroic at all. To lie to oneself about one's own potential development is another cause of guilt. It is one of the most insidious daily inner gnawings a person can experience. Guilt, remember, is the bind that man experiences when he is humbled and stopped in ways that he does not understand, when he is overshadowed in his energies by the world. But the misfortune of man is that he can experience this guilt in two ways: as bafflement from without and from within—by being stopped in relation to his own potential development. Guilt results from unused life, from "the unlived in us."[6]

More sensational are those other familiar miscarriages of lies about reality, what we call obsessions and compulsions, phobias of all kinds. Here we see the result of too much fetishization or partialization, too much narrowing-down of the world for action. The result is that the person gets stuck in the narrowness. It is one thing to ritually wash one's hands three times; it is another to wash them until the hands bleed and one is in the bathroom most of the day. Here we see in pure culture, as it were, what is at stake in all human repression: the fear of life and death. Safety in the face of the real terror of creature existence is becoming a real problem for the person. He feels vulnerable—which is the truth! But he reacts too totally, too inflexibly. He fears going out in the street, or up in elevators, or into transportation of any kind. At this extreme it is as though the person says to himself "If I do anything at all . . . I will die."[7]

We can see that the symptom is an attempt to live, an attempt to unblock action and keep the world safe. The fear of life and death is encapsulated in the symptom. If you feel vulnerable it is because you feel bad and inferior, not big or strong enough to face up to the terrors of the universe. You work out your need for perfection (bigness, invulnerability) in the symptom—say, hand-washing or the avoidance of sex in marriage. We might say that the symptom itself represents the locus of the performance of heroism. No wonder that one cannot give it up: that would release all by itself the whole flood of terror that one is trying to deny and overcome. When you put all your eggs in one basket you must clutch that basket for dear life. It is as though one were to take the whole world and fuse it into a single object or a single fear. We immediately recognize this as the same creative dynamic that the person uses in transference, when he fuses all the terror and majesty of creation in the transference-object. This is what Rank meant when he said that neurosis represents creative power gone astray and confused. The person doesn't really know what the problem is, but he hits on an ingenious way to keep moving past it. Let us note, too, that Freud himself used the expression "transference-neurosis" as a collective term for hysterical fears and compulsion neuroses.[8] We can say that Rank and modern psychiatry merely simplify and carry through this basic insight, but now putting the burden of explanation on life-and-death fears, not merely on Oedipal dynamics. One young psychiatrist has recently summed up the whole matter beautifully, in the following words:

It must be clear that the despair and anguish of which the patient complains is not the result of such symptoms but rather are the reasons for their existence. It is in fact these very symptoms that shield him from the torment of the profound contradictions that lie at the heart of human existence. The particular phobia or obsession is the very means by which man . . . eases the burden of his life's tasks . . . is able to . . . assuage his sense of insignificance. . . . Thus, neurotic symptoms serve to reduce and narrow—to magically transform the world so that he may be distracted from his concerns of death, guilt, and meaninglessness. The neurotic preoccupied with his symptom is led to believe that his central task is one of confrontation with his particular obsession or phobia. In a sense his neurosis allows him to take control of his destiny—to transform the whole of life's meaning into the simplified meaning emanating from his self-created world.[9]

The ironic thing about the narrowing-down of neurosis is that the person seeks to avoid death, but he does it by killing off so much of himself and so large a spectrum of his action-world that he is actually isolating and diminishing himself and becomes as though dead.[10] There is just no way for the living creature to avoid life and death, and it is probably poetic justice that if he tries too hard to do so he destroys himself.

But we still haven't exhausted the range of behaviors that we can call neurotic. Another way of approaching neurosis is from the opposite end of the problem. There is a type of person who has difficulty fetishizing and narrowing-down; he has a vivid imagination, takes in too much experience, too large a chunk of the world—and this too must be called neurotic.[11] We introduced this type in the last chapter where we talked about the creative person. We saw that these people feel their isolation, their individuality. They stick out, are less built-into normal society, less securely programmed for automatic cultural action. To have difficulty partializing experience is to have difficulty living. Not to be able to

fetishize makes one susceptible to the world as a total problem—
with all the living hell that this exposure raises. We said that
partializing the world is biting off what an animal can chew. Not to
have this talent means constantly biting off more than one can chew.
Rank puts it this way:

The neurotic type . . . makes the reality surrounding him a part of his
ego, which explains his painful relation to it. For all outside processes,
however unmeaningful they may be in themselves, finally concern him
. . . he is bound up in a kind of magic unity with the wholeness of life
around him much more than the adjusted type who can be satisfied with
the role of a part within the whole. The neurotic type has taken into
himself potentially the whole of reality.[12]

Now we can see how the problem of neurosis can be laid out
along the lines of the twin ontological motives: on the one hand,
one merges with the world around him and becomes too much a
part of it and so loses his own claim to life. On the other hand, one
cuts oneself off from the world in order to make one's own *complete*
claim and so loses the ability to live and act in the world on its
terms. As Rank put it, some individuals are unable to separate and
others are unable to unite. The ideal of course is to find some
balance between the two motives, such as characterize the better
adjusted person; he is at ease with both. The neurotic represents
precisely "an extreme at one end or the other"; he feels that one or
the other is a burden.[13]

The question for a characterology is why some people cannot
balance their ontological urges, why they hug at the extremes. The
answer must obviously go back to the personal life history. There
are those who shrink back from experience out of greater life-and-
death anxieties. They grow up not giving themselves freely to the
cultural roles available to them. They can't lose themselves thoughtlessly in the games that others play. One reason is that they have
trouble relating to others; they haven't been able to develop the
necessary interpersonal skills. Playing the game of society with automatic ease means playing with others without anxiety. If you are
not involved in what others take for granted as the nourishment of
their lives, then your own life becomes a total problem. At its extreme this describes the schizoid type par excellence. Classically

this state was called the "narcissistic neurosis" or psychosis. The psychotic is the one who cannot shut out the world, whose repressions are all on the surface, whose defenses no longer work; and so he withdraws from the world and into himself and his fantasies. He fences himself off and becomes his own world (narcissism).

It may seem courageous to take in the whole world, instead of just biting off pieces and acting on them, but as Rank points out, this is also precisely a defense against engagement in it:

. . . this apparent egocentricity originally is just a defense mechanism against the danger of reality. . . . [The neurotic] seeks to complete his ego constantly . . . without paying for it.[14]

To live is to engage in experience at least partly on the terms of the experience itself. One has to stick his neck out in the action without any guarantees about satisfaction or safety. One never knows how it will come out or how silly he will look, but the neurotic type wants these guarantees. He doesn't want to risk his self-image. Rank calls this very aptly the "self-willed over-valuation of self" whereby the neurotic tries to cheat nature.[15] He won't pay the price that nature wants of him: to age, fall ill or be injured, and die. Instead of living experience he ideates it; instead of arranging it in action he works it all out in his head.

We can see that neurosis is par excellence the danger of a symbolic animal whose body is a problem to him. Instead of living biologically, then, he lives symbolically. Instead of living in the partway that nature provided for he lives in the total way made possible by symbols. One substitutes the magical, all-inclusive world of the self for the real, fragmentary world of experience. Again, in this sense, everyone is neurotic, as everyone holds back from life in some ways and lets his symbolic world-view arrange things: this is what cultural morality is for.[16] In this sense, too, the artist is the most neurotic because he too takes the world as a totality and makes a largely symbolic problem out of it.

If this neurosis characterizes everyone to a certain extent and the artist most of all, where do we cross the line into "neurosis" as a clinical problem? One way, as we saw, is by the production of a crippling symptom or a too-constricting life style. The person has tried to cheat nature by restricting his experience, but he remains sensitive to the terror of life at some level of his awareness. Besides, he can't arrange his triumph over life and death in his mind or in his narrow heroics without paying some price: the symptom or a bogging down in guilt and futility because of an unlived life.

A second way of crossing the line into clinical neurosis follows naturally from everything we have said. Rank asked why the artist so often avoids clinical neurosis when he is so much a candidate for it because of his vivid imagination, his openness to the finest and broadest aspects of experience, his isolation from the cultural world-view that satisfies everyone else. The answer is that he takes in the world, but instead of being oppressed by it he reworks it in his own personality and recreates it in the work of art. The neurotic is precisely the one who cannot create—the "artiste-manqué," as Rank so aptly called him. We might say that both the artist and the neurotic bite off more than they can chew, but the artist spews it back out again and chews it over in an objectified way, as an external, active, work project. The neurotic can't marshal this creative response embodied in a specific work, and so he chokes on his introversions. The artist has similar large-scale introversions, but he uses them as material.[17] In Rank's inspired conceptualization, the difference is put like this:

. . . it is this very fact of the ideologization of purely psychical conflicts that makes the difference between the productive and the unproductive types, the artist and the neurotic; for the neurotic's creative power, like the most primitive artist's, is always tied to his own self and exhausts itself in it, whereas the productive type succeeds in changing this purely subjective creative process into an objective one, which means that through ideologizing it he transfers it from his own self to his work.[18]

The neurotic exhausts himself not only in self-preoccupations like hypochondriacal fears and all sorts of fantasies, but also in *others:* those around him on whom he is dependent become his therapeutic work project; he takes out his subjective problems on them. But people are not clay to be molded; they have needs and counter-wills of their own. The neurotic's frustration as a failed artist can't be remedied by anything but an objective creative work of his own. Another way of looking at it is to say that the more totally one takes in the world as a problem, the more inferior or "bad" one is going to feel inside oneself. He can try to work out this "badness" by striving for perfection, and then the neurotic symptom becomes his "creative" work; or he can try to make himself perfect by means of his partner. But it is obvious to us that the only way to work on perfection is in the form of an objective work that is fully under your control and is perfectible in some real ways. Either you eat up yourself and others around you, trying for perfection; or you *objectify that imperfection in a work,* on which you then unleash your creative powers. In this sense, some kind of objective creativity is the only answer man has to the problem of life. In this way he satisfies nature, which asks that he live and act objectively as a vital animal plunging into the world; but he also satisfies his own distinctive human nature because he plunges in on his own *symbolic* terms and not as a reflex of the world as given to mere physical sense experience. He takes in the world, makes a total problem out of it, and then gives out a fashioned, human answer to that problem. This, as Goethe saw in Faust, is the highest that man can achieve.

From this point of view the difference between the artist and the neurotic seems to boil down largely to a question of talent. It is like the difference between an illiterate schizophrenic and a Strindberg: one ends up on the backwards and the other becomes a culture hero—but both experience the world in similar ways and only the quality and the power of the reaction differ. If the neurotic feels vulnerable in the face of the world he takes in, he reacts by criticizing himself to excess. He can't endure himself or the isolation that his individuality plunges him into. On the other hand, he still needs to be a hero, still needs to earn immortality on the basis of his unique qualities, which means that he still must glorify himself in some ways. But he can glorify himself only *in fantasy,* as he cannot fashion a creative work that speaks on his behalf by virtue of its objective perfection. He is caught in a vicious circle because he experiences the unreality of fantasied self-glorification. There is really no conviction possible for man unless it comes from others or from outside himself in some way—at least not for long. One simply cannot justify his own heroism in his own inner symbolic fantasy, which is what leads the neurotic to feel more unworthy and inferior. This is pretty much the situation of the adolescent who has not discovered his inner gifts. The artist, on the other hand, overcomes his inferiority and glorifies himself *because he has the talent* to do so.[19]

From all this we can see how interchangeably we can talk about neurosis, adolescence, normality, the artist—with only varying degrees of difference or with a peculiar additive like "talent" making all the difference. Talent itself is usually largely circumstantial, the result of luck and work, which makes Rank's view of neurosis true to life. Artists are neurotic as well as creative; the greatest of them can have crippling neurotic symptoms and can cripple those around them as well by their neurotic demands and needs. Look what Carlyle did to his wife. There is no doubt that creative work is itself done under a compulsion often indistinguishable from a purely clinical obsession. In this sense, what we call a creative gift is merely the social license to be obsessed. And what we call "cultural routine" is a similar license: the proletariat demands the obsession of work in order to keep from going crazy. I used to wonder how people could stand the really demonic activity of working behind those hellish ranges in hotel kitchens, the frantic whirl of waiting on a dozen tables at one time, the madness of the travel agent's office at the height of the tourist season, or the torture of working with a jack-hammer all day on a hot summer street. The answer is so simple that it eludes us: the craziness of these activities is exactly that of the human condition. They are "right" for us because the alternative is natural desperation. The daily madness of these jobs is a repeated vaccination against the madness of the asylum. Look at the joy and eagerness with which workers return from vacation to their compulsive routines. They plunge into their work with equanimity and lightheartedness because it drowns out something more ominous. Men have to be protected from reality. All of which poses another gigantic problem to a sophisticated Marxism, namely: What is the nature of the obsessive denials of reality that a utopian society will provide to keep men from going mad?

The Problem of Illusion

We have looked at neurosis as a problem of character and have seen that it can be approached in two ways: as a problem of too much narrowness toward the world or of too much openness. There are those who are too narrowly built-into their world, and there are those who are floating too freely apart from it. Rank makes a special type out of the hypersensitive, open neurotic; and if we put him on the schizoid continuum this is probably true. But it is very risky to try to be hard and fast about types of personality; there are all kinds of blends and combinations that defy precise compartmental-ization. After all, one of the reasons we narrow down too much is that we must sense on some level of awareness that life is too big and threatening a problem. And if we say that the average man narrows down "just about right," we have to ask who this average man is. He may avoid the psychiatric clinic, but somebody around has to pay for it. We are reminded of those Roman portrait-busts that stuff our museums: to live in this tight-lipped style as an average good citizen must have created some daily hell. Of course we are not talking only about daily pettinesses and the small sadisms that are practised on family and friends. Even if the average man lives in a kind of obliviousness of anxiety, it is because he has erected a massive wall of repressions to hide the problem of life and death. His anality may protect him, but all through history it is the "normal, average men" who, like locusts, have laid waste to the world in order to forget themselves.

Perhaps this blending-in of normalcy and neurosis becomes even clearer if we look at the problem not only as one of character but also under another general aspect: as a question of reality and illu-sion. Here again Rank has scored a triumph of insight. In terms of everything we have said so far, this way of looking at neurosis will be easy to grasp. We have seen that what we call the human character is actually a lie about the nature of reality. The *causa-sui* project is a pretense that one is invulnerable because protected by the power of others and of culture, that one is important in nature and can do something about the world. But in back of the *causa-sui* project whispers the voice of possible truth: that human life may not be more than a meaningless interlude in a vicious drama of flesh and bones that we call evolution; that the Creator may not care any more for the destiny of man or the self-perpetuation of individual men than He seems to have cared for the dinosaurs or the Tasmanians. The whisper is the same one that slips incon-gruously out of the Bible in the voice of Ecclesiastes: that all is vanity, vanity of vanities.

Some people are more sensitive to the lie of cultural life, to the illusions of the *causa-sui* project that others are so thoughtlessly and trustingly caught up in. The neurotic is having trouble with the balance of cultural illusion and natural reality; the possible horrible truth about himself and the world is seeping into his consciousness. The average man is at least secure that the cultural game *is* the truth, the unshakable, durable truth. He can earn his immortality in and under the dominant immortality ideology, period. It is all so simple and clear-cut. But now the neurotic:

[He] perceives himself as unreal and reality as unbearable, because with him the mechanisms of illusion are known and destroyed by self consciousness. He can no longer deceive himself about himself and disillusions even his own ideal of personality. He perceives himself as bad, guilt laden, inferior, as a small, weak, helpless creature, which is the truth about mankind, as Oedipus also discovered in the crash of his heroic fate. All other is illusion, deception, but necessary deception in order to be able to bear one's self and thereby life.[20]

In other words, the neurotic isolates himself from others, cannot engage freely in their partialization of the world, and so cannot live by their deceptions about the human condition. He lifts himself out of the "natural therapy" of everyday life, the active, self-forgetful engagement in it; and so the illusions that others share seem unreal to him. This is forced.[21] Neither can he, like the artist, *create new illusions*. As Anaïs Nin put it graphically: "The caricature aspect of life appears whenever the drunkenness of illusion wears off."[22] And don't some people drink to head off the despair of reality as they sense it truly is? Man must always imagine and believe in a "second" reality or a better world than the one that is given him by nature.[23] In this sense, the neurotic symptom is a communication about truth: that the illusion that one is invulnerable is a lie. Let me quote another piece of Rank's powerful summing-up of this problem of illusion and reality:

With the truth, one cannot live. To be able to live one needs illusions, not only outer illusions such as art, religion, philosophy, science and love afford, but inner illusions which first condition the outer [i.e., a secure sense of one's active powers, and of being able to count on the powers of others]. The more a man can take reality as truth, appearance as essence, the sounder, the better adjusted, the happier will he be . . . this constantly effective process of self-deceiving, pretending and blundering, is no psychopathological mechanism. . . .[24]

Rank calls this a paradoxical but deep insight into the essence of neurosis, and he sums it up in the words we have used as an epigraph to this chapter. In fact, it is this and more: it absolutely shakes the foundations of our conceptualization of normality and health. It makes them entirely a relative value problem. The neurotic opts out of life because he is having trouble maintaining his illusions about it, which proves nothing less than that life is possible only with illusions.

And so, the question for the science of mental health must become an absolutely new and revolutionary one, yet one that reflects the essence of the human condition: On what level of illusion does one live?[25] We will see the import of this at the close of this chapter, but right now we must remind ourselves that when we talk about the need for illusion we are not being cynical. True, there is a great deal of falseness and self-deception in the cultural *causa-sui* project, but there is also the necessity of this project. Man needs a "second" world, a world of humanly created meaning, a new reality that he can live, dramatize, nourish himself in. "Illusion" means creative play at its highest level. Cultural illusion is a necessary ideology of self-justification, a heroic dimension that is life itself to the symbolic animal. To lose the security of heroic cultural illusion is to die—that is what "deculturation" of primitives means and what it does. It kills them or reduces them to the animal level of chronic fighting and fornication. Life becomes possible only in a continual alcoholic stupor. Many of the older American Indians were relieved when the Big Chiefs in Ottawa and Washington took control and prevented them from warring and feuding. It was a relief from the constant anxiety of death for their loved ones, if not for themselves. But they also knew, with a heavy heart, that this eclipse of their traditional hero-systems at the same time left them as good as dead.[26]

Neurosis as Historical

Our third general approach to the problem of neurosis is that of the historical dimension. It is the most important of all, really, because it absorbs the others. We saw that neurosis could be looked at at a basic level as a problem of character and, at another level, as a problem of illusion, of creative cultural play. The historical level is a third level into which these two merge. The quality of cultural play, of creative illusion, varies with each society and historical period. In other words, the individual can more easily cross the line into clinical neurosis precisely where he is thrown back on himself and his own resources in order to justify his life. Rank could validly raise the issue of neurosis as a historical problem and not a clinical one. If history is a succession of immortality ideologies, then the problems of men can be read directly against those ideologies—how embracing they are, how convincing, how easy they make it for men to be confident and secure in their personal heroism. What characterizes modern life is the failure of all traditional immortality ideologies to absorb and quicken man's hunger for self-perpetuation and heroism. Neurosis is today a widespread problem because of the disappearance of convincing dramas of heroic apotheosis of man.[27] The subject is summed up succinctly in Pinel's famous observation on how the Salpêtrière mental hospital got cleared out at the time of the French Revolution. All the neurotics found a ready-made drama of self-transcending action and heroic identity. It was as simple as that.

It begins to look as though modern man cannot find his heroism in everyday life any more, as men did in traditional societies just by doing their daily duty of raising children, working, and worshipping. He needs revolutions and wars and "continuing" revolutions to last when the revolutions and wars end. That is the price modern man pays for the eclipse of the sacred dimension. When he dethroned the ideas of soul and God he was thrown back hopelessly on his own resources, on himself and those few around him. Even lovers and families trap and disillusion us because they are not substitutes for absolute transcendence. We might say that they are poor illusions in the sense that we have been discussing.[28]

Rank saw that this hyper-self-consciousness had left modern man to his own resources, and he called him aptly "psychological man." It is a fitting epithet in more than one sense. Modern man became psychological because he became isolated from protective collective ideologies. He had to justify himself from within himself. But he also became psychological because modern thought itself evolved that way when it developed out of religion. The inner life of man had always been portrayed traditionally as the area of the soul. But in the 19th century scientists wanted to reclaim this last domain of superstition from the Church. They wanted to make the inner life of man an area free of mystery and subject to the laws of causality. They gradually abandoned the word "soul" and began to talk about the "self" and to study how it develops in the child's early relationship with his mother. The great miracles of language, thought, and morality could now be studied as social products and not divine interventions.[29] It was a great breakthrough in science that culminated only with the work of Freud; but it was Rank who saw that this scientific victory raised more problems than it solved. Science thought that it had gotten rid forever of the problems of the soul by making the inner world the subject of scientific analysis. But few wanted to admit that this work still left the soul perfectly intact as a word to explain the inner energy of organisms, the mystery of the creation and sustenance of living matter. It really doesn't matter if we discover that man's inner precepts about himself and his world, his very self-consciousness in language, art, laughter, and tears, are all socially built into him. We still haven't explained the inner forces of evolution that have led to the development of an animal capable of self-consciousness, which is what we still must mean by "soul"—the mystery of the meaning of organismic awareness, of the inner dynamism and pulsations of nature. From this point of view the hysterical reaction of 19th-century believers against Darwin only shows the thinness and unimaginativeness of their faith. They were not open to plain and ordinary awe and wonder; they took life too much for granted; and when Darwin stripped them of their sense of "special wondrousness" they felt as good as dead.

But the triumph of scientific psychology had more equivocal

effects than merely leaving intact the soul that it set out to banish. When you narrow down the soul to the self, and the self to the early conditioning of the child, what do you have left? You have the individual man, and you are stuck with him. I mean that the promise of psychology, like all of modern science, was that it would usher in the era of the happiness of man, by showing him how things worked, how one thing caused another. Then, when man knew the causes of things, all he had to do was to take possession of the domain of nature, including his own nature, and his happiness would be assured. But now we come up against the fallacy of psychological self-scrutiny that Rank, almost alone among the disciples of Freud, understood. The doctrine of the soul showed man *why* he was inferior, bad, and guilty; and it gave him the means to get rid of that badness and be happy. Psychology also wanted to show man why he felt this way; the hope was that if you found men's motives and showed to man why he felt guilty and bad, he could then accept himself and be happy. But actually psychology could only find *part* of the reason for feelings of inferiority, badness, and guilt—the part caused by the objects—trying to be good for them, fearing them, fearing leaving them, and the like. We don't want to deny that this much is a lot. It represents a great liberation from what we could call "false badness," the conflicts artificially caused by one's own early environment and the accidents of birth and place. As this research reveals one part of the *causa-sui* lie, it does unleash a level of honesty and maturity that puts one more in control of oneself and does make for a certain level of freedom and the happiness that goes with it.

But now the point that we are driving at: early conditioning and conflicts with objects, guilt toward specific persons, and the like are only part of the problem of the person. The *causa-sui* lie is aimed at the whole of nature, not only at the early objects. As the existentialists have put it, psychology found out about neurotic guilt or circumstantial, exaggerated, unscrutinized personal guilts; but it did not have anything to say about real or natural creature guilt. It tried to lay a total claim on the problem of unhappiness, when it had only a part-claim on the problem. This is what Rank meant when he said that:

. . . psychology, which is gradually trying to supplant religious and moral ideology, is only partially qualified to do this, because it is a preponderantly negative and disintegrating ideology. . . .[30]

Psychology narrows the cause for personal unhappiness down to the person himself, and then he is stuck with himself. But we know that the universal and general cause for personal badness, guilt, and inferiority is the natural world and the person's relationship to it as a symbolic animal who must find a secure place in it. All the analysis in the world doesn't allow the person to find out *who he is* and why he is here on earth, why he has to die, and how he can make his life a triumph. It is when psychology pretends to do this, when it offers itself as a full explanation of human unhappiness, that it becomes a fraud that makes the situation of modern man an impasse from which he cannot escape. Or, put another way, psychology has limited its understanding of human unhappiness to the personal life-history of the individual and has not understood how much individual unhappiness is itself a historical problem in the larger sense, a problem of the eclipse of secure communal ideologies of redemption. Rank put it this way:

In the neurotic in whom one sees the collapse of the whole human ideology of God it has also become obvious what this signifies psychologically. This was not explained by Freud's psychoanalysis which only comprehended the destructive process in the patient from his personal history without considering the cultural development which bred this type.[31]

If you fail to understand this you risk making the neurotic even worse off by closing him off from the larger world-view that he needs. As Rank put it:

. . . it was finally the understanding psychoanalyst who sent the self-conscious neurotic back to the very self-knowledge from which he wanted to escape. On the whole, psychoanalysis failed therapeutically because it aggravated man's psychologizing rather than healed him of his introspection.[32]

Or better, we would say, psychoanalysis failed therapeutically where it fetishized the causes of human unhappiness as sexuality, and when it pretended to be a total world-view in itself. We can conclude with Rank that religion is "just as good a psychology" as the psychology that pretended to replace it.[33] In some ways it is of course even better because it gets at the actual causes of universal guilt; in some ways it is much worse, because it usually reinforces the parental and social authorities and makes the bind of circumstantial guilt even stronger and more crippling.

There is no way to answer Rank's devastating relativization of modern psychology.[34] We have only to look around at the growing number of psychological gurus in the marketplace in order to get the lived historical flavor of the thing. Modern man started looking inward in the 19th century because he hoped to find immortality in a new and secure way. He wanted heroic apotheosis as did all other historical men—but now there is no one to give it to him except his psychological guru. He created his own impasse. In this sense, as Rank said (with what has to be a touch of ironic humor): psychotherapists "are, so to say, the neurotic's product due to his illness."[35] Modern man needs a "thou" to whom to turn for spiritual and moral dependence, and as God was in eclipse, the therapist has had to replace Him—just as the lover and the parents did. For generations now, the psychoanalysts, not understanding this historical problem, have been trying to figure out why the "termination of the transference" in therapy is such a devilish problem in many cases. Had they read and understood Rank, they would quickly have seen that the "thou" of the therapist is the new God who must replace the old collective ideologies of redemption. As the individual cannot serve as God he must give rise to a truly *devilish* problem.[36]* Modern man is condemned to seek the meaning of his life in psychological introspection, and so his new confessor has to be the

* One exception is Alan Wheelis, who discusses these very things: the need for transference, the problem of historical change and neurosis, the insufficiency of psychoanalytic therapy for finding an identity, and so on. (*The Quest for Identity* [N.Y.: Norton, 1958], pp. 159–173). The whole discussion is pure Rank, although Wheelis evidently arrived at his views independently.

supreme authority on introspection, the psychoanalyst. As this is so, the patient's "beyond" is limited to the analytic couch and the world-view imparted there.†

In this sense, as Rank saw with such deep understanding, psychoanalysis actually stultifies the emotional life of the patient. Man wants to focus his love on an absolute measure of power and value, and the analyst tells him that all is reducible to his early conditioning and is therefore relative. Man wants to find and experience the marvelous, and the analyst tells him how matter-of-fact everything is, how clinically explainable are our deepest ontological motives and guilts. Man is thereby deprived of the absolute mystery he needs, and the only omnipotent thing that then remains is the man who explained it away.[37] And so the patient clings to the analyst with all his might and dreads terminating the analysis.‡

† If psychology represents the analytic breakdown and dissipation of the self and usually limits the world to the scientific ideology of the therapist, we can see some of the reasons Jung developed his own peculiar ideas. His work represents in part a reaction to the very limitations of psychological analysis. For one thing, he revitalized the inner dimensions of the psyche to secure it *against* the self-defeating analytic breakdown of it. He deepened it beyond the reaches of analysis by seeing it as a source of self-healing archetypes, of natural renewal, if the patient will only allow it. For another thing, he broadened the psyche beyond its individual base, by turning it into a "collective unconscious." No matter what the individual did to his psyche he was transcended as an individual by it. In these two ways the person could get his heroic justification from within his own psyche even by analyzing it, in fact, especially by analyzing it! In this way Jung's system is an attempt to have the advantages of psychological analysis and to negate and transcend them at the same time; to have his cake and eat it too. As Rieff has so compellingly argued, dissatisfaction with and criticism of Jung must stem largely from the impossibility of achieving the psychological redemption of psychological man—as we will conclude in Part III (Philip Rieff, *The Triumph of the Therapeutic: Uses of Faith After Freud* [N.Y.: Harper Torchbooks, 1966], Chap. 5).

‡ The emotional impoverishment of psychoanalysis must extend also to many analysts themselves and to psychiatrists who come under its ideology. This fact helps to explain the terrible deadness of emotion that one experiences in psychiatric settings, the heavy weight of the character armor erected against the world.

Rank and Kierkegaard: The Merger of Sin and Neurosis

The further one pushes his study of Rank the more his writings blur into those of Kierkegaard—all the more remarkably, as we now fully appreciate, because of the far greater sophistication of clinical psychoanalysis. By now it should be clear that this blurring of Rank and Kierkegaard is not a weak surrender to ideology but an actual scientific working-through of the problem of human character. Both men reached the same conclusion after the most exhaustive psychological quest: that at the very furthest reaches of scientific description, psychology has to give way to "theology"— that is, to a world-view that absorbs the individual's conflicts and guilt and offers him the possibility for some kind of heroic apotheosis. Man cannot endure his own littleness unless he can translate it into meaningfulness on the largest possible level. Here Rank and Kierkegaard meet in one of those astonishing historical mergers of thought: that sin and neurosis are two ways of talking about the same thing—the complete isolation of the individual, his disharmony with the rest of nature, his hyperindividualism, his attempt to create his own world from within himself. Both sin and neurosis represent the individual blowing himself up to larger than his true size, his refusal to recognize his cosmic dependence. Neurosis, like sin, is an attempt to force nature, to pretend that the *causa-sui* project really suffices. In sin and neurosis man fetishizes himself on something narrow at hand and pretends that the whole meaning and miraculousness of creation is limited to that, that he can get his beatification from that.[38]

Rank's summing-up of the neurotic world-view is at the same time that of the classic sinner:

The neurotic loses every kind of collective spirituality, and makes the heroic gesture of placing himself entirely within the immortality of his own ego, as the observations and cosmic fantasies of psychotics so clearly show.[39]

But we know that this attempt is doomed to failure because man simply cannot justify his own heroism; he cannot fit himself into his own cosmic plan and make it believable. He must live with agonizing doubts if he remains in touch at all with the larger reality. Only when he loses this touch do the doubts vanish—and that is the definition of psychosis: a wholly unreal belief in the self-justification of cosmic heroism. "*I* am Christ." In this sense, as Rank said, neurosis represents the striving for an "individual religion," a self-achieved immortality.[40]

Sin and neurosis have another side: not only their unreal self-inflation in the refusal to admit creatureliness but also a penalty for intensified self-consciousness: the failure to be consoled by shared illusions. The result is that the sinner (neurotic) is hyperconscious of the very thing he tries to deny: his creatureliness, his miserableness and unworthiness.[41] The neurotic is thrown back on his true perceptions of the human condition, which caused his isolation and individuation in the first place. He tried to build a glorified private inner world because of his deeper anxieties, but life takes its revenge. The more he separates and inflates himself, the more anxious he becomes. The more he artificially idealizes himself, the more exaggeratedly he criticizes himself. He alternates between the extremes of "I am everything" and "I am nothing."[42] But it is clear that if one is going to be *something* he has to be a secure part of something else. There is no way to avoid paying the debt of dependency and yielding to the larger meaning of the rest of nature, to the toll of suffering and the death that it demands; and there is no way to justify this payment from within oneself, no matter how mightily one tries.

But now we see the historical difference between the classical sinner and the modern neurotic: both of them experience the naturalness of human insufficiency, only today the neurotic is stripped of the symbolic world-view, the God-ideology that would make sense out of his unworthiness and would translate it into heroism. Traditional religion turned the consciousness of sin into a condition for salvation; but the tortured sense of nothingness of the neurotic qualifies him now only for miserable extinction, for merciful release in lonely death. It is all right to be nothing *vis-à-vis* God, who alone can make it right in His unknown ways; it is another thing to be nothing to oneself, who is nothing. Rank summed it up this way:

The neurotic type suffers from a consciousness of sin just as much as did his religious ancestor, without believing in the conception of sin. This is precisely what makes him "neurotic"; he feels a sinner without the religious belief in sin for which he therefore needs a new rational explanation.[43]

Thus the plight of modern man: a sinner with no word for it or, worse, who looks for the word for it in a dictionary of psychology and thus only aggravates the problem of his separateness and hyperconsciousness. Again, this impasse is what Rank meant when he called psychology a "preponderantly negative and disintegrating ideology."

Health as an Ideal

We have now covered the three aspects of the problem of neurosis: as a result of character-formation, as a problem of reality versus illusion, and as a result of historical circumstances. All three of course merge into one. Man lives his contradictions for better or worse in some kind of cultural project in a given historical period. Neurosis is another word for the total problem of the human condition; it becomes a clinical word when the individual bogs down in the face of the problem—when his heroism is in doubt or becomes self-defeating. Men are naturally neurotic and always have been, but at some times they have it easier than at others to mask their true condition. Men avoid clinical neurosis when they can trustingly live their heroism in some kind of self-transcending drama. Modern man lives his contradictions for the worse, because the modern condition is one in which convincing dramas of heroic apotheosis, of creative play, or of cultural illusion are in eclipse. There is no embracing world-view for the neurotic to depend on or merge with to mask his problems, and so the "cure" for neurosis is difficult in our time.[44]

This is Rank's devastating Kierkegaardian conclusion: if neurosis is sin, and not disease, then the only thing which can "cure" it is a world-view, some kind of affirmative collective ideology in which the person can perform the living drama of his acceptance as a creature ·Only in this way can the neurotic come out of his isolation to become part of such a larger and higher wholeness as religion has always represented. In anthropology we called these the myth-ritual complexes of traditional society. Does the neurotic lack something outside him to absorb his need for perfection? Does he eat himself up with obsessions? The myth-ritual complex is a social form for the channelling of obsessions. We might say that it places creative obsession within the reach of everyman, which is precisely the function of ritual. This function is what Freud saw when he talked about the obsessive quality of primitive religion and compared it to neurotic obsession. But he didn't see how natural this was, how all social life is the obsessive ritualization of control in one way or another. It automatically engineers safety and banishes despair by keeping people focussed on the noses in front of their faces. The defeat of despair is not mainly an intellectual problem for an active organism, but a problem of self-stimulation via movement. Beyond a given point man is not helped by more "knowing," but only by living and doing in a partly self-forgetful way. As Goethe put it, we must plunge into experience and then reflect on the meaning of it. All reflection and no plunging drives us mad; all plunging and no reflection, and we are brutes. Goethe wrote maxims like these precisely at the time when the individual lost the protective cover of traditional society and daily life became a problem for him. He no longer knew what were the proper doses of experience. This safe dosage of life is exactly what is prescribed by traditional custom, wherein all the important decisions of life and even its daily events are ritually marked out. Neurosis is the contriving of private obsessional ritual to replace the socially-agreed one now lost by the demise of traditional society. The customs and myths of traditional society provided a whole interpretation of the meaning of life, ready-made for the individual; all he had to do was to accept living it as true. The modern neurotic must do just this if he is to be "cured": he must welcome a living illusion.[45]

It is one thing to imagine this "cure," but it is quite another thing to "prescribe" it to modern man. How hollow it must ring in his ears. For one thing, he can't get living myth-ritual complexes, the deep-going inherited social traditions that have so far sustained men, on a prescription form from the corner pharmacy. He can't even get them in mental hospitals or therapeutic communities. The modern neurotic cannot magically find the kind of world he needs, which is one reason he tries to create his own. In this very crucial sense neurosis is the modern tragedy of man; historically he is an orphan.

A second reason for the hollowness of our prescription for neurosis follows. If there are no ready-made traditional world-views into which to fit oneself with dependency and trust, religion becomes a very personal matter—so personal that faith itself seems neurotic, like a private fantasy and a decision taken out of weakness. The one thing modern man cannot do is what Kierkegaard prescribed: the lonely leap into faith, the naïve personal trust in some kind of transcendental support for one's life. This support is now independent of living external rituals and customs: the church and the community do not exist, or do not carry much conviction. This situation is what helps make faith fantastic. In order for something to seem true to man, it has to be visibly supported in some way— lived, external, compelling. Men need pageants, crowds, panoplies, special days marked off on calendars—an objective focus for obsession, something to give form and body to internal fantasy, something external to yield oneself to. Otherwise the neurotic is brought back to the point of his departure: how is he to believe in his lonely, inner sense of specialness? §

A third problem is that modern man is the victim of his own disillusionment; he has been disinherited by his own analytic strength. The characteristic of the modern mind is the banishment of mystery, of naïve belief, of simple-minded hope. We put the accent on the visible, the clear, the cause-and-effect relation, the logical—always the logical. We *know* the difference between dreams and reality, between facts and fictions, between symbols and bodies. But right away we can see that these characteristics of the modern mind are

---

§ I think this helps explain the intensive evangelism of so many converts. Offhand we may wonder why they must continually buttonhole us in the street to tell us how to be as happy as they. If they are so happy, we muse, why are they bugging us? The reason, according to what we have said, must be that they need the conviction of numbers in order to strengthen and externalize something that otherwise remains very private and personal—and so risks seeming fantastic and unreal. To see others like oneself is to believe in oneself.

exactly those of neurosis. What typifies the neurotic is that he "knows" his situation *vis-à-vis* reality. He has no doubts; there is nothing you can say to sway him, to give him hope or trust. He is a miserable animal whose body decays, who will die, who will pass into dust and oblivion, disappear forever not only in this world but in all the possible dimensions of the universe, whose life serves no conceivable purpose, who may as well not have been born, and so on and so forth. He knows Truth and Reality, the motives of the entire universe.

It was G. K. Chesterton who kept alive the spirit of Kierkegaard and naïve Christianity in modern thought, as when he showed with such style that the characteristics the modern mind prides itself on are precisely those of madness.[46] There is no one more logical than the lunatic, more concerned with the minutiae of cause and effect. Madmen are the greatest reasoners we know, and that trait is one of the accompaniments of their undoing. All their vital processes are shrunken into the mind. What is the one thing they lack that sane men possess? The ability to be careless, to disregard appearances, to relax and laugh at the world. They can't unbend, can't gamble their whole existence, as did Pascal, on a fanciful wager. They can't do what religion has always asked: to believe in a justification of their lives that seems absurd. The neurotic knows better: he is the absurd, but nothing else is absurd; it is "only too true." But faith asks that man expand himself trustingly into the nonlogical, into the truly fantastic. This spiritual expansion is the one thing that modern man finds most difficult, precisely because he is constricted into himself and has nothing to lean on, no collective drama that makes fantasy seem real because it is lived and shared.

Let me hasten to assure the reader that I am not developing an apologia for traditional religion but only describing the impoverishment of the modern neurotic and some of the reasons for it. I want to give some background for understanding how centrally Rank himself stands in the tradition of Pascal, Kierkegaard, and Chesterton on the problem of faith and illusion or creative play. As we have learned from Huizinga and more recent writers like Josef Pieper and Harvey Cox, the only secure truth men have is that which they themselves create and dramatize; to live is to play at the meaning of life. The upshot of this whole tradition of thought is that it teaches us once and for all that childlike foolishness is the calling of mature men. Just this way Rank prescribed the cure for neurosis: as the "need for legitimate foolishness."[47] The problem of the union of religion, psychiatry, and social science is contained in this one formula.

We said earlier that the question of human life is: on what level of illusion does one live? This question poses an absolutely new question for the science of mental health, namely: What is the "best" illusion under which to live? Or, what is the most legitimate foolishness? If you are going to talk about life-enhancing illusion, then you can truly try to answer the question of which is "best." You will have to define "best" in terms that are directly meaningful to man, related to his basic condition and his needs. I think the whole question would be answered in terms of how much freedom, dignity, and hope a given illusion provides. These three things absorb the problem of natural neurosis and turn it to creative living.

We have to look for the answer to the problem of freedom where it is most absent: in the transference, the fatal and crushing enslaver of men. The transference fetishizes mystery, terror, and power; it holds the self bound in its grip. Religion answers directly to the problem of transference by expanding awe and terror to the cosmos where they belong. It also takes the problem of self-justification and removes it from the objects near at hand. We no longer have to please those around us, but the very source of creation— the powers that created us, not those into whose lives we accidentally fell. Our life ceases to be a reflexive dialogue with the standards of our wives, husbands, friends, and leaders and becomes instead measured by standards of the highest heroism, ideals truly fit to lead us on and beyond ourselves. In this way we fill ourselves with independent values, can make free decisions, and, most importantly, can lean on powers that really support us and do not oppose us.[48] The personality can truly begin to emerge in religion because God, as an abstraction, does not oppose the individual as others do, but instead provides the individual with all the powers necessary for independent self-justification. What greater security than to lean confidently on God, on the Fount of creation, the most terrifying power of all? If God is hidden and intangible, all the better: that allows man to expand and develop by himself.

The problem of transference is thus—like all things human—partly a value problem, a question of ideals. Freud tried to keep it wholly scientific by showing how exaggerated and false transference perceptions of reality were, which to a great extent is of course true. But what is the norm of "true" perception? Here Freud himself had to hedge. What is more unreal than the perceptions of a normal person in love, who is carried into rapture and expansion of being by his very exaggerations?[49] Van der Leeuw, that great psychologist of religion, saw the problem of transference introjections more broadly than Freud. He cites an ancient Egyptian text in which a certain Paheri discusses his inner conscience as the voice of God dwelling within man; and then Van der Leeuw says:

Now it is possible, certainly, with Nietzsche and Freud, to ascribe the "strangeness" of the voice, which warns us to avoid, to infantilism; "not the voice of God in the heart of man, but the voice of some men in man" [says Nietzsche].

But Van der Leeuw concludes on a surprising note: "We may however prefer the Egyptian description; on this point phenomenology has no decision to make."[50] In other words, we may prefer it for the larger expansiveness of being that it represents, as more imaginatively it links the person with higher mysterious powers. God-consciousness is not only regressive transference but also creative possibility. But unlike Van der Leeuw we are arguing that on this matter psychology does have a decision to make: it can talk about less-constricting forms of transference.

Best of all, of course, religion solves the problem of death, which no living individuals can solve, no matter how they would support us. Religion, then, gives the possibility of heroic victory in freedom and solves the problem of human dignity at its highest level. The two ontological motives of the human condition are both met: the need to surrender oneself in full to the rest of nature, to become a part of it by laying down one's whole existence to some higher meaning; and the need to expand oneself as an individual heroic personality. Finally, religion alone gives hope, because it holds open the dimension of the unknown and the unknowable, the fantastic mystery of creation that the human mind cannot even begin to approach, the possibility of a multidimensionality of spheres of existence, of heavens and possible embodiments that make a mockery of earthly logic—and in doing so, it relieves the absurdity of earthly life, all the impossible limitations and frustrations of living matter. In religious terms, to "see God" is to die, because the creature is too small and finite to be able to bear the higher meanings of creation. Religion takes one's very creatureliness, one's insignificance, and makes it a condition of hope. Full transcendence of the human condition means limitless possibility unimaginable to us.[51]

What is the ideal for mental health, then? A lived, compelling illusion that does not lie about life, death, and reality; one honest enough to follow its own commandments: I mean, not to kill, not to take the lives of others to justify itself. Rank saw Christianity as a truly great ideal foolishness in the sense that we have been discussing it: a childlike trust and hope for the human condition that left open the realm of mystery. Obviously, all religions fall far short of their own ideals, and Rank was talking about Christianity not as practiced but as an ideal. Christianity, like all religions, has in practice reinforced the regressive transference into an even more choking bind: the fathers are given the sanction of divine authority. But as an ideal, Christianity, on all the things we have listed, stands high, perhaps even highest in some vital ways, as people like Kierkegaard, Chesterton, the Niebuhrs, and so many others have compellingly argued.[52] The curious thing—as we can now fully appreciate—is that Rank, after a lifetime of work, drew the circle of psychoanalysis itself on this tradition of thought. In this he stands side by side with Jung, as Progoff so well showed.[53] ‖

‖ There are many other names one could mention in the synthesis of psychoanalytic, existential, and theological thought. We have already noted Waldman's work, which carries the synthesis all the way back to Adler, as Progoff also showed. Thus we are not talking about an accidental convergence or unusual similarity but about a solid cumulative achievement of several major strands of thought. Igor A. Caruso's important book *Existential Psychology: From Analysis to Synthesis* (New York: Herder and Herder, 1964) is an excellent "Rankian" statement on neurosis. See also Wilfried Daim, "On Depth-Psychology and Salvation," *Journal of Psychotherapy as a Religious Process,* 1955, 2: 24–37, for another part of the modern movement of the closure of psychoanalysis on Kierkegaard. One of the first modern attempts in this direction—perhaps the first—was that of Freud's friend the Reverend Oskar Pfister,

Finally, if mental health is a problem of ideal illusion, we are left with one large question on the matter of human character. If we are talking about the "best" ideal, then we should also talk about the costs of lesser ideals. What is the toll taken on the human personality by a failure to fully meet the twin ontological needs of man? Again we are back to the problem of Freud's life: what is the cost of the denial of absolute transcendence, of the attempt to fabricate one's own religion? When a man fails to draw the powers of his existence from the highest source, what is the cost to himself and those around him? We haven't even begun to discuss questions like this in characterology, but it seems to me that they are basic and necessary, the key questions, without which we cannot even talk about mental health intelligently. Rank posed the basic question: he asked whether the individual is able at all "to affirm and accept himself from himself." But he quickly sidestepped it by saying that it "cannot be said." Only the creative type can do this

---

who wrote a massive work on anxiety, translated as *Christianity and Fear* (London: Allen and Unwin, 1948). It took anxiety as a mainspring of conduct from John through Kierkegaard, Heidegger, and Freud; his intent was to show that anxiety is best overcome through the immortality ideology of Christian love. This is not the place to assess Pfister's extensive study and argument, but it is important to note that the work is vitiated by a curious failure to understand that the anxiety of life and death is a universal characteristic of man. He sides with those who believe that a healthy development of the child can take place without guilt, and that a full expression of love can banish fear: ". . . nor is it true that this pre-disposition to fear must necessarily be called into play by existence in the world as such. . . . That existence in the world as such causes fear is true only of persons who have been disposed to fear by various 'dammings'. . . ." (p. 49). He says that Kierkegaard had a fear neurosis based on his difficult childhood—hence his morbidity. The curious thing is that Pfister failed to get behind the cultural immortality ideology that absorbs and transmutes fear, even while he recognized it: "Many persons, not only children and the aged, find it possible to face death. They may even welcome it as a friend and be ready to die for a great cause." *Ibid.* This is true but, as we now know, it is also trivial because it does not come to grips with the transference transmutations of reality and power. The result is a book that offers a sort of Wilhelm Reich-Norman Brown thesis of the possibilities of unrepressed living, with Christ as the focus for Eros. All of which leads to the rumination that when liberal Christianity seizes upon Freud to try to make the world the cheerfully "*right* place," such unusual partners in such an un-Christian venture are bound to produce something false.

to some extent, he reasoned, by using his work as a justification for his existence.[54] I myself have posed this question as a central one for the science of man, in ignorance of the work of Rank.[55] I think it can be answered as Rank himself elsewhere answered it, as we saw in the last chapter: even the creative type should ideally surrender to higher powers than himself.[56] It was Jung, with his analytical penetration, who saw also the reason, which is that the unusual person takes his transference projections back into himself. As we said in the last chapter, one reason for his creativity is that he sees the world on his own terms and relies on himself. But this leads to a dangerous kind of megalomania because the individual becomes too full with his own meanings. Furthermore, if you don't fetishize the world by transference perceptions, totalities of experience put a tremendous burden on the ego and risk annihilating it. The creative person is too full both of himself and of the world.[57] Again, as the creative person has the same personality problems as the neurotic and the same biting off of the wholeness of experience, he needs some kind of resolution in a new and greater dependency —ideally, a freely chosen dependency, as Rank said.

As we saw so poignantly with Freud, the strongest among us faint away like children when pushed to take the whole meaning of life on themselves, to support it with their own meager creature powers. We said at the end of Chapter Six that Freud couldn't take the step from scientific to religious creatureliness. As Jung understood only too well, that would have meant Freud's abandoning of his own peculiar passion as a genius. Jung must have understood it from within his own experience: he himself could never bring himself to visit Rome because—as he admitted—Rome raised questions "which were beyond my powers to handle. In my old age— in 1949—I wished to repair this omission, but was stricken with a faint while I was buying tickets. After that, the plans for a trip to Rome were once and for all laid aside."[58] What are we to make of all these giants fainting at the prospect of what to us seems simple tourism? Freud, too, had not been able to visit Rome until later in life and turned back each time he approached the city.

I think we can fully understand this problem now that we have discussed Rank's closure on Kierkegaard, especially his psychology of the artist. These men had problems that no simple tourist knows:

they were innovators who tried to give a whole new meaning to creation and history, which meant that they had to support and justify all previous meanings and all possible alternative ones on their shoulders alone. Probably Rome epitomized these meanings in herself, her ruins and her history, and so she made their legs quiver. How much human blood was soaked into her soil; how many human dramas were played out there with what must seem, in the perspective of history, such unfeeling and extravagant wastefulness? It raises a problem just like that of the dinosaurs that troubled Freud or of the deformed infants that mocked Luther, only now on the level of all human beings. We mentioned in Chapter Six that when Freud himself came to analyze his reluctances about Rome and his strange experience on the Acropolis, he saw that somehow the memory of his father stood in judgment of his own achievements; he said he was troubled by a feeling of "piety" for him. I think if we push the analysis to its ultimate point we have to say that each earthly father accuses us of our impotence if we become truly creative personalities; they remind us that we are born of men and not gods. No living person can give genius the powers it needs to shoulder the meaning of the world.

Yet, what are we to say about this problem if even Jung, who always relied on God, could still faint away with the burden of life? Probably in the last analysis only this: that all men are here to use themselves up and the problem of ideal illusion doesn't spare any man from that. It only addresses the question of the best quality of work and life that men can achieve, depending on the beliefs they have and the powers they lean on. And this subject, as we said, is a matter for discussion by the empirical science of psychology itself. We have to reason about the highest actualization that man can achieve. At its ultimate point the science of psychology meets again the questioning figure of Kierkegaard. What world-view? What powers? For what heroism?

CHAPTER TEN

A General View of Mental Illness

> ... the essential, basic arch-anxiety (primal
> anxiety) [is] innate to all isolated, individual
> forms of human existence. In the basic anxiety
> human existence is afraid of as well as anxious
> about its "being-in-the-world". . . . Only if we
> understand ... [this can we] conceive of the
> seemingly paradoxic phenomenon that people
> who are afraid of living are also
> especially frightened of death.
> —MÉDARD BOSS[1]

I remember one of my college professors—a man very much admired as a teacher of medieval history—confessing that the more he learned about the period the less he was prepared to say: the epoch was so complex, so diversified that no general statement could safely be made about it. The same thing can surely be said about the theory of mental illness. How dare someone try to write a chapter entitled "A general view" of such a complex and varied phenomenon—especially someone who is not himself a psychiatrist? In fact, I have had an unusually difficult time forcing myself to sit down and write this chapter, even though I feel it belongs in the book. The literature is there for all to see: the record of lifetimes of work by some of the greatest psychologists who ever lived, men possessing the richest personal sensitivities, work reflecting unusual theoretical gifts and based on the most extensive and varied clinical materials. Why should someone try to rake this area over again, in what can only be a superficial and simple-minded way?

Probably for that very reason: today we need simple-mindedness in order to be able to say anything at all; this is the other side of the coin of the confession of the medievalist. The great characteristic of our time is that we know everything important about human nature that there is to know. Yet never has there been an age in which so little knowledge is securely possessed, so little a part of the common understanding. The reason is precisely the advance of specialization, the impossibility of making safe general statements, which has led to a general imbecility. What I would like to do in these few pages is to run the risk of simple-mindedness in order to make some dent in the unintended imbecility brought about by specialization and its mountains of fact. Even if I succeed only poorly, it seems like a worthwhile barter. In such a stifling and crushing scientific epoch someone has to be willing to play the fool in order to relieve the general myopia.

Right away the expert will say that it is presumptuous to talk about a general theory of mental illness, that this is something far in the future, a distant and perhaps unattainable goal—as if we didn't already have such a theory securely lodged in the countless volumes that crowd our libraries and bookstores. The gigantic figures of modern psychology have given us a thorough understanding of human behavior in both its neurotic and psychotic aspects, as well as its perversions of all types. The problem is, as we said, how to put some kind of general order into this wealth of insight and knowledge. One way is to make the most general statements about it, the same kind of statements that we have used so far in this book to tie together diverse areas of fact. Is man an animal who fears death, who seeks self-perpetuation and heroic transcendence of his fate? Then, failure for such an animal is failure to achieve heroic transcendence. As Adler put it so succinctly in the epigraph we have borrowed for this part of the book, mental illness is a way of talking about people who have lost courage, which is the same as saying that it reflects the failure of heroism. This conclusion follows logically from the discussion of the problem of neurosis in the previous chapter. We saw there that the neurotic was one who especially could not stand his own creatureliness, who couldn't surround his anality with convincing illusion. It was Adler who saw that low self-esteem was the central problem of mental illness. When does the person have the most trouble with his self-esteem? Precisely when his heroic transcendence of his fate is most in doubt, when he doubts his own immortality, the abiding value of his life; when he is not convinced that his having lived really makes any cosmic difference. From this point of view we might well say that mental illness represents styles of bogging-down in the denial of creatureliness.

Depression

We would not get very far with general statements like these if we could not show how they sum up the *specifics* of each syndrome. Fortunately, we can do just that. Adler had already revealed how perfectly depression or melancholia is a problem of courage; how it develops in people who are afraid of life, who have given up any semblance of independent development and have been totally immersed in the acts and the aid of others.[2] They have lived lives of "systematic self-restriction," and the result is that the less you do the less you can do, the more helpless and dependent you become. The more you shrink back from the difficulties and the darings of life, the more you naturally come to feel inept, the lower is your self-evaluation. It is ineluctable. If one's life has been a series of "silent retreats,"[3] one ends up firmly wedged into a corner and has nowhere else to retreat. This state is the bogging-down of depression. Fear of life leads to excessive fear of death, as Boss too reminds us in the epigraph we have borrowed for this chapter. Finally, one doesn't dare to move—the patient lies in bed for days on end, not eating, letting the housework pile up, fouling the bed.

The moral of this example of failure of courage is that in some way one must pay with life and consent daily to die, to give oneself up to the risks and dangers of the world, allow oneself to be engulfed and used up. Otherwise one ends up *as though dead* in trying to avoid life and death. This is how modern existentialist psychiatrists understand depression, exactly as Adler did at the beginning of this century. Médard Boss sums it up in a few lines:

It is always the whole existence of the melancholic patient which has failed to take over openly and responsibly all those possibilities of relating to the world which actually would constitute his own genuine self.

Consequently, such an existence has no independent standing of its own but continually falls prey to the demands, wishes and expectations of others. Such patients try to live up to these foreign expectations as best they can, in order not to lose the protection and love of their surroundings. [But they go more deeply into debt.] Hence the terrible guilt feelings of the melancholic . . . derive from his existential guilt.[4]

The interesting scientific question here is why we have had so much trouble getting agreement on the simple dynamics of depression, when it had been revealed so early and so lucidly by Adler and now again by the school of existential psychiatry. One of the reasons is that the dynamics are not so simple as they appear. They go very deeply into the heart of the human condition, and we have not been able to read this heart in any straightforward or easy way. For one thing, we ourselves had so effectively banished the idea of the fear of death and life; we were not sufficiently impressed by the terror of the living creature; and so we could not understand the torturings and turnings of anguished people who were jerked about by these terrors. For example, despite Adler's excellent and early general theory, he put us off somewhat by talking about the selfishness and the pamperedness of the depressed person, the "spoiled child" who refuses to grow up and accept the responsibility for his life, and so on. Of course these things are true to some extent, and Adler fully realized that nature herself had made man a weakling in the animal kingdom. But the accent is important. Adler should have stressed more the sheer terror of individuation, of difference, of being alone, of losing support and delegated power. He revealed to us the "life-lie" that people use in order to live, but we tended to overlook how necessary this lie is in some form or other for most men; how men simply do not have their own powers to rely on. When we remind ourselves again how giants like Freud and Jung shrink and faint while buying simple travel tickets, perhaps we can get some correct feeling for the magnitude of the task of poor Mr. Average Man, just daily trying to negotiate a semblance of tranquil heroism by embedding himself in the powers of others. When these tactics fail and he is threatened with the exposure of his life-lie, how logical it is that he give way to his own version of fainting by bogging down in a depressive withdrawal.

Another complexity of the dynamics of depression that we over-looked was the one that Rank taught us: the urge to immortaliza-tion and self-perpetuation by pleasing the other, by conforming to the code of behavior that he represents.[5] People hunger for im-mortality and get it where they can: in the small family circle or in the single love object. The transference object is the locus of our conscience, of our whole cosmology of good and evil. It is not some-thing we can simply break away from, as it embodies our whole hero-system. We saw how complete and complex the transference can be. We obey our authority figures all our lives, as Freud showed, because of the anxiety of separation. Every time we try to do something other than what they wanted, we awaken the anxiety connected with them and their possible loss. To lose their powers and approval is thus to lose our very lives. Also, we saw that the transference object in itself embodies the *mysterium tremendum* of existence. It *is* the primary miracle. In its concrete existence it tran-scends mere symbolic commands, and what is more natural than conforming to this miraculousness? We must add, with Rank, what is more natural than continuing to strive for immortality by fulfilling the moral code represented by the object? Transference is the posi-tive use of the object for eternal self-perpetuation. This explains the durability of transference and its strength, even after the death of the object: "I am immortal by continuing to please this object who now may not be alive but continues to cast a shadow by what it has left behind and may even be working its powers from the invisible spirit world." This is a part of the psychology of ancient ancestor worshippers as well as of moderns who continue to live according to family codes of honor and conduct.

Depression, then, sums up both the terror of life and death and the hunger for self-perpetuation; how heroic can one get? It is so natural to try to be heroic in the safe and small circle of family or with the loved one, to give in to a "silent retreat" now and then to keep this heroics secure. How many people have an independent gift to give to the cosmos in order to assure their special im-mortality? Only the creative person can manage that. When the average person can no longer convincingly perform his safe heroics or cannot hide his failure to be his own hero, then he bogs down in the failure of depression and its terrible guilt. I particularly like

Gaylin's insight that the bogging-down into total helplessness and dependency in depression is itself the last and most natural defense available to the mammalian animal:

Dependency is the basic survival mechanism of the human organism. . . . When the adult gives up hope in his ability to cope and sees himself incapable of either fleeing or fighting, he is "reduced" to a state of depression. This very reduction with its parallel to the helplessness of infancy becomes . . . a plea for a solution to the problem of survival via dependency. The very stripping of one's defenses becomes a form of defensive maneuver.[6]

Boss says that the terrible guilt feelings of the depressed person are existential, that is, they represent the failure to live one's own life, to fulfill one's own potential because of the twisting and turning to be "good" in the eyes of the other. The other calls the tune to one's eligibility for immortality, and so the other takes up one's unlived life. Relationship is thus always slavery of a kind, which leaves a residue of guilt. A modern therapist like Frederick Perls actively worked against this tyranny by reminding his patients that "they were not in the world to please their partner, nor he to please them." It was a way of cutting into the morality of "personal-performance for immortality." All this is very good, but it can hardly sum up all the guilt that the patient feels, or at least accuses himself of. To judge by his own self-accusations of worthlessness, the patient feels an immense burden of guilt. We have to understand this self-accusation not only as a reflection of guilt over unlived life but also as a *language* for making sense out of one's situation. In short, even if one is a very guilty hero he is at least a hero in the same hero-system. The depressed person uses guilt to hold onto his objects and to keep his situation unchanged. Otherwise he would have to analyze it or be able to move out of it and transcend it. Better guilt than the terrible burden of freedom and responsibility, especially when the choice comes too late in life for one to be able to start over again. Better guilt and self-punishment when you cannot punish the other—when you cannot even dare to accuse him, as he represents the immortality ideology with which you have identified. If your god is discredited, you yourself die; the evil must be in yourself and not in your god, so that you may live. With guilt you lose some of your life but avoid the greater evil of death.[7] The depressed person exaggerates his guilt because it unblocks his dilemma in the safest and easiest way.[8] He also, as Adler pointed out, gets the people around him to respond to him, to pity him, and to value him and take care of him. He controls them and heightens his own personality by his very self-pity and self-hatred.[9] All these things, then, make obsessive guilt prominent in the depression syndrome.

We can thus see some of the complexities of the dynamics of depression that have made it hard for us to understand it in an agreed and straightforward way, even though it is rather simple when conceptualized as the natural bogging-down of an unheroic human life. One of the things that hinders us, too, was Freud's language and world-view. The Freudians said the menopausal depression, for example, was triggered by a re-experiencing of the early castration anxiety. It was easy to scoff at this explanation; it seemed that the Freudians were intent on once again reducing the problems of an adult life to the Oedipal period and to their own patriarchal world-view. Here she was again, the poor castrated woman paying the debt of her natural disadvantages. I myself reacted to this a decade ago with the temerity that comes with inexperience and brashness and offered a theory to counter it, a theory that went to the very opposite extreme and focussed on the failure of social role and that alone. I saw that often menopausal women in psychiatric hospitals were there because their lives were no longer useful. In some cases their role as wives had failed because of a late divorce; in others this circumstance combined with the expiration of their role as mothers because their children had grown up and married, and they were now alone with nothing meaningful to do. As they had never learned any social role, trade, or skill outside of their work in the family, when the family no longer needed them they were literally useless. That their depression coincided with the time of menopause I thought was an excellent illustration that the failure of useful social role could alone be called upon to explain the illness.

We encounter the Freudian world-view and language at almost every turn as a peculiar scientific problem: it contains a powerful truth that is phrased in such a manner as to be untrue. And we ourselves often get hung up ridiculously trying to untangle the two; or, we throw the truth out with the untrue accent. I suppose one has to be brash to do anything at all in the present state of proliferation of specialists, but it is dangerous. An occasional scoffer cannot wish away a half-century of clinical observation and thought. A constant danger in science is that each gain risks abandoning ground that was once securely annexed. Nowhere is this more true than in the present "role-theories" of mental illness that threaten to abandon the Freudian formulations based on *bodily* facts.

The fact is that the woman's experience of a repetition of castration at menopause is a real one—not in the narrow focus that Freud used, but rather in the broader sense of Rank, the existentialists, and Brown. As Boss so well said, "castration fear" is only an inroad or an aperture whereby the anxiety inherent in all existence may break into one's world.[10] It will be easy for us to understand at this point that menopause simply reawakens the horror of the body, the utter bankruptcy of the body as a viable *causa-sui* project—the exact experience that brings on the early Oedipal castration anxiety. The woman is reminded in the most forceful way that she is an animal thing; menopause is a sort of "animal birthday" that specifically marks the physical career of degeneration. It is like nature imposing a definite physical milestone on the person, putting up a wall and saying "You are not going any further into life now, you are going toward the end, to the absolute determinism of death." As men don't have such animal birthdays, such specific markers of a physical kind, they don't usually experience another stark discrediting of the body as a *causa-sui* project. Once has been enough, and they bury the problem with the symbolic powers of the cultural worldview. But the woman is less fortunate; she is put in the position of having all at once to catch up psychologically with the physical facts of life. To paraphrase Goethe's aphorism, death doesn't keep knocking on her door only to be ignored (as men ignore their aging), but kicks it in to show himself full in the face.*

---

* We might interject here that from this point of view, one of the crucial projects of a person's life, of true maturity, is to resign oneself to the process of aging. It is important for the person gradually to assimilate his true age, to stop protesting his youth, pretending that there is no end to his life. Eliot Jacques, in his truly superb little essay "Death and the Mid-Life Crisis," in

Once again we see that psychoanalysis has to be broadened to take in the fear of death rather than fears of punishment from the parents. It is not the parents who are the "castrators" but nature herself. Probably the guilt feelings of the patient also express the new *real* self-evaluation over being merely a fecal animal, dirty and truly worthless. But now we see too how the Freudian view and the sociological view merge naturally into one. Normally the cultural *causa-sui* project masks the re-experience of castration anxiety; but it is precisely the failure of the social role, the cultural project, that then reinforces the natural animal helplessness. Both projects, the bodily one and the cultural one, join in a mutual, resounding failure. No wonder, then, that menopausal depression is peculiarly a phenomenon of those societies in which aging women are deprived of some continuing useful place, some vehicle for heroism that transcends the body and death. No wonder, too, that instead of the eternity of life that one has a right to take for granted under the umbrella of a secure schema of self-perpetuation, the depressed person feels instead condemned to an eternity of destruction.[11] From this vantage point, we have to admit that after all is said and done, the accent on social role as the key to the syndrome is correct because it is the superordinate level of the problems that absorbs the

---

H. M. Ruitenbeek, ed., *Death: Interpretations* (New York: Delta Books, 1969), Chapter 13, beautifully develops the idea of the need for "self-mourning," the mourning of one's own eventual death, and thus the working of it out of one's unconscious where it blocks one's emotional maturity. One must, so to speak, work himself out of his own system. By a study of these dynamics we see how important it is for man to resign himself to his earthly condition, his creatureliness; and we seem to have put full scientific closure on James's early insight on the place of inner emotional collapse in personal growth (James, *Varieties*, p. 99). We might say that in this sense Freud developed the dynamics for the total resignation that he could not himself quite manage. His ingenious discovery of the process called "mourning labor" can now be understood as basic to the resignation of the person himself. (See Perls's important appreciation in *Ego, Hunger, and Aggression* [New York: Vintage Books], pp. 96–97, which reaffirms the total bodily character of this process.) We can also better understand how cultural forces conspire to produce menopausal depression in any society that lies to the person about the stages of life, that has no provision in its world-view for the mourning of one's creatureliness, and that does not provide some kind of larger heroic design into which to resign oneself securely, as we will see.

bodily level. Heroism transmutes the fear of death into the security of self-perpetuation, so much so that people can cheerfully face up to death and even court it under some ideologies.

Furthermore, it is more realistic from a practical point of view to put the accent on the supportive social role because we cannot really expect people at large to emerge from their lifelong object-embeddedness and to attain self-reliance and self-sustaining power without some continued vehicle for heroism. Existence is simply too much of a burden; object-embeddedness and bodily decay are universally the fate of men. Without some kind of "ideology of justification" people naturally bog down and fail. Here again we can see how correctly Rank emphasized the historical dimension of mental illness: the question is never about nature alone but also about the social ideologies for the transcendence of nature. If you can't be a hero within a communal ideology, then you must be a nagging, whining failure in your family. From this perspective the problem of heroism and of mental illness would be "who nags whom?" Do men harangue the gods, the armies of other nations, the leaders of their own state, or their spouses? The debt to life has to be paid somehow; one has to be a hero in the best and only way that he can; in our impoverished culture even—as Harrington so truly put it—"if only for his skill at the pinball machine."[12]

Schizophrenia

From the historical perspective the schizophrenic psychosis becomes more richly understandable. There is a type of person for whom life is a more insurmountable problem than for others, for whom the burden of anxiety and fear is almost as constant as his daily breath. Rank used the term "neurotic" for one type of person who was without illusion, who saw things as they were, who was overwhelmed by the fragility of the human enterprise; and in this sense the term describes perfectly the schizophrenic type. He is the "realist" that William James talked about when he said that the right reaction to the horrors of organismic life on this planet is the psychotic one.[13] But this kind of "realism," as Rank said, is the most self-defeating of all.

Adler very early showed how the schizophrenic was crippled by the fear of life and its demands, by a low self-evaluation in the face of them. He mistrusts not only himself but also the knowledge and ability of others; nothing seems to him to be able to overcome the inevitable horrors of life and death—except perhaps the fantastic ideational system that he fabricates for his own salvation.[14] His feelings of magical omnipotence and immortality are a reaction to the terror of death by a person who is totally incapable of opposing this terror with his own secure powers. We might even say that the psychotic uses blatantly, openly, and in an exaggerated way the same kinds of thought-defenses that most people use wishfully, hiddenly, and in a more controlled way, just as the melancholic uses blatantly the defenses of the milder, more "normal" depressions of the rest of us: an occasional giving in to despair, a secret hatred of our loved ones, a quiet self-accusation and sorrowful guilt. In this sense the psychoses are a caricature of the life styles of all of us—which is probably part of the reason that they make us so uncomfortable.

Adler's line of thought was developed by many people. Some of them are among the most profound and subtle students of the human condition who have ever lived: H. S. Sullivan, H. F. Searles, and R. D. Laing—to mention the nearest few. The result is that we have today an excellent general theory of schizophrenia in the scientific record for anyone to read. Here I want only to mention the main characteristic of the syndrome—why it is that the schizophrenic is in such an extraordinary state of terror. It took a long time for us to understand this state because we were dealing with a phenomenon so strange it seems truly like science fiction. I mean the fact that human experience is split into two modes—the symbolic self and the physical body—and that these two modes of experience can be quite distinct. In some people they are so distinct as to be unintegrated, and these are the people we call schizophrenic. The hypersensitive individual reacts to his body as something strange to himself, something utterly untrustworthy, something not under his secure control.[15]

Right away we can see that the schizophrenic is burdened, like all of us, with an "alien" animal body. What makes his burden greater is that he is not securely rooted in his body. In his early childhood development he did not develop a secure "seating" in his body: as a result his self is not anchored intimately in his neuro-anatomy. He cannot make available to himself the natural or-ganismic expansion that others use to buffer and absorb the fear of life and death. He does not feel this natural animal plenitude. We might say with Santayana that the healthy "Animal Faith" is denied him, which is why he has to develop complex ideational systems of thought. We know today that the cultural sense of space, time, and perception of objects are literally built into the neural struc-ture.[16] As the cultural immortality ideology comes to be grounded in one's muscles and nerves, one lives it naturally, as a secure and confident part of one's daily action. We can say that the schizo-phrenic is deprived precisely of this neurological-cultural security against death and of programming into life. He relies instead on a hypermagnification of mental processes to try to secure his death-transcendence; he has to try to be a hero almost entirely idea-tionally, from within a bad body-seating, and in a very personal way. Hence the contrived nature of his efforts. No one understood better than Chesterton how freakish men become when they must rely on thoughts alone, separate from generous emotions in an ex-pansive and secure body.[17]

Schizophrenia takes the risk of evolution to its furthest point in man: the risk of creating an animal who perceives himself, reflects on himself, and comes to understand that his animal body is a menace to himself. When you are not even securely anchored in this body it really becomes a problem. Terror becomes unabsorb-able by anything neural, anything fleshy in the spot where you stand; your symbolic awareness floats at maximum intensity all by itself. This is really a cursed animal in evolution, an animal gone astray beyond natural limits. We cannot imagine an animal com-pletely open to experience and to his own anxieties, an animal utterly without programmed neurophysical reactivity to segments of the world. Man alone achieves this terrifying condition which we see in all its purity at the extremes of schizophrenic psychosis. In this state each object in the environment presents a massive prob-lem because one has no response within his body that he can marshal to dependably respond to that object. At least we could wish that an animal without instincts would be able to sink back at will into a friendly mass of flesh that he can call his own intimate and basic possession, even if it doesn't "tell" him what response to make. The schizophrenic cannot even do that. His body has completely "happened" to him, it is a mass of stench and decay. The only thing intimate about it is that it is a direct channel of vulnerability, the direct toehold that the outer world has on his most inner self. The body is his betrayal, his continually open wound, the object of his repulsion—as Catherine Deneuve portrayed so well in Polanski's "Repulsion." No wonder this "disease" is the one that most intrigues and fascinates man. It pushes his own protest over his dualistic condition to its limits. It represents neurotic openness carried to its extreme of helplessness. Freud very aptly called the syndrome "narcissistic neurosis": the ballooning of the self in fantasy, the complete megalomanic self-inflation as a last defense, as an attempt at *utter symbolic power* in the absence of lived physical power. Again, this is what cultural man everywhere strove to achieve, but the "normal" person is neurally programmed so that he feels at least that his body is his to use with confidence.

By pushing the problem of man to its limits, schizophrenia also reveals the nature of creativity. If you are physically unprogrammed in the cultural *causa-sui* project, then you have to invent your own: you don't vibrate to anyone else's tune. You see that the fabrications of those around you are a lie, a denial of truth—a truth that usually takes the form of showing the terror of the human condition more fully than most men experience it. The creative person becomes, then, in art, literature, and religion the mediator of natural terror and the indicator of a new way to triumph over it. He reveals the darkness and the dread of the human condition and fabricates a new symbolic transcendence over it. This has been the function of the creative deviant from the shamans through Shakespeare.

But if the neurotic is the "artiste manqué," what is the schizophrenic who has no talent, who is not creative? He must be a completely inverted and pathetic failure, as the wards in our mental hospitals attest. An impoverished and powerless person—even when he is a perceiver of truth—has no gift to offer to his fellows or to himself. The uncreative psychotic is simply totally crippled by life-and-death fears. This is not the place to toss off in a few words such a complex matter, so little understood, especially as I have not studied the problem in depth or detail. The plain fact, however, is that the matter revolves around one simple question: whether one has an ego with which to control his subjective experiences, no matter how unusual they are. If he does, then he gives form to his unique perceptions; he takes the energetic life process as it functions on the frontier of evolution—in the dualistic mode of human life—and he channels and contains it as a response to that mode. It becomes the work of genius. We seem to be able to pointedly sum up the problem like this: The schizophrenic is not programmed neurally into automatic response to social meanings, but he cannot marshal an ego response, a directive control of his experiences. His own erupting meanings cannot be given any creative form. We might say that because of his exaggerated helplessness he uses his symbolic inner experiences alone as an experiential anchor, as something to lean on. He exists reflexively toward them, comes to be controlled by them instead of reshaping and using them. The genius too is not programmed in automatic cultural meanings; but he has the resources of a strong ego, or at least a sufficient one, to give his own personal meanings a creative form. No one to my knowledge has understood this difference between the genius and the schizophrenic better than Reich,[18] at least in these gross terms.

In schizophrenia, like depression, we see the problem of heroics in its stark nudity. How does one become a hero from a position in which he has hardly any resources at all?—a position from which he sees more clearly than anyone else the menacing dangers of life and death and yet has no solid feeling of inner glory to oppose to them? He has to fabricate such a feeling in the best way he can, which will be a clumsy, crippled, and inverted way. No wonder that psychotic transferences are so total, so intense, so all-absorbing, so frightening (when they are not pathetic). The only way for a lonely cripple to attempt a heroic transcendence of death is through the complete servitude of personal idolatry, the total constriction of the self in the person of the other. One has so little personal "ballast" —to use Adler's excellent expression[19]—that he has to suck in an entire other human being to keep from disappearing or flying away.

Perversion

It would be foolhardy to write about the perversions today if one wanted to say something new; the literature is so immense— big, thick volumes like Reik's on Masochism, sets of volumes like

Stekel's on all the perversions, whole shelves on homosexuality; and in the professional journals, one article after another piling up insights and clinical facts. The problem is covered from all aspects and in a wealth of detail, a century's accumulation of scientific research. To my mind the best single book, summing up the key arguments of various schools and adding its own brilliant contribution, is Médard Boss's.[20] After Erwin Straus's lifelong contributions, culminating in his recent essay on "The Miser,"[21] we have the clearest and richest general theory that a science could hope for. But again, the danger is that one can't see the forest for the trees, that it has become impossible to say anything about the perversions without saying everything. Some kind of simple-minded, general statement is in order, one that is not itself polemical but tries to combine all the major viewpoints into one clear perspective. For the most part the Freudians, the existentialists, the Adlerians, and the behaviorists continue to talk past each other. Let us then see if we can pick out the crucial ingredients of the problem of perversion. It will give us an excellent review and summary of the problem of human nature and the heroic, so that we can finally move on to the conclusion of our study.

The reason that it is worth dwelling on so seemingly an esoteric and marginal matter as the perversions is that they are not marginal at all. So much has been written on them precisely because they are the core problem of human action. They reveal what is at stake in that action better than any other behavior because they narrow it down to its essentials. In this sense the perversions are truly the sub-atomic theory of the human sciences, the nucleus where the basic particles and energies are concentrated. This is why, too, they are usually reserved for the advanced and sophisticated student. But now, after we have covered so much ground, our summary will really be a review of everything we have discussed and so should be understandable with ease.

We saw earlier in several examples that Freud's genius opened up whole new territories to the understanding, and yet he phrased his formulations in such narrow and single-minded terms that they obscured matters and caused a continued scientific debate long past the need for such debate. Nowhere is this more true than on the problem of the perversions. Freud made possible the conquest of this most difficult terrain, and yet once again he caused us to shrug in disbelief. Take fetishism, which is surely the paradigm of perversion and which Freud himself used as a kind of epitome of his whole theoretical system. Why is it that the fetishist needs some object like a shoe or a corset before he can begin to make love to a woman? Freud answered:

To put it plainly: the fetish is a substitute for the woman's (mother's) phallus which the little boy once believed in and does not wish to forego —we know why.[22]

Note the utter assurance of that last phrase. The "reason" is that the female genitals prove the reality of castration and awaken the horror of it for oneself. The only way to triumph over this threat is to "give" the woman a phallus, however artificially and symbolically; and the fetish is precisely the "token of triumph over the threat of castration and a safeguard against it. . . ." With it, the fetishist can proceed to have intercourse. The fetish "saves the fetishist from being a homosexual by endowing women with the attribute which makes them acceptable as sexual objects." In a word, the fetish gives him the courage to be a man. Freud was so confident of his formulation that he said categorically:

Probably no male human being is spared the terrifying shock of threatened castration at the sight of the female genitals. . . . [And he concluded triumphantly:] Investigations into fetishism are to be recommended to all who still doubt the existence of the castration complex. . . .[23]

When a man of Freud's stature makes such triumphant closure on his whole work in a writing coming so late in his career, we have to accept that it contains an indubitable truth. But again he has engulfed us in the peculiar paradox of psychoanalysis—the phrasing of the most acute truth in a language of such concrete narrowness as to make that truth unrecognizable. Let us, then, try to pull it apart. The way out of the paradox was shown to us by thinkers like Adler, Jung, Rank, Boss, Straus, and Brown. The horror of castration is not the horror of punishment for incestuous sexuality, the threat of the Oedipus complex; it is rather the existential anxiety of life and death finding its focus on the animal body. This much is secure. But Freud stuck to the idea of the mother's body, specifically, the idea of the phallic mother that the child wants to believe in. All through the later psychoanalytic literature this idea occurs again and again in the fantasies of patients, and Robert Bak reaffirmed Freud's basic idea in a most recent writing, in the same categorical terms.

. . . in all perversions the dramatized or ritualized denial of castration is acted out through the regressive revival of the fantasy of the maternal or female phallus.[24]

And here is a perfect description of the typical fantasy from May Romm's rich paper:

At times the patient would fantasy during masturbation that he was able to take his penis in his mouth and in so doing he would be a *complete circle.* At this period he dreamed that he was looking at his body and discovered that he had breasts like a woman and male genitals. . . . The Greek priest, in his cassock with his hair flowing over his shoulders, represented to him a neuter person, celibate and bisexual.[25]

The Hermaphroditic Image

The hermaphroditic image is an idea that goes right to the heart of the human condition and reveals to us the dynamic of the perversions and what is at stake in the desperate efforts of crippled people to find some kind of animal satisfaction in this world. The hermaphroditic symbol is no mystery after the writings of Rank, Jung, and many others. The problem has been, again, to strip it of its narrow sexual connotations; it is not a sexual problem but a human problem. The self finds itself in a strange body casing and cannot understand this dualism. Man is aghast at the arbitrary nature of genitality, the accidentality of his separate sexual emergence. He can't accept the impermanence of the body casing or its incompleteness—now male, now female. The body makes no sense to us in its physical thingness, which ties us to a particular kind of fate, a one-sided sexual role. The hermaphroditic image represents a striving for wholeness, a striving that is not sexual but ontological. It is the desire of being for a recapture of the (Agape) unity with the rest of nature, as well as for a completeness in oneself. It is a desire for a healing of the ruptures of existence, the dualism of self and body, self and other, self and world. Add the desire of the self for self-perpetuation outside of and beyond the body, and we can understand how the partialness of the sexual identity is a further limitation and danger.

Freud was right to see the centrality of the image of the phallic mother and to connect it directly with the castration complex. But he was wrong to make the sexual side of the problem the central core of it, to take what is derivative (the sexual) and make it primary (the existential dilemma). The wish for the phallic mother, the horror of the female genitals, may well be a universal experience of mankind, for girls as well as boys. But the reason is that the child wants to see the omnipotent mother, the miraculous source of all his protection, nourishment, and love, as a really godlike creature complete beyond the accident of a split into two sexes. The threat of the castrated mother is thus a threat to his whole existence in that his mother is an animal thing and not a transcendent angel. The fate that he then fears, that turns him away from the mother in horror, is that he too is a "fallen" bodily creature, the very thing that he fights to overcome by his anal training. The horror of the female genitals, then, is the shock of the tiny child who is all at once—before the age of six—suddenly turned into a philosopher, a tragedian who must be a man long before his time and who must draw on reserves of wisdom and strength that he doesn't have. Again, this is the burden of the "primal scene": not that it awakens unbearable sexual desires in the child or aggressive hate and jealousy toward the father, but rather that it thoroughly confuses him about the nature of man. Romm observed on her patient:

His distrust of everyone he attributed mostly to the disappointment consequent to his discovery of the sexual relationship between his parents. The mother, who was supposed to be an angel, turned out to be human and carnal.[26]

This is perfect: how can you trust people who represent the priority of the cultural code of morality, the "angelic" transcendence of the decay of the body, and yet who cast it all aside in their most intimate relations? The parents are the gods who set the standards for one's highest victory; and the more unambiguously they themselves embody it, the more secure is the child's budding identity. When they themselves engage in grunting and groaning animal activities, the child finds it "disgusting": the experience of disgust arises when straightforward meanings are undermined. This is why—if he has never witnessed the primal scene—the child often resists the revelation by his street friends that his parents engage in sexual intercourse as everyone else. How apt was Tolstoy's observation that so much separates him from the newborn babe, and so little from the child of five; in those five years the child must shoulder the whole existential burden of the human condition. There is really little more for him to learn about his basic fate during the remainder of his life.

Jung saw the wishful meaning and centrality of the hermaphroditic image with great clarity and historical sweep,[27] as did Rank all through his work, Boss,[28] and Brown.[29] Nothing is more eloquent and to the point than the words of a psychoanalytic patient, a female fetishist who "condemned the abhorrent envelope of her body" by saying: "I wish I could tear this skin off. If I didn't have this stupid body, I would be as pure outside as I feel inside."[30]

The body is definitely the hurdle for man, the decaying drag of the species on the inner freedom and purity of his self. The basic problem of life, in this sense, is whether the species (body) will predominate over one's individuality (inner self). This explains all hypochondria, the body being the major threat to one's existence as a self-perpetuating creature. It explains too such dreams of children as that their hands are turning into claws. The emotional message is that they have no control over their fate, that the accidentality of the body form inhibits and restricts their freedom and determines them. One of the favorite games of childhood is "pinning the tail on the donkey." What better way to work off anxiety about the accidentality of the forms of things than to rearrange nature playfully with the same casualness with which she seems to have placed bodily appendages? At heart children are Picassos protesting the arbitrariness of external forms and affirming the priority of the inner spirit.[31] Anxiety over the body shows up too in all "anal" dreams, when people find themselves soiled by overflowing toilets, someone's splashing urine—in the midst of the most important affairs and all dressed up in their social finery. No mistake —the turd is mankind's real threat. We see this confusion between symbolic transcendence and anal function throughout the psychoanalytic literature. Romm's patient, "Whenever he felt socially, financially or sexually insecure . . . developed flatulence and diarrhea." Or again: "He dreamed of seeing his father making a speech to an audience. Suddenly he notices that his father's penis was exposed."[32]

What, in other words, is the truth about the human condition? Is it in bodies or in symbols? If it is not straightforward, then there must be some lie somewhere, which is the threat. Another patient collected books, "and always wanted to defecate when he entered a book-shop."[33] His own literary work was inhibited by his bodily fears. As we remarked several times, children really toilet train themselves because of the existential anxiety of the body. It is often pathetic how broken up they get when they accidentally wet their pants, or how quickly and easily they give in to public morality and will not urinate or defecate any more in the street "where someone might see." They do this quite on their own, even after being raised by the most unashamed parents. It is obvious that they are shamed by their own bodies. We can conclude quite categorically that hypochondrias and phobias are focalizations of the terror of life and death by an animal who doesn't want to be one.

It was already plain in Freud's early paper on the "Rat-man" that death and decay are central themes in the syndrome of obsession, and recently this was developed beautifully and with finality in the work of the European existential psychiatrists, notably Straus.[34] The psychoanalytic literature on fetishism, after Freud, shows very clearly what Rank had already argued: that the child is really bothered by bodies. Phyllis Greenacre provided the conclusive clinical closure on this in a series of very important papers that agreed that the castration anxiety long precedes the actual Oedipal period; it is a problem of global vulnerability rather than a specifically sexual one. This is an important development out of

Freud. In their favorite technical language the psychoanalysts say that the castration anxiety is "specifically weighted . . . with a strong admixture of oral and anal trends."[35] In other words, it is a problem of the whole bodily orientation to reality. In the history of fetishists we see again and again that they are subjected to early traumas about bodily decay and death.

The traumas which are most significant are those which consist of the witnessing of some particularly mutilating event: a mutilating death or accident, operation, abortion, or birth in the home. . . . If we take Freud's 1938 paper in which he outlines the development of a case of fetishism, and emphasizes the sight of the female genitals coincidental with masturbation and threats of castration just at the beginning of the phallic phase, and substitute for "threat of castration" "sight of mutilated and bleeding body," I think we may envision what happens in a certain number of children.[36]

This would hold true naturally—and especially—if the child himself had had a traumatic illness or painful operation.[37] One of Fenichel's patients had a prolapsed rectum that his mother had to press back into place each time he moved his bowels. It is no surprise, then, that he was haunted by the fear that his intestine might fall into the lavatory-pan.[38] Imagine being so vulnerable as to have to be pressed back into place. No wonder he was obsessed with a fear of death, that his castration anxiety was overwhelming, that he thought that his dead mother or his sister's penis could have gone down the drain just as turds and bathwater do or just as his intestine might. The world is not particular about what it flushes away of bodies; things just mysteriously disappear. One of Lorand's patients, a boy of four, could not understand why a girl he had seen at camp had no fingers on her hand or why one of his relatives was missing a leg. He could not enter the same room with the man and ran away screaming at the sound of his voice. He asked the doctor, quietly and with fear in his eyes: "You won't make me disappear, will you?"[39] Here again we see the child as philosopher, voicing the concern of Whitehead over one of the two great evils of organismic life: that "things fade."

One of the main conclusions that Greenacre arrived at about

fetishists was that their faulty early development was due to a number of similar things: excessive traumas, disturbed mother-child relations, ruptured home life with absent fathers, or very weak fathers who present a poor model for the child's strength. These kinds of disturbance lead to one main disturbance: these people were weak in their body confidence—to put it in nonclinical terms. Simon Nagler, in an important paper, traced the whole problem of fetishism to low self-esteem, the sense of inadequacy, and hence fear of the male role. These accents are important modifications on Freud because they stress the role of development rather than instinct. Freud lacked the rich developmental theory that has accumulated since his time, which is why it had to be a mystery to him why some people become homosexuals and others fetishists and yet the great majority of men become neither, but transcend the horror of the female genitals.[40] If the matter was one of instinct relatively unaffected by developmental experience, then truly these things would be a mystery. This focus on uniform instinct rather than differential development was one of the main shortcomings of Freud's early work. Simon Nagler, in fact, goes so far as to want to throw out the fear of castration entirely; he also questions the idea of the phallic mother.[41] I once agreed with him in some of my own immodest and incomplete attempts to understand fetishism;[42] but now it is clear that this overemphasis is foolish. A rounded theory of fetishism has to recognize the centrality of the invulnerable phallic mother, the hermaphroditic image; it has to accept the generalized castration fear as the basic sense of vulnerability of the body; and it has to include the developmental history that makes some people weaker and more anxious than others in the face of experience.

The idea of low self-esteem is of course crucial, but we have to remember that self-esteem is not at first a symbolic problem but an active, organismic one. It takes root in the elemental physical experience of the infant, when his experience gives him a confident narcissism, a sense of invulnerability. High self-esteem means such a sense of invulnerability, and one gets it in three basic ways. It derives first from the power of the other—from the mother when she is a dependable support and does not interfere too much with the child's own activity and from a strong father with whom the child can identify. The second source of power to overcome vulnerability is one we have mentioned, the secure possession of one's own body as a safe locus under one's control. We see that this security can be weakened by traumas, as well as by the quality of the early family environment. A third way one obtains power is of course from the cultural *causa-sui* project, the symbols and dramatizations of our transcendence of animal vulnerability. (We will see shortly how important this third source is in fetishism.) Only these three things taken together can give us a coherent view of the dynamics of fetishism.

The Problem of Personal Freedom versus Species Determinism

Most people, then, avoid extreme fetishism because somehow they get the power to use their bodies "as nature intended." They fulfill the species role of intercourse with their partner without being massively threatened by it. But when the body does present a massive threat to one's self, then, logically, the species role becomes a frightening chore, a possibly annihilating experience. If the body is so vulnerable, then one fears dying by participating fully in its acts. I think this idea sums up simply what the fetishist experiences. From this vantage point we could look at all perversion as a protest against the submergence of individuality by species standardization.

Rank developed this idea all through his work. The only way in which mankind could actually *control* nature and rise above her was to convert sexual immortality into individual immortality. Rank sums up the implications of this in a very powerful and suggestive way:

. . . in essence sexuality is a collective phenomenon which the individual at all stages of civilization wants to individualize, that is, control. This explains all [!] sexual conflicts in the individual, from masturbation to the most varied perversions and perversities, above all the keeping secret of everything sexual by individuals as an expression of a personal tendency to individualize as much as possible collective elements in it.[43]

In other words, perversion is a protest against species sameness, against submergence of the individuality into the body. It is even a focus of personal freedom *vis-à-vis* the family, one's own secret way of affirming himself against all standardization. Rank even makes the breathtaking speculation that the Oedipus complex in the classic Freudian understanding may be an attempt by the child to resist the family organization, the dutiful role of son or daughter, the absorption into the collective, by affirming his own ego.[44] Even in its biological expression, then, the Oedipus complex might be an attempt to transcend the role of obedient child, to find freedom and individuality through sex through a break-up of the family organization. In order to understand it we must once again emphasize the basic motive of man, without which nothing vital can be understood —self-perpetuation. Man is divided into two distinct kinds of experience—physical and mental, or bodily and symbolic. The problem of self-perpetuation thus presents itself in two distinct forms. One, the body, is standardized and given; the other, the self, is personalized and achieved. How is man going to succeed himself, how is he going to leave behind a replica of himself or a part of himself to live on? Is he going to leave behind a replica of his body or of his spirit? If he procreates bodily he satisfies the problem of succession, but in a more or less standardized species form. Although he perpetuates himself in his offspring, who may resemble him and may carry some of his "blood" and the mystical quality of his family ancestors, he may not feel that he is truly perpetuating his own inner self, his distinctive personality, his spirit, as it were. He wants to achieve something more than a mere animal succession. The distinctive human problem from time immemorial has been the need to spiritualize human life, to lift it onto a special immortal plane, beyond the cycles of life and death that characterize all other organisms. This is one of the reasons that sexuality has from the beginning been under taboos; it had to be lifted from the plane of physical fertilization to a spiritual one.

By approaching the problem of succession or self-perpetuation in its fully dualistic nature, Rank was able to understand the deeper meanings of Greek homosexuality:

Seen in this light, boy-love, which, as Plato tells us, aimed perpetually at the improvement and perfection of the beloved youth, appears definitely as . . . a spiritual perfecting in the other person, who becomes transferred into the worthy successor of oneself here on earth; and that, not on the basis of the biological procreation of one's body, but in the sense of the spiritual immortality-symbolism in the pupil, the younger.[45]

In other words, the Greek sought to impress his inner self, his spirit or soul, upon the beloved youth. This spiritual friendship was designed to produce a son in whom one's soul would survive:

In boy-love, man fertilized both spiritually and otherwise the living image of his own soul, which seemed materialized in an ego as idealized and as much like his own body as was possible.[46]

This brilliant speculation enables us to understand some of the ideal motives for homosexuality, not only of the Greeks, but of especially individualized and creative persons like Michelangelo. For such a one, apparently, homosexuality has nothing to do with the sex organs of the beloved but rather represents a struggle to create one's own rebirth in the "closest possible likeness," which, as Rank says, is obviously to be found in one's own sex.[47] In terms of our discussion we can see that this attempt represents the complete *causa-sui* project: to create all by oneself a spiritual, intellectual, and physically similar replica of oneself: the perfectly individualized self-perpetuation or immortality symbol.

If the castration complex represents the admission by the child that his animal body is a bankrupt *causa-sui* project, what better way to defy the body than by abandoning its sexual role entirely? In this sense perversions would equal a total freedom from the castration complex; they are a hyperprotest against species sameness. But Rank was so intent on accenting the positive, the ideal side of perversion that he almost obscured the overall picture. We are no longer ancient Greeks, and very few of us are Michelangelos; in a word, we are not dominated by ideal motives nor do we possess the highest powers of genius. Routine perversions are protests out of weakness rather than strength; they represent the bankruptcy of talent rather than the quintessence of it. If the neurotic is the "artiste manqué," all the more is the usual homosexual the "Greek manqué," the Michelangelo without secure power and talent. The pervert is the clumsy artist trying desperately for a counter-illusion that preserves his individuality—but from within a limited talent and powers: hence the fear of the sexual role, of being gobbled up by the woman, carried away by one's own body, and so on. As F. H. Allen—an earlier follower of Rank—pointed out, the homosexual is often one who chooses a body like his own because of his terror of the difference of the woman, his lack of strength to support such a difference.⁴⁸ In fact, we might say that the pervert represents a striving for individuality precisely because he does not feel individual at all and has little power to sustain an identity. Perversions represent an impoverished and ludicrous claim for a sharply defined personality by those least equipped by their early developmental training to exercise such a claim. If, as Rank says, perversions are a striving for freedom, we must add that they usually represent such a striving by those least equipped to be able to stand freedom. They flee the species slavery not out of strength but out of weakness, an inability to support the purely animal side of their nature. As we saw above, the childhood experience is crucial in developing a secure sense of one's body, firm identification with the father, strong ego control over oneself, and dependable interpersonal skills. Only if one achieves these can he "do the species role" in a self-forgetful way, a way that does not threaten to submerge him with annihilation anxiety.

When we sum up this whole problem we can see that there are several ways to overcome the sense of sex as a species-standardization threat to oneself, most of which lie on a spectrum of desperation and ingenuity, rather than self-confidence and control. The most ideal way, the "highest" way, is of course in the experience of love. Here, one identifies with the partner totally and banishes the threat of separateness, helplessness, anxious self-consciousness *vis-à-vis* the body. The lover gives himself in joy and self-forgetful fulfillment, the body becomes the treasured vehicle for one's apotheosis, and one experiences real gratitude precisely *to* the species sameness. One is glad to have a standardized body because it permits the love union. But even without ideal love, one can give in to strong physical desire and allow himself to be "carried away" in a self-forgetful manner, so that the species is no threat to one's distinctive inner self. We see this in phallic narcissism and in some forms of what is called "nymphomania." Here the person seems to give in to the species identity with a vengeance, to submerge himself in it totally. Perhaps this activity gives the person a relief from the burdens of his self and his dualism. It may often be what the psychoanalysts call a "counter-phobic" attitude: to embrace wholeheartedly just what one dreads, as a means of protesting that it holds no anxiety. In many forms of sado-masochism it must also represent the plunging into the "truth" of the body, the affirmation of the physical as the primary area of reality, as Fromm has so well speculated. Finally, in schizoid persons, the anxiety connected with the species body is so great that they can simply dissociate themselves from their bodies, even during the act of sexual intercourse. In this way they preserve the sanctity of their own inner selves against the degradations of the body. Prostitutes, too, are said to actively practice this kind of self-body dissociation to keep their personal identities intact and pure no matter how degraded they may feel physically. As one schizophrenic girl remarked, in the most offhand manner, "I *think* I was raped on the way here." This is an affirmation, with a vengeance, of the transcendence of the inner spirit, a complete freedom from contamination by the body. Once again we see that schizophrenia represents the extreme frontier of the human condition, a desperate solution of the problem of dualism that evolution has saddled us with. This kind of desperation partakes necessarily of caricature: man cannot get rid of his body even if he throws it away—to paraphrase Goethe. There can be no absolute transcendence of the species role while men live. When even the greatest talents of a Michelangelo leave us filled with some doubts about human victory, what are we to say of the pathetic efforts of lesser beings who must still drag their bodies through the span of life and use them to relate to others?

The Fetish Object and the Dramatization

Once we understand the problems of hermaphroditic wholeness, self and body, strength and weakness, species determinism and personal freedom, we can begin to get some idea of what the fetishists are trying to do. This is surely the most fascinating area of this problem, as we can see by exploring it even a little.

One of the main puzzles has been what the fetish object represented, what the meaning was of a shoe or a corset, leather and furs, or even an artificial leg.[49] Freud and his followers maintained steadfastly that it represented "a quite special penis"—the mother's.[50] It was also argued that the fetish represented a denial of the penis, a vagina, feces, and the like. All of which seems to indicate that what it represented was not clear, that it could represent many things to many different fetishists, which is surely the truth of the matter. But another thing is sure, which is that the fetish had to do with a problem posed by the sexual act. Boss showed this in a most brilliant manner.[51] Out of his study, as well as from the excellent succession of papers by Greenacre, has come a new and fuller understanding of the fetish object. If fetishism represents the anxiety of the sexual act, the danger of species functioning for a symbolic animal, what must the fetish be if not some sort of magical charm? The fetish object represents the magical means for transforming animality into something transcendent and thereby assuring a liberation of the personality from the standardized, bland, and earthbound flesh. Such a liberation gives one the courage to perform the sexual act, as he is not bound to it in an animal way but already transcends it symbolically. Freud was right when he said that the fetish saved the person from homosexuality, but not because it was a penis—except perhaps, as Boss says,[52] for the weakest men. Rather, the fetish is a way of transforming reality. Boss says of one of his patients:

Whenever he saw or touched [ladies boots] "the world changed miraculously," he said. What had just appeared as "grey and senseless within the dreary, lonely and unsuccessful everyday, then suddenly drifts away from me, and light and glamour radiate from the leather to me." These leather objects seemed to have "a strange halo" shedding its light upon all other things. "It is ridiculous, but it feels like being a fairy prince. An incredible power, Mana, emanates from these gloves, furs and boots, and completely enchants me." . . . Naked women or a woman's hand without a glove or especially a woman's foot without a shoe . . . seemed to be like lifeless pieces of meat in a butcher shop. In fact, a woman's naked foot was really repulsive to him. . . . However, when the woman wore a glove, a piece of fur, or a riding boot, she was at once "raised above her arrogant, too humanly personal level." She then grew above the "pettiness and vicious concreteness of the common female" with her "abhorrent genitals" and she was raised into the super individual sphere, "the sphere where superhuman and subhuman blend into universal godliness."[53]

Not much more needs to be said after such an astonishingly probing revelation. The fetish takes "species meat" and weaves a magic spell around it. The impersonal, concrete, animal demand is arrogant, insulting: you are confronted by a body and obliged to relate to that body wholly on its terms, terms entirely given by its flesh and sex. Boss's patient says: "Somehow I always think that sexual intercourse is a great disgrace for humans."[54] The fetish changes all this by transforming the whole quality of the relationship. Everything is spiritualized, etherealized. The body is no longer flesh, no longer an impersonal demand by the species; it has a halo, emanates light and freedom, becomes a really personal, individual thing.[55]

As Greenacre so well argued, pills and pellets are forms of fetishes too, ways of overcoming anxiety, the terror of the body, in a reassuring magical way.[56] Fetishism exists on a gamut running from pills all the way to furs, leather, silks, and shoes. We then have full-blown articles for the exercise of a kind of symbolic magic: the person hypnotizes himself with the fetish and creates his own aura of fascination that completely transforms the threatening reality.[57] In other words, men use the fabrications of culture, in whatever form, as charms with which to transcend natural reality. This is really the extension of the whole problem of childhood: the abandonment of the body as *causa-sui* project, in favor of the new magic of cultural transcendence. No wonder fetishism is universal, as Freud himself remarked: all cultural contrivances are self-hypnotic devices—from motorcars to moon rockets—ways that a sorely limited animal can drum up to fascinate himself with the powers of transcendence over natural reality. As no one can be exactly comfortable in the species submergence of his distinctive inner self, all of us use a bit of magical charming in our relations to the world.

If the fetish object is a magical charm, then it naturally partakes of the qualities of magic, that is, it must have some of the properties of the thing that it seeks to control. To control the body, then, it must show some intimate relationship to the body—have an impress of its form, possess some of its smell, testify to its concreteness and animality. This is why, I think, the shoe is the most common fetish. It is the closest thing *to* the body and yet is not *the* body, and it is associated with what almost always strikes fetishists as the most ugly thing: the despised foot with its calloused toes and yellowed toenails. The foot is the absolute and unmitigated testimonial to our degraded animality, to the incongruity between our proud, rich, lively, infinitely transcendent, free inner spirit and our earth-bound body. Someone I know summed it up perfectly: "The foot is such a dumb-looking thing." Freud thought that the shoe was fetishized because, as it was the last thing the child saw before looking up at the dreaded genitals, he could safely stop there for his denial.[58] But the foot is its own horror; what is more, it is accompanied by its own striking and transcending denial and contrast—the shoe. The genitals and breasts, it is true, are contrasted by underclothing and stiff corsets, which are popular as fetishes, but nothing equals the foot for ugliness or the shoe for contrast and cultural contrivance. The shoe has straps, buckles, the softest leather, the most elegant curved arch, the hardest, smoothest, shiniest heel.[59] There is nothing like the spiked high heel in all of nature, I venture. In a word, here is the quintessence of cultural contrivance and contrast, so different from the body that it takes one a safe world away from it even while remaining intimately associated to it.

Also, if the fetish is a charm it has to be a very personal and secret charm, as Greenacre argues. We have long known, from sociology and the writings of Simmel, how important the secret is for man. The secret ritual, the secret club, the secret formula—these create a new reality for man, a way of transcending and transforming the everyday world of nature, giving it dimensions it would not otherwise possess and controlling it in arcane ways. The secret implies, above all, power to control the given by the hidden and thus power to transcend the given—nature, fate, animal destiny. Or, as Greenacre put it, " . . . the secret relates at its most primitive level to body organs and processes . . . it contains more fundamentally the struggle with the fear of death. . . ."[60]

The secret, in other words, is man's illusion par excellence, the

denial of the bodily reality of his destiny. No wonder man has always been in search of fountains of youth, holy grails, buried
treasures—some kind of omnipotent power that would instantly
reverse his fate and change the natural order of things. Greenacre
recalls, too, with brilliant appositeness, that Hermann Goering hid
capsules of poison in his anus, using them to take his own life in
a final gesture of defiant power.[61] This is the reversal of things with
a vengeance: using the locus of animal fallibility as the source of
transcendence, the container for the secret amulet that will cheat
destiny. And yet this, after all, is the quintessential meaning of
anality: it is the protest of all of man's cultural contrivances as anal
magic to prove that of all animals he alone leads a charmed life because of the splendor of what he can imagine and fashion, what he
can symbolically spin out of his anus.

The final characteristic of mysterious rituals is that they be
dramatized; and the activities of fetishists and allied perverts such
as transvestites have always fascinated observers precisely because
of that. They stage a complicated drama in which their gratification
depends on a minutely correct staging of the scene; any small detail or failure to conform to the precise formula spoils the whole
thing. The right words have to be pronounced at the right time, the
shoes arranged in a certain way, the corset put on and laced correctly, and so on.[62] The fetishist prepares for intercourse in *just the
right way* to make it safe. The castration anxiety can be overcome
only if the *proper forms* of things prevail. This pattern sums up the
whole idea of ritual—and again, of all of culture: the manmade
forms of things prevailing over the natural order and taming it,
transforming it, and making it safe.

It is in transvestism that we see an especially rich staging of the
drama of transcendence. Nowhere do we see the dualism of culture
and nature so strikingly. Transvestites believe that they can transform animal reality by dressing it in cultural clothing—exactly as
men everywhere do who dress pompously to deny, as Montaigne
put it, that they sit "on their arse" just like any animal, no matter
how grandiose the throne. The clinical transvestite, however, is even
more dedicated than the average man, more simple-minded it seems,
completely obsessed by the power of clothing to create an identity.
Often there is a past history of dressing dolls or of playing games
with one's sister in which clothing was exchanged and with it the

identity of each one.[63] It is obvious that for these people "the play is the thing," and they are as dedicated as stage personalities to actually being what their clothes make them.

What do they want to be? It seems that they want to refute the castration complex, overcome the species identity, the separation into sexes, the accidentality of the single sex and its confining fate, the incompleteness within each of us, the fact that we are a fragment not only of nature but even of a complete body. The transvestite seems to want to prove the reality of hermaphroditism by possessing a penis and yet appearing as a woman.[64] "I want to be my sister and yet to retain my penis," said one patient:

When indulging in his perverse practices, it was his custom, as soon as ejaculation had taken place, to tear the borrowed clothes off as quickly as possible. In connection with this he had the association that he had been warned that, if one made faces and the clock struck, one's face would stay so. Thus he was afraid that he might actually "remain stuck" in his feminine role, and this would involve his forfeiting his penis.[65]

Obviously, this is one way of affirming that the game is for keeps, the play is the reality, and if one gets caught when the clock strikes twelve he is apt to lose everything. Bak reports similarly on his patient:

Dressing up and undressing in front of a mirror dominated his practice for a long time. The penis was bandaged and very forcefully tied backward, and the testes pushed back into the inguinal canal. Such episodes were followed by intense castration anxiety—he feared that the shaft was broken, that the penis had become crooked, that the spermal duct was torn and he would be sterile.[66]

The dramatic play-control of sex does not absorb the anxiety completely, probably again because the danger of it heightens the sense of the reality of the games and because of the inevitable sense of guilt from the fact that the self is now completely overshadowed by the body in *both* its sexual forms, which can only mean that individuation is completely stunted.

There is no doubt about the simple-minded dedication to the magical efficacy of clothing. Fenichel's patient, on one occasion when he caught sight of a crippled boy, "felt an impulse to change clothes with him. The implication was a denial that the boy really was a cripple."[67] But often these fantasies can be turned to reality. One of Greenacre's patients had many fantasies of changing boys into girls and vice versa and went on to become an endocrinologist![68] From which we can conclude that the transvestite and the fetishist do not live entirely in illusion. They have glimpsed the truth that all men live, that culture can indeed transform natural reality. There is no hard and fast line between cultural and natural creativity. Culture is a symbol system that actually does give power to overcome the castration complex. Man can partly create himself. In fact, from this point of view, we can understand transvestism as the perfect form of *causa sui*, the direct sexual relationship *to* oneself, without having to go via the "circuitous" route of a female partner. As Buckner pointed out in a stimulating essay, the transvestite seems to develop a female personality within himself; this gives him an internal two-person relationship, actually an "internal marriage."[69] He is not dependent on anyone for sexual gratification since he can enact his own "counter-role." This is the logical consequence of the hermaphroditic completeness, the becoming of a whole world unto oneself.

Nowhere is there a better example of the blurring of the line between fetishist creativity and cultural creativity than in the ancient Chinese practice of binding the feet of females. This practice mutilated the feet, which were then an object of veneration by the men even though deformed. Freud himself remarked on this practice in relation to fetishism and observed that the "Chinese man seems to want to thank the woman for having submitted to castration."[70] Again, a profound insight conceptualized and phrased slightly beside the point. We should rather say that this practise represents the perfect triumph of cultural contrivance over the animal foot— exactly what the fetishist achieves with the shoe. The veneration, then, is the same: gratitude for the transformation of natural reality. The mutilated foot is a testimonial and token sacrifice to the efficacy of culture. The Chinese are then revering themselves, their culture, in the foot, which has now become sacred precisely because it has left the given and bland reality of the everyday animal world.

But somewhere we have to draw the line between creativity and failure, and nowhere is this line more clear than in fetishism. The anal protest of culture can be self-defeating, especially if we like our women to walk or if we want to relate to them as full human beings. That is precisely what the fetishist cannot do. Secret magic and private dramatization may be a hold on reality, the creation of a personal world, but they also separate the practitioner from reality, just as cultural contrivances do on a more standardized level. Greenacre has understood this very acutely, remarking that the secret is Janus-faced, a subterfuge that weakens the person's relationships to others.[71] The transvestite in his secret internal marriage actually does without the marriage relationship entirely. In all of this we must not forget the general impoverishment of the fetishist and transvestite: the insecure identification with the father, the weak body-ego.[72] Perversion has been called a "private religion"— and that it really is, but it testifies to fear and trembling and not to faith. It is an idiosyncratic, symbolic protest of control and safety by those who can rely on nothing—neither their own powers nor the shared cultural map for interpersonal action. This is what makes their ingenuity pathetic. As the fetishist, unlike the matter-of-fact cultural performer, is not secure in his repressions and body-ego, he is still overwhelmed by the sexual act, the demand that he do something *responsible* to someone else with his entire body. Romm says of her patient: "While he had a very sensitive need for his wife's sexual compliance, all desire left him whenever his wife indicated any sexual drive."[73] We can look at this as the refusal of the impersonal, instrumental species role, but it is a refusal based in insecurity, when one is *called upon* to perform. Remember we said, with Rank, that a major characteristic of neurosis was seeing the world as it is, in all its superordinacy, power, overwhelmingness. The fetishist must feel the truth of his helplessness *vis-à-vis* the ponderous object and the task he has to perform. He is not securely enough "programmed" neurally by solid repressions and body-ego, to be able to *falsify* his real situation and hence act his animal role with indifference. The object must be overwhelming in its massiveness of hair, pendulous breasts, buttocks, and stomach. What attitude to take toward all this "thingness" when one feels so empty in himself? One of the reasons that the fetish object is itself so splendid and fascinating to the fetishist must be that he transfers to it the awesomeness of the other human presence. The fetish is then the manageable miracle, while the partner is not. The result is that the fetish becomes supercharged with a halo-like effect.

Romm's patient saw things in their pristineness and never got over the effect:

The patient's earliest recollection was of his mother washing her hair. When drying her hair in the sun she would throw it over her face. He was both fascinated and horrified at not being able to see her face, and relieved when it was again visible. Her hair combings held a great fascination for him.[74]

On one level we might understand this as expressing the anxiety of the child that the most personal and human part of the object —the face—can be eclipsed by the animal hair. But the whole feeling of the scene is one of awesomeness at the miracle of the created object. Most of us manage to get over the hypnotic quality of natural objects, and we do it, I think, in two related ways. One is by achieving a sense of our own power and so establishing a kind of balance between ourselves and the world. We can then ply our desires on the object without being thrown off balance by them. But a second thing must also be done: desire itself has to be fetishized. We cannot relate to the total object as it is, and thus we need standardized definitions of sexual attractiveness. These we get in the form of "cues" that serve to cut the object down to manage-able size: we look at the breast or the black underwear, which allow us not really to have to take account of the total person we are relating to.[75] In these two ways we strip the partner of awesome-ness and power and so overcome our general helplessness in the face of her. One of Greenacre's patients conveys the problem per-fectly:

If he continued to see the girl she would become increasingly repulsive to him, especially as his attention seemed inevitably focussed on her body orifices. Even then the pores of her skin began to be too conspicuous, to loom larger and become repellent. . . . Gradually he found too that he could be more successful if he approached a girl from the rear and did not have to be visually or tactually too aware of the difference between them.[76]

(I think here, too, of Rousseau's famous account of his repulsion from the breath-taking Venetian whore, when he noticed a slight imperfection on her breast.) When the overwhelming object cannot be shrunken as a straightforward vehicle of desire, it could become repulsive because its animal qualities become disengaged from it and begin to loom larger and larger. This, I think, might explain the paradox that the fetishist is overwhelmed by the awesomeness of the object, the superordinacy of it, and yet finds it repulsive in its animality. The foot only becomes a problem in itself as a paradigm of ugliness when we cannot fuse it into the body under the secure rush of our own desire and will. Otherwise it is a neutral part of an attractive woman. The fetishist's difficulty, then, is like the child's exactly: the inability to master pragmatic action situations with the requisite equanimity. I think this helps explain, too, why the typical phallic-narcissist, the Don Juan character, often takes any object—ugly or beautiful—that comes along, with the same unconcern: he does not really take account of it in its total personal qualities.†

All perversions, then, can truly be seen as "private religions," as

† This brings up the longstanding problem of why so few females are fetishists, a problem that has been solved by Greenacre and Boss. Their point is that the male, in order to fulfill his species role, has to perform the sexual act. For this he needs secure self-powers and also cues to arouse and channelize his desires. In this sense, the male is naturally and inevitably a fetishist of some kind and degree. The less self-power, the more terror of the looming female body, the more fetish narrowness and symbolism is necessary. The female does not have this problem because her role is passive; we might say that her fetishism is absorbed in the surrender of her body. As Boss says, women who shrink at the physical aspect of love, at the concreteness of the partner, can simply react with total frigidity (*Sexual Perversions*, pp. 53–54). Or, as Greenacre observed as well: "The sense of failure due to frigidity in the female is softened by the possibility of concealment" ("Further Considerations," p. 188, note). "Frigidity can be covered up to a degree which is not possible with disturbances of potency in the man" ("Further Notes," p. 192). Also, the woman, in her passive, submissive role, often gets her security by identifying with the power of the male; this overcomes the problem of vulnerability by receiving delegated powers—both of the penis itself and of the cultural world-view. But the male fetishist is precisely the one who does not have secure delegated powers from any source and cannot get them by passive submission to the female (Cf. Greenacre, "Certain Relationships," p. 95). We might sum this all up by saying that the frigid woman is one who submits but is not convinced that she is safe in the power of the male; she does not need to fetishize anything as she does not have to perform an act. The impotent male is also not convinced that he is safe, but it does not suffice for him to lie passively in order to fulfill his species role. He creates the fetish, then, as a locus of denial-power so that he can perform the act; the woman denies with her whole body. Using an artfully apt term of Von Gebsattel's, we could say that frigidity is the woman's form of "passive autofetishism" (Cf. Boss, *Sexual Perversions*, p. 53).

attempts to heroically transcend the human condition and to achieve some kind of satisfaction in that condition. That is why perverts are forever saying how superior and life-enhancing their particular approach is, how they cannot understand why anyone would not prefer it. It is the same sentiment that animates all true believers, the trumpeting of who is the true hero and what is the only genuine path to eternal glory.

At this point perversions and so-called normality meet. There is no way to experience all of life; each person must close off large portions of it, must "partialize," as Rank put it, in order to avoid being overwhelmed. There is no way to surely avoid and transcend death, for all organisms perish. The biggest, warmest, most secure, courageous spirits can still only bite off pieces of the world; the smallest, meanest, most frightened ones merely bite off the smallest possible pieces. I recall the episode of the illustrious Immanuel Kant when a glass was broken at one of his gatherings; how carefully he weighed the alternatives for a perfect place in the garden where the fragments could safely be buried so that no one would be injured by them accidentally. Even our greatest spirits must indulge in the fetishist's magical, ritual drama to banish accident because of animal vulnerability.

The Naturalness of Sado-Masochism

Although there is nothing new to say on this problem, with all the vast writings that have covered it, I want to again stress the naturalness of these perversions. Sadism and masochism seem like frighteningly technical ideas, secrets about the inner recesses of man only fully revealed to practicing psychoanalysts. Even more than that, they seem like rare and grotesque aberrations of normal human conduct. Both these suppositions are false. Masochism comes naturally to man, as we have seen again and again in these pages. Man is naturally humble, naturally grateful, naturally guilty, naturally transcended, naturally a sufferer; he is small, pitiful, weak, a passive taker who tucks himself naturally in a beyond of superior, awesome, all-embracing power. Sadism likewise is the natural activity of the creature, the drive toward experience, mastery, pleasure, the need to take from the world what it needs in order to increase itself and thrive;[77] what is more, a human creature who has to forget himself, resolve his own painful inner contradictions. The hyphenated word sado-masochism expresses a natural complementarity of polar opposites: no weakness without intensive focus of power and no use of power without falling back on a secure merger with a larger source of power. Sado-masochism, then, reflects the general human condition, the daily lives of most people. It reflects man living by the nature of the world and his own nature as it has been given to him. Actually, then, it reflects "normal" mental health.[78]

Do we wonder, for example, that rape is on the increase in today's confused world? People feel more and more powerless. How can they express their energies, get things more in balance between overwhelming input and feeble output? Rape gives a feeling of personal power in the ability to cause pain, to totally manipulate and dominate another creature. The autocratic ruler, as Canetti so well observes, gets the ultimate in the experience of domination and control by turning all persons into animals and treating them as chattels. The rapist gets the same kind of satisfaction in what seems a perfectly natural way; there are very few situations in life in which people can get a sense of the perfect appropriateness of their energies: the quickened vitality that comes when we prove that our animal bodies have the requisite power to secure their dominion in this world—or at least a living segment of it.‡

‡ This explains, too, the naturalness of the connection between sadism and sexuality without putting them on an instinctive basis. They represent a mutually reinforcing sense of appropriate power, of heightened vitality. Why, for example, does a boy masturbate with fantasies on such a gory story as the "Pit and the Pendulum" (Greenacre, "Certain Relationships," p. 81)? We have to imagine that the fantasy gives him a sense of power that the masturbation reinforces; the experience is a denial of impotence and vulnerability. It is much more than a simple sexual experience; it is much less than an expression of gratuitous destructive drives. Most people secretly respond to sado-masochistic fantasies not because everyone is instinctively perverse but because these fantasies do represent the perfect appropriateness of our energies as well as our limitations as animal organisms. No higher satisfaction is possible for us than to dominate entirely a sector of the world or to give in to the powers of nature by surrendering ourselves completely. Very fittingly these fantasies usually take place when people are having trouble with the stress of symbolic affairs of the everyday world, and one may wonder why—at a meeting concerning business or academic strategy—he can't shut out images from Luis Buñuel's "Belle de Jour."

Have we always been puzzled by how willingly the masochist experiences pain? Well, for one thing pain calls the body to the forefront of experience. It puts the person back into the center of things forcefully as a feeling animal. It is thus a natural complement to sadism. Both are techniques for experiencing forceful self-feeling, now in outer-directed action, now in passive suffering. Both give intensity in the place of vagueness and emptiness. Furthermore, to experience pain is to "use" it with the possibility of controlling it and triumphing over it. As Irving Bieber argued in his important paper, the masochist doesn't "want" pain, he wants to be able to identify its source, localize it, and so control it.[79] Masochism is thus a way of taking the anxiety of life and death and the overwhelming terror of existence and congealing them into a small dosage. One then experiences pain from the terrifying power and yet lives through it without experiencing the ultimate threat of annihilation and death. As Zilboorg so penetratingly observed, the sado-masochistic combination is the perfect formula for transmuting the fear of death.[80] Rank called masochism the "small sacrifice," the "lighter punishment," the "placation" that allows one to avoid the arch-evil of death. When applied to sexuality, masochism is thus a way of taking suffering and pain, "which in the last analysis are symbols of death," and transmuting them into desired sources of pleasure.[81] As Henry Hart also observed so well, this is a way of taking self-administered, homeopathic doses; the ego controls total pain, total defeat, and total humiliation by experiencing them in small doses as a sort of vaccination.[82] From still another point of view, then, we see the fascinating ingenuity of the perversions: the turning of pain, the symbol of death, into ecstasy and the experience of more-life.§

But again, the limits of the ingenuity of perversion are obvious. If you fix the terror of life and death magically on one person as the source of pain, you control that terror, but you also overinflate that person. This is a private religion that "makes believe" too much and so humiliates the masochist by placing him in the power of another

---

§ Boss assigns an even more creative intent to sado-masochism, at least in some of its forms (see pp. 104 ff.). I don't know how far to follow his generalizations on the basis of the few cases he cites. And I am a little uncomfortable with what seems to be his inclination to accept his patients' rationalizations as really ideal motives. I think this has to be weighed more carefully.

person. No wonder sado-masochism is ultimately belittling, a hot-house drama of control and transcendence played by pint-sized characters. All heroism is relative to some kind of "beyond"; the question is, which kind? This question reminds us of something we discussed earlier: the problem of too-limited beyonds. From this point of view, perversions are merely a demonstration of the severe limitation of the beyonds one chooses for his drama of heroic apotheosis. The sado-masochist is someone who plays out his drama of heroism *vis-à-vis* one person only; he is exercising his two onto-logical motives—Eros and Agape—on the love object alone. On the one hand, he is using that object to expand his sense of his own full-ness and power; on the other, giving vent to his need to let go, abandon his will, find peace and fulfillment by a total merger with something beyond him. Romm's patient showed perfectly this shrinkage of a cosmic problem to the single partner:

In an attempt to relieve his severe tension he struggled between the wish to be a dominant male, aggressive and sadistic toward his wife, and the desire to give up his masculinity, be castrated by his wife and thus return to a state of impotence, passivity and helplessness.[83]

How easy it would be if we could satisfy the yearnings of the whole human condition safely in the bedroom of our cottage. As Rank put it, we want the partner to be like God, all-powerful to support our desires, and all-embracing to merge our desires into—but this is impossible.

If, then, sado-masochism reflects the human condition, the acting out of our twin ontological motives, we can truly talk about honest masochism, or mature masochism, exactly as Rank did in his unusual discussion in *Beyond Psychology*.[84] It was one of Freud's limitations that he could not quite push his thought to this kind of conclusion, even though he brushed it repeatedly. He was so impressed by the intensity, depth, and universality of sadism and masochism that he termed them instincts. He saw truly that these drives went right to the heart of the human creature. But he drew a pessimistic conclu-sion, lamenting the fact that mankind could not get rid of these drives. Again, he was stuck with his instinct theory, which made him see these drives as remnants of an evolutionary condition and as tied to specific sexual appetites. Rank, who saw more truly, could transform sadism and masochism from clinically negative to humanly positive things. The maturity of masochism, then, would depend on the object toward which it was directed, on how much in possession of himself the mature masochist was. In Rank's view, a person would be neurotic not because he was masochistic but because he was not really submissive, but only wanted to make believe that he was.[85] Let us dwell on this type of failure briefly, because it sums up the whole problem of mental illness that we have broached.

Mental Illness as Failed Heroics

One very interesting and consistent conclusion emerges from our overview of mental illness: that Adler was right to say that the mentally ill all have a basic problem of courage. They cannot assume responsibility for their own independent lives; they are hyperfearful of life and death. From this vantage point the theory of mental illness is really a general theory of the failures of death-transcendence. The avoidance of life and the terror of death become enmeshed in the personality to such an extent that it is crippled—unable to exercise the "normal cultural heroism" of other members of the society. The result is that the person cannot permit himself the routine heroic self-expansion nor the easy yielding to the superordinate cultural world-view that other members can. This is why he becomes a burden on others in some way. Mental illness, then, is also a way of talking about those people who burden others with their hyperfears of life and death, their own failed heroics.

As we have seen, the depressed person is one who has embedded himself so comfortably in the powers and protection of others that he has forfeited his own life. As Adler taught us long ago, the people around the depressed person have to pay for it. Guilt, self-torture, and accusations are also ways of coercing others.[86] What is more coercive than the magical transference of the schizophrenic, which reflects so excellently the failure of courage? Or paranoia, where the person is so weak and so alone that he creates imaginary objects of hatred in order to have any relationship at all?[87] We have to consent to be hated in order that the paranoid can feel some small measure of vitality. This is the ultimate of "laying one's trip" on someone else. It is truly a "trip" through life and towards death that weak and frightened people lay especially hard upon others. The point is that *we* are coerced by the magical transference and the paranoia—and they may not be *our* problems.ǁ

In the specific perversions we see this coercion in an almost pure culture, where it becomes negation of ourselves as whole persons. The reason women object to perverse relationships and are offended at the artificial aid that the fetishist uses is precisely that it denies their existence as whole persons, or as persons at all.[88] What links all the perversions is the inability to be a responsible human animal. Erich Fromm had already well described masochism as an attempt to get rid of the burden of freedom.[89] Clinically we find that some people are so weak in the face of responsibility that they even fear

---

ǁ Nowhere is this clearer than in Waite's highly researched and carefully thought-out paper on Hitler ("Adolf Hitler's Guilt Feelings," *Journal of Interdisciplinary History*, 1971, 1, No. 2: 229–249), in which he argues that six million Jews were sacrificed to Hitler's personal sense of unworthiness and hypervulnerability of the body to filth and decay. So great were Hitler's anxieties about these things, so crippled was he psychically, that he seems to have had to develop a unique perversion to deal with them, to triumph over them. "Hitler gained sexual satisfaction by having a young woman—as much younger than he as his mother was younger than his father—squat over him to urinate or defecate on his head" (Ibid., p. 234). This was his "private religion": his personal transcendence of his anxiety, the hyperexperience and resolution of it. This was a personal trip that he laid not only on the Jews and the German nation but directly on his mistresses. It is highly significant that each of them committed suicide or tried to do so, and more than a simple coincidence. It might very possibly be that they could not stand the burden of his perversion; the whole of it was on them, it was theirs to live with— not in itself, as a simple and disgusting physical act, but in its shattering absurdity and massive incongruity with Hitler's public role. The man who is the object of all social worship, the hope of Germany and the world, the victor over evil and filth, is the same one who will in an hour plead with you in private to "be nice" to him with the fullness of your excretions. I would say that this discordance between private and public esthetics is possibly too much to bear, unless one can get some kind of commanding height or vantage point from which to mock it or otherwise dismiss it, say, as a prostitute would by considering her client a simple pervert, an inferior form of life.

the freedom of being in a good state of health and vigor, as Bieber reminded us.[90] In the most extreme perversion, necrophilia, we see the most extreme fear of life and of persons, as Fromm has described.[91] One of Brills' patients was so afraid of corpses that when he overcame this fear he became a necrophile because he was fascinated by his new-won freedom; we might say that he used necrophilia as his heroics and that undertakers' parlors were the stage for his drama of apotheosis. Corpses are perfect in their helplessness: they can't possibly hurt you or disgrace you; you don't have to worry about their safety or their responses.[92]

Boss has described a coprophiliac whose existence was so shrunken that he could find creative heroics only in the products of the rectum.[93] Here we see perfectly the terror of the species role, the inability to relate to the body of the sexual partner. In this patient they are so great that they risk cutting him off entirely from expressing his desires in an interpersonal relationship. He is in effect "saved" by feces and by his ingenious rationalization that they are the true source of life. Little does it matter to him that the needs of his particular heroics have reduced his wife to nothing more than a rectum. Nothing could be more graphic than the perversions in showing how fear and weakness lead to unlived life and what crippled heroics result. Straus goes so far as to connect necrophilia with miserliness and involutional depression, as part of the same problem of the general retreat from life.[94] We have no argument with this formulation.

At this time with our sure theoretical understanding we can skip lightly and almost anecdotally over the whole spectrum of mental illness and perversion without much risk: they all refer to the terror of the human condition in people who can't bear up under it. Precisely at this point our discussion of the perversions as failed heroics once again and finally makes a circle on the whole problem of human nature in its ideal dimensions. Heroism, is, after all, an ideal matter. The problem of mental illness, since Kierkegaard and through Scheler, Hocking, Jung, Fromm, and many others, has been inseparable from the problem of idolatry.[95] In what cosmology is one going to perform his heroics? If—as we have argued—even the strongest person has to exercise his Agape motive, has to lay the burden of his life somewhere beyond him, then we are brought once again to the great questions: What is the highest reality, the true ideal, the really great adventure? What kind of heroism is called for, in what kind of drama, submission to what kind of god? The religious geniuses of history have argued that to be really submissive means to be submissive to the highest power, the true infinity and absolute—and not to any human substitutes, lovers, leaders, nation-states.

From this point of view the problem of mental illness is one of not knowing what kind of heroics one is practising or not being able—once one does know—to broaden one's heroics from their crippling narrowness. Paradoxical as it may sound, mental illness is thus a matter of weakness and stupidity. It reflects ignorance about how one is going about satisfying his twin ontological motives. The desire to affirm oneself and to yield oneself are, after all, very neutral: we can choose any path for them, any object, any level of heroics. The suffering and the evil that stems from these motives are not a consequence of the nature of the motives themselves, but of our stupidity about satisfying them. This is the deeper meaning of one of Rank's insights, which otherwise would seem flippant. In a letter of 1937 he wrote:

Suddenly . . . while I was resting in bed it occurred to me what really was (or is) "Beyond Psychology." You know what? Stupidity! All that complicated and elaborate explanation of human behavior is nothing but an attempt to give a meaning to one of the most powerful motives of behavior, namely stupidity! I began to think that it is even more powerful than badness, meanness—because many actions or reactions that appear mean are simply stupid and even calling them bad is a justification.[96]

Finally, then, we can see how truly inseparable are the domains of psychiatry and religion, as they both deal with human nature and the ultimate meaning of life. To leave behind stupidity is to becomes aware of life as a problem of heroics, which inevitably becomes a reflection about what life ought to be in its ideal dimensions. From this point of view we can see that the perversions of "private religions" are not "false" in comparison to "true religions." They are simply less expansive, less humanly noble and responsible. All living organisms are condemned to perversity, to the narrowness of being mere fragments of a larger totality that overwhelms them, which they cannot understand or truly cope with—yet must still live and struggle in. We still must ask, then, in the spirit of the wise old Epictetus, what kind of perversity is fitting for man.#

I cannot leave this chapter without calling attention to one of the richest little essays on the perversions that I have yet come upon—too late to discuss here unfortunately, but tying into and deepening these views in the most suggestive and imaginative ways: Avery D. Weisman's "Self-Destruction and Sexual Perversion," in *Essays in Self-Destruction*, edited by E. S. Shneidman, (New York: Science House, 1967). Note especially the case of the patient whose mother had given her the message: "If you have sex you will jeopardize your whole life." The result was that the patient hit upon the technique of half-strangling or half-suffocating herself in order to be able to experience orgasm. In other words, *if she paid the price of almost dying*, she could have pleasure without crushing guilt; to be a victim in the sexual act became the fetish that permitted it to take place. All of Weisman's patients had an image of reality and death that was medieval: they saw the world as evil, as overwhelmingly dangerous; they equated disease, defeat, and depravity, just like medieval penitents; and like them, too, they had to become victims in order to deserve to remain alive, to buy off death. Weisman calls them aptly "virginal romantics," who cannot stand the blatancy of physical reality and seek to transform it into something more idealized by means of the perversion.

PART III

RETROSPECT AND CONCLUSION: THE DILEMMAS OF HEROISM

CHAPTER ELEVEN

Psychology and Religion:
What Is the Heroic Individual?

*If there is any science man really needs it is the
one I teach, of how to occupy properly that
place in creation that is assigned to man, and how
to learn from it what one must be
in order to be a man.*
—IMMANUEL KANT

When we are young we are often puzzled by the fact that each person we admire seems to have a different version of what life ought to be, what a good man is, how to live, and so on. If we are especially sensitive it seems more than puzzling, it is disheartening. What most people usually do is to follow one person's ideas and then another's, depending on who looms largest on one's horizon at the time. The one with the deepest voice, the strongest appearance, the most authority and success, is usually the one who gets our momentary allegiance; and we try to pattern our ideals after him. But as life goes on we get a perspective on this, and all these different versions of truth become a little pathetic. Each person thinks that he has the formula for triumphing over life's limitations and knows with authority what it means to be a man, and he usually tries to win a following for his particular patent. Today we know that people try so hard to win converts for their point of view because it is more than merely an outlook on life: it is an immortality formula. Not everyone, of course, has the authority of Kant speaking the words we have used in our epigraph to this chapter, but in matters of immortality everyone has the same self-righteous conviction. The thing seems perverse because each diametrically opposed view is put forth with the same maddening certainty; and authorities who are equally unimpeachable hold opposite views!

Take, for example, Freud's seasoned thoughts on human nature, and his idea of where he stood on the pyramid of struggling mankind:

. . . I have found little that is "good" about human beings on the whole. In my experience most of them are trash, no matter whether they publicly subscribe to this or that ethical doctrine or none at all. . . . If we are to talk of ethics, I subscribe to a high ideal from which most of the human beings I have come across depart most lamentably.[1]

When perhaps the greatest psychologist who ever lived lets drop the stock phrase "in my experience," it has the authority of a Papal Bull during medieval times. Of course, he also implies that if most people are trash, some aren't, and we can surmise who is one of the few exceptions. We are reminded of those once-popular books on eugenics that always carried a handsome frontispiece photograph of the author beaming his vitality and personality as the ideal type for the book's argument.

As we would expect, Freud's self-evaluation would hardly be agreed upon by everyone; almost each of his major dissenting disciples could find something to look down upon him for, with a certain condescending pity. Wilhelm Reich once remarked that Freud was caught in the psychoanalytic movement, trapped by his disciples and his own creation, that his very cancer was the result of being shut in upon himself, unable to speak as a free agent.[2] There's our problem again, you see: Reich's judgment would have carried more authority if it had come from a god instead of from a man who was even more caught up in his own movement and who was more decisively and ignominiously undone by it. Jung, too, thought Freud had great limitations, but he saw these limitations as a necessary part of Freud's *diamon,* of his genius and peculiar message. But maybe this understanding was actually a reflection of Jung's own demonic drivenness into alchemy, of the almost shamanistic quality of his inner life.[3] No less a student of man than Erich Fromm has written the bitterest lines on Jung, denouncing him as an enemy of science. Pity the layman scurrying under the feet of all these giants dropping their weighty pronunciamentos on one another.

I haven't even mentioned Rank's powerful views on Freud's limitations. In Rank's system of thought the most generous judgment that might probably be made about Freud's limitations was that he shared the human weakness of the neurotic: he lacked the capacity for illusion, for a creative myth about the possibilities of creation. He saw things too "realistically," without their aura of miracle and infinite possibility. The only illusion he allowed himself was that of his own science—and such a source is bound to be a shaky support because it comes from one's own energies and not from a powerful beyond. This is the problem of the artist generally: that he creates his own new meanings and must, in turn, be sustained by them. The dialogue is too inverted to be secure. And hence Freud's lifelong ambivalence about the value of posterity and fame, the security of the whole panorama of evolution. We touched on all these questions in our comparison of Freud and Kierkegaard, and now we are back to it. One can only talk about an *ideal* human character from a perspective of absolute transcendence. Kierkegaard would say that Freud still had pride, that he lacked the creature consciousness of the *truly* analyzed man, that he had not fully served his apprenticeship in the school of anxiety. In Kierkegaard's understanding of man, the *causa-sui* project is the Oedipus complex, and in order to be a man one has to abandon it completely. From this point of view Freud still had not analyzed away his Oedipus complex, no matter how much he and the early psychoanalysts prided themselves that they had. He could not yield emotionally to superordinate power or conceptually to the transcendental dimension. He lived still wholly in the dimension of the visible world and was limited by what was possible in that dimension only; therefore, all his meanings had to come from that dimension.

Kierkegaard had his own formula for what it means to be a man. He put it forth in those superb pages wherein he describes what he calls "the knight of faith."[4] This figure is the man who lives in faith, who has given over the meaning of life to his Creator, and who lives centered on the energies of his Maker. He accepts whatever happens in this visible dimension without complaint, lives his life as a duty, faces his death without a qualm. No pettiness is so petty that it threatens his meanings; no task is too frightening to be beyond his courage. He is fully in the world on its terms and wholly beyond the world in his trust in the invisible dimension. It is very much the old Pietistic ideal that was lived by Kant's parents. The great strength of such an ideal is that it allows one to be open, generous, courageous, to touch others' lives and enrich them and open them in turn. As the knight of faith has no fear-of-life-and-death trip to lay onto others, he does not cause them to shrink back upon themselves, he does not coerce or manipulate them. The knight of faith, then, represents what we might call an ideal of mental health, the continuing openness of life out of the death throes of dread.

Put in these abstract terms the ideal of the knight of faith is surely one of the most beautiful and challenging ideals ever put forth by man. It is contained in most religions in one form or another, although no one, I think, has described it at length with such talent at Kierkegaard. Like all ideals it is a creative illusion, meant to lead men on, and leading men on is not the easiest thing. As Kierkegaard said, faith is the hardest thing; he placed himself between belief and faith, unable to make the jump. The jump doesn't depend on man after all—there's the rub: faith is a matter of grace. As Tillich later put it: religion is first an open hand to receive gifts (grace) and then a closed hand to give them. One cannot give the gifts of the knight of faith without first being dubbed a knight by some Higher Majesty. The point I am driving at is that if we take Kierkegaard's life as a believing Christian and place it against Freud's as an agnostic, there is no balance sheet to draw. Who is to tally up which one caused others to shrink up more or to expand more fully? For every shortcoming that we can point to in Freud, we can find a corresponding one in Kierkegaard. If Freud can be said to have erred on the side of the visible, then Kierkegaard can surely be said to have equally erred on the side of the invisible. He turned away from life partly from his fear of life, he embraced death more easily because he had failed in life; his own life was not a voluntary sacrifice undertaken in free will, but a pathetically driven sacrifice. He did not live in the categories in which he thought.[5]

I am talking matter-of-factly about some of the surest giants in the history of humanity only to say that in the game of life and death no one stands taller than any other, unless it be a true saint, and only to conclude that sainthood itself is a matter of grace and not of human effort. My point is that for man not everything is possible. What is there to choose between religious creatureliness and scientific creatureliness? The most one can achieve is a certain relaxedness, an openness to experience that makes him less of a driven burden on others. And a lot of this depends on how much talent he has, how much of a *daimon* is driving him; it is easier to lay down light burdens than heavy ones. How does a man create from all his living energies a system of thought, as Freud did, a system directed wholly to the problems of this world, and then just give it up to the invisible one? How, in other words, can one be a saint and still organize scientific movements of world-historical importance? How does one lean on God and give over everything to Him and still stand on his own feet as a passionate human being? These are not rhetorical questions, they are real ones that go right to the heart of the problem of "how to be a man"—a problem that no one can satisfactorily advise anyone else on, as the wise William James knew. The whole thing is loaded with ambiguity impossible to resolve. As James said, each person sums up a whole range of very personal experiences so that his life is a very unique problem needing very individual kinds of solutions. Kierkegaard had said that same thing when he answered those who objected to his life style: he said it was singular because it was the one singularly designed to be what he needed in order to live; it is as simple and as final as that.

James, again, knew how difficult it was to live astride both worlds, the visible and the invisible. One tended to pull you away from the other. One of his favorite precepts, which he often repeated, was: "Son of man, stand upon your own feet so that I may speak with you." If men lean too much on God they don't accomplish what they have to in this world on their own powers. In order to do anything one must first be a man, apart from everything else. This throws the whole splendid ideal of sainthood into doubt because there are many ways of being a good man. Was Norman Bethune any less a saint than Vincent de Paul? That, I suppose, is another way of saying that in this world each organism lives to be consumed by its own energies; and those that are consumed with the most relentlessness, and burn with the brightest flame, seem to serve the purposes of nature best, so far as accomplishing anything on this planet is concerned. It is another way, too—with Rank—of talking about the priority of the "irrational" life force that uses organismic forms only to consume them.

The Impossible Heroism

In the light of all this ambiguity we can take an understanding look at some of the modern prophets on human nature. I have been saying that a man cannot evolve beyond his character, that he is stuck with it. Goethe said that a man cannot get rid of his nature even if he throws it away; to which we can add—even if he tries to throw it to God. Now it is time to see that if a man cannot evolve beyond his character, he surely can't evolve *without* character. This brings up one of the great debates in contemporary thought. If we talk about the irrational life force living the limitations of organisms, we are not going to take the next step and get carried away into abstractions that are so popular today, abstractions in which the life force suddenly and miraculously seems to emerge from nature without any limits. I am referring, of course, to the new propheticism of people like Marcuse, Brown, and so many others, on what man may achieve, what it really means to be a man. I promised at the beginning of this book to linger a bit on the details of this problem, and now is the time for it.

Take Norman Brown's *Life Against Death:* rarely does a work of this brilliance appear. Rarely does a book so full of closely reasoned argument, of very threatening argument, achieve such popularity; but like most other foundation-shaking messages, this one is popular for all the wrong reasons. It is prized not for its shattering revelations on death and anality, but for its wholly non-sequitur conclusions: for its plea for the unrepressed life, the resurrection of the body as the seat of primary pleasure, the abolition of shame and guilt. Brown concludes that mankind can only transcend the terrible toll that the fear of death takes if it lives the body fully and does not allow any unlived life to poison existence, to sap pleasure, and to leave a residue of regret. If mankind would do this, says Brown, then the fear of death will no longer drive it to folly, waste, and destruction; men will have their apotheosis in eternity by living fully in the now of experience.[6] The enemy of mankind is basic repression, the denial of throbbing physical life and the spectre of death. The prophetic message is for the wholly unrepressed life, which would bring into birth a new man. A few lines of Brown's own words give us his key message:

If we can imagine an unrepressed man—a man strong enough to live and therefore strong enough to die, and therefore what no man has ever been, an individual—such a man [would have] . . . overcome guilt and anxiety. . . . In such a man would be fulfilled on earth the mystic hope of Christianity, the resurrection of the body, in a form, as Luther said, free from death and filth. . . . With such a transfigured body the human soul can be reconciled, and the human ego become once more what it was designed to be in the first place, a body-ego and the surface of a body. . . . The human ego would have to become strong enough to die; and strong enough to set aside guilt. . . . [F]ull psychoanalytic consciousness would be strong enough to cancel the debt [of guilt] by deriving it from infantile fantasy.[7]

What is one to say about such an eloquent program when it flies in the face of everything we know about man and most of what Brown himself has written about human character in the preceding almost 300 pages? These few lines contain fallacies so obvious that one is shocked that a thinker of Brown's power could even let them linger in his mind, much less put them down as reasoned arguments. Once again and always we are back to basic things that we have not shouted loud enough from the rooftops or printed in big-enough block letters: guilt is not a result of infantile fantasy but of self-conscious adult reality. There is no strength that can overcome guilt unless it be the strength of a god; and there is no way to overcome creature anxiety unless one is a god and not a creature. The child denies the reality of his world as miracle and as terror; that's all there is to it. Wherever we turn we meet this basic fact that we must repeat one final time: guilt is a function of real overwhelmingness, the stark majesty of the objects in the child's world. If we, as adults, are well dulled and armored against all this, we have only to read poets such as Thomas Traherne, Sylvia Plath, or R. L. Stevenson, who haven't blunted their receptors to raw experience:

As I go on in this life, day by day, I become more of a bewildered child; I cannot get used to this world, to procreation, to heredity, to sight, to hearing; the commonest things are a burthen. The prim, obliterated, polite surface of life, and the broad, bawdy, and orgiastic—or maenadic —foundations, form a spectacle to which no habit reconciles me.[8]

Brown's whole vision of some future man falls flat on the one failure to understand guilt.[9] It does not derive from "infantile fantasy" but from reality.

In other words—and this too is crucial enough to bear stressing one final time—the child "represses himself." He takes over the control of his own body as a reaction to the totality of experience, not only to his own desires. As Rank so exhaustively and definitively argued the child's problems are existential: they refer to his total world—what bodies are for, what to do with them, what is the meaning of all this creation.[10] Repression fulfills the vital function of allowing the child to act without anxiety, to take experience in hand and develop dependable responses to it. How could we ever get a new man without guilt and anxiety if each child, in order to become human, necessarily puts limits on his ego? There can be no birth in "second innocence"[11] because we would get a repetition of the very dynamics that Brown deplores, dynamics that rule out the possibility of the terrors of innocence. These are the necessary dynamics of humanization, of ego development.

Brown plunges with both feet into Aristotelian first causes and claims to know what the human ego "was designed to be in the first place, a body-ego. . . ." Now Brown is not the first to claim to see that evolution of the human animal is some kind of mishap; he has prominent predecessors like Trigant Burrow and L. L. Whyte, and now he has to be included with them for the nonsense as well as the good things that they have written. How can we say that evolution has made a mistake with man, that the development of the forebrain, the power to symbolize, to delay experience, to bind time, was not "intended" by nature and so represents a self-defeat embodied in an improbable animal? The ego, on the contrary, represents the immense broadening of experience and potential control, a step into a true kind of sub-divinity in nature. Life in the body is not "all we have"[12] if we have an ego. And the ego represents, as far as we can judge, a natural urge by the life force itself toward an expansion of experience, toward more life. If the urge toward more life is an evolutionary blunder, then we are calling into question all of creation and fitting it into the narrow mold of our own preferences about what "more-life" ought to be. Admittedly, when evolution gave man a self, an inner symbolic world of experience, it split him in two, gave him an added burden. But this burden seems to be the price that had to be paid in order for organisms to attain more life, for the development of the life force on the furthest reach of experience and self-consciousness. Brown claims that the "reunification of the ego and the body is not a dissolution but a strengthening of the human ego."[13] But this one phrase in passing rings hollow because it is truly empty chatter that avoids facing everything we know about the ego. To talk about a "new man" whose ego merges wholly with his body is to talk about a subhuman creature, not a superhuman one.

The ego, in order to develop at all, must deny, must bind time, must stop the body. In other words, the kind of new man that Brown himself wants would have to have an ego in order to experience his body, which means that the ego has to disengage itself from the body and oppose it. That is another way of saying that the child must be blocked in his experience in order to be able to register that experience. If we don't "stop" the child he develops very little sense of himself, he becomes an automaton, a reflex of the surface of his world playing upon his own surface. Clinically we have huge documentation for this character type whom we call the psychopath; phenomenologically we have understood this since Dewey's *Experience and Nature*.[14] Brown's whole thesis falls then, on a twin failure: not only on his failure to understand the real psychodynamics of guilt, but also his turning his back on how the child registers experience on his body: the need to develop in a dualistic way in order to be a rich repository of life.[15]

For a thinker of Brown's breadth and penetration these failures are rather uncanny, and we realize them with a sense of reluctance, of unwillingness to find such glaring lapses in what is really a thinker of heroic dimensions. I am less upset when I find similar lapses in Marcuse, who is a much less daring reinterpreter of Freud but who puts forth a similar call for a new kind of unrepressed man. On the one hand Marcuse calls for a revolution of unrepression because he knows that it is not enough to change the structure of society in order to bring a new world into being; the psychology of man also has to be changed. But on the other hand, he admits that unrepression is impossible, because there is death: "The brute fact of death denies once and for all the reality of a non-repressive existence."[16] The closing pages of his book are a realistic and regretful admission that the ego has to spread itself beyond the pleasures of the body in order for men to be men. But the dedicated social revolutionary who wants a new world and a new man more than anything else can't accept the reality that he himself sees. He still believes in the possibility of some kind of "final liberation," which also rings like the hollow, passing thought that it is. Marcuse even turns his back wholly on living experience and gets carried away by his abstractions: "Men can die without anxiety if they know that what they love is protected from misery and oblivion [by the new utopian society]."[17] As if men could ever know that, as if you and I can be sure at any instant that our children will not be obliterated by a senseless accident or that the whole planet will not be smashed by a gigantic meteor.

Why do brilliant thinkers become so flaccid, dissipate so carelessly their own careful arguments? Probably because they see their task as a serious and gigantic one: the critique of an entire way of life; and they see themselves in an equally gigantic prophetic role: to point to a way out once and for all, in the most uncompromising terms. This is why their popularity is so great: they are prophets and simplifiers. Like Brown, Marcuse wants a sure indicator of alienation, a focal point in nature, and finds it in the ideology and fear of death. Being a true revolutionary he wants to change this in his lifetime, wants to see a new world born. He is so committed to this fulfillment that he cannot allow himself to stop in midstream and follow out the implications of his own reservations on unrepression, his own admissions about the inevitable grip of death; fear of death is obviously deeper than ideology. To admit this would make his whole thesis ambiguous—and what revolutionary wants that? He would have to put forth a program that is not totally revolutionary, that allows for repression, that questions what men may become, that sees how inevitably men work against their own better interests, how they must shut out life and pleasure, follow irrational hero-systems—that there is a demonism in human affairs that even the greatest and most sweeping revolution cannot undo. With an admission like this Marcuse would be an anomaly—a "tragic revolutionary"—and would dissipate his role as a straightforward prophet. Who can expect him to do that?

There is no point in lingering on the fallacies of the revolutionaries of unrepression; one could go on and on, but everything would come back to the same basic thing: the impossibility of living without repression. No one has argued this impossibility with more authority and style than Philip Rieff in his recent work, and so far as I can see it should lay the matter to rest.[18] He turns the whole movement on end: repression is not falsification of the world, it is "truth"—the only truth that man can know, because he cannot experience everything. Rieff is calling us back to basic Freudianism, to a stoical acceptance of the limits of life, the burdens of it and of ourselves. In a particularly beautiful phrase, he puts it this way:

The heaviest crosses are internal and men make them so that, thus skeletally supported, they can bear the burden of their flesh. Under the sign of this inner cross, a certain inner distance is achieved from the infantile desire to be and have everything.[19]

Rieff's point is the classical one: that in order to have a truly human existence there must be limits; and what we call culture or the superego sets such limits. Culture is a compromise with life that makes human life possible. He quotes Marx's defiant revolutionary phrase: "I am nothing and should be everything." For Rieff this is the undiluted infantile unconscious speaking. Or, as I would prefer to say with Rank, the neurotic consciousness—the "all or nothing" of the person who cannot "partialize" his world. One bursts out in boundless megalomania, transcending all limits, or bogs down into wormhood like a truly worthless sinner. There is no secure ego balance to limit the intake of reality or to fashion the output of one's own powers.

If there is tragic limitation in life there is also possibility. What we call maturity is the ability to see the two in some kind of balance into which we can fit creatively. As Rieff put it: "Character is the restrictive shaping of possibility."[20] It all boils down, again, to the fact that the prophets of unrepression simply have not understood human nature; they envisage a utopia with perfect freedom from inner constraint and from outer authority. This idea flies in the face of the fundamental dynamism of unfreedom that we have discovered in each individual: the universality of transference. This fact is hardly lost on Rieff, who realizes that men need transference because they like to see their morality embodied, need some kind of points of support in the endless flux of nature:

Abstractions will never do. God-terms have to be exemplified. . . . Men crave their principles incarnate in enactable characters, actual selective mediators between themselves and the polytheism of experience.[21]

This failure to push the understanding of psychodynamics to its limits is the hurdle that none of the utopians can get over; it finally vitiates their best arguments. I am thinking here, too, of Alan Harrington's tremendously effective writing on fear of death as the mainspring of human conduct. Like Brown he pins an entirely fanciful and self-defeating thesis onto the most penetrating and damaging insights. Is fear of death the enemy? Then the cure is obvious: abolish death. Is this fanciful? No, he answers, science is working on the problem; admittedly, we may not be able to abolish death entirely, but we can prolong life to a great extent—who knows how much eventually. We can envisage a utopia wherein people will have such long lives that the fear of death will drop away, and with it the fiendish drivenness that has haunted man so humiliatingly and destructively all through his history and now promises to bring him total self-defeat. Men will then be able to live in an "eternal now" of pure pleasure and peace, become truly the godlike creatures that they have the potential to be.[22]

Again, the modern utopians continue the one-sided Enlightenment dream. Condorcet had already had the identical vision in 1794:

. . . a period must one day arrive when death will be nothing more than the effect either of extraordinary accidents, or of the slow and gradual decay of the vital powers: and that the duration of the interval between the birth of man and his decay will have itself no assignable limit.[23]

But Choron offers a caution on this vision that goes right to heart of it and demolishes it: that the "postponement of death is not a solution to the problem of the fear of death . . . there still will remain the fear of dying prematurely."[24] The smallest virus or the stupidest accident would deprive a man not of 90 years but of 900—and would be then 10 times more absurd. Condorcet's failure to understand psychodynamics was forgivable, but not Harrington's today. If something is 10 times more absurd it is 10 times more threatening. In other words, death would be "hyperfetishized" as a source of danger, and men in the utopia of longevity would be even less expansive and peaceful than they are today!

I see this utopia in one way resembling the beliefs of many primitive societies. They denied that death was the total end of experience and believed instead that it was the final ritual promotion to a higher form of life. This meant too that invisible spirits of the dead had power over the living, and if someone died prematurely it was thought to be the result of malevolent spirits or the breach of taboos. Premature death did not come as an impersonal accident. This reasoning meant that primitive man put the highest priority on ways to avoid bad will and bad action, which is why he seems to have circumscribed his activities in often compulsive and phobic ways.[25] Tradition has laid a heavy hand over men everywhere. Utopian man might live in the same "eternal now" of the primitives, but undoubtedly too with the same real compulsivity and phobia. Unless one is talking about real immortality one is talking merely about an intensification of the character defenses and superstitions of man. Curiously, Harrington himself seems to sense this, when he speculates on what kind of gods the utopians would worship:

... the children of eternity may worship variations of Luck, or That Which Cannot Be Controlled. ... Luck will be ... the only thing that can kill them, and for this reason they may go down on their knees before it. ... [They] may conduct ceremonies before the future equivalent of a giant slot machine or roulette wheel.[26]

Some godlike creatures! The fallacy in all this sterile utopianism is that fear of death is not the only motive of life; heroic transcendence, victory over evil for mankind as a whole, for unborn generations, consecration of one's existence to higher meanings—these motives are just as vital and they are what give the human animal his nobility even in the face of his animal fears. Hedonism is not heroism for most men. The pagans in the ancient world did not realize that and so lost out to the "despicable" creed of Judeo-Christianity. Modern men equally do not realize it, and so they sell their souls to consumer capitalism or consumer communism or replace their souls—as Rank said—with psychology. Psychotherapy is such a growing vogue today because people want to know why they are unhappy in hedonism and look for the faults within themselves. Unrepression has become the only religion after Freud—as Philip Rieff so well argued in a recent book; evidently he did not realize that his argument was an updating and expansion of exactly what Rank had maintained about the historical role of psychology.[27]

The Limits of Psychotherapy

As we have already covered this problem in Chapter Four where we first broached the dilemma of life, let us refresh our memories here. We saw that there really was no way to overcome the real dilemma of existence, the one of the mortal animal who at the same time is conscious of his mortality. A person spends years coming into his own, developing his talent, his unique gifts, perfecting his discriminations about the world, broadening and sharpening his appetite, learning to bear the disappointments of life, becoming mature, seasoned—finally a unique creature in nature, standing with some dignity and nobility and transcending the animal condition;

no longer driven, no longer a complete reflex, not stamped out of any mold. And then the real tragedy, as André Malraux wrote in *The Human Condition:* that it takes sixty years of incredible suffering and effort to make such an individual, and then he is good only for dying. This painful paradox is not lost on the person himself—least of all himself. He feels agonizingly unique, and yet he knows that this doesn't make any difference as far as ultimates are concerned. He has to go the way of the grasshopper, even though it takes longer.

We said that the point was that even with the highest personal development and liberation, the person comes up against the real despair of the human condition. Indeed, because of that development his eyes are opened to the reality of things; there is no turning back to the comforts of a secure and armored life. The person is stuck with the full problem of himself, and yet he cannot rely on himself to make any sense out of it. For such a person, as Camus said, "the weight of days is dreadful." What does it mean, then, we questioned in Chapter Four, to talk fine-sounding phrases like "Being cognition," "the fully centered person," "full humanism," "the joy of peak experiences," or whatever, unless we seriously qualify such ideas with the burden and the dread that they also carry? Finally, with these questions we saw that we could call into doubt the pretensions of the whole therapeutic enterprise. What joy and comfort can it give to fully awakened people? Once you accept the truly desperate situation that man is in, you come to see not only that neurosis is normal, but that even psychotic failure represents only a little additional push in the routine stumbling along life's way. If repression makes an untenable life liveable, self-knowledge can entirely destroy it for some people. Rank was very sensitive to this problem and talked about it intimately. I would like to quote him at length here in an unusually mature and sober psychoanalytic reflection that sums up the best of Freud's own stoical world-picture:

A woman comes for consultation; what's the matter with her? She suffers from some kind of intestinal symptoms, painful attacks of some kind of intestinal trouble. She had been sick for eight years, and has tried every kind of physical treatment. . . . She came to the conclusion it must be some emotional trouble. She is unmarried, she is thirty-five. She appears to me (and admits it herself) as being fairly well adjusted. She lives with a sister who is married; they get along well. She enjoys life, goes to the country in the summer. She has a little stomach trouble; why not keep it, I tell her, because if we are able to take away those attacks that come once in a fortnight or so, we do not know what problem we shall discover beneath it. Probably this defense mechanism is her adjustment, probably that is the price she has to pay. She never married, she never loved, and so never fulfilled her role. One cannot ever have everything, probably she has to pay. After all, what difference does it make if she occasionally gets these attacks of indigestion? I get it occasionally, you do too, probably, and not for physical reasons, as you may know. One gets headaches. In other words, it is not so much a question as to whether we are able to cure a patient, whether we can or not, but whether we should or not.[28]

No organismic life can be straightforwardly self-expansive in all directions; each one must draw back into himself in some areas, pay some penalty of a severe kind for his natural fears and limitations. It is all right to say, with Adler, that mental illness is due to "problems in living,"— but we must remember that life itself is the insurmountable problem.

This is not to say that psychotherapy cannot give great gifts to tortured and overwhelmed people and even added dignity to anyone who values and can use self-knowledge. Psychotherapy can allow people to affirm themselves, to smash idols that constrict the self-esteem, to lift the load of neurotic guilt—the extra guilt piled on top of natural existential guilt. It can clear away neurotic despair—the despair that comes from a too-constricted focus for one's safety and satisfactions. When a person becomes less fragmented, less blocked and bottled up, he does experience real joy: the joy of finding more of himself, of the release from armor and binding reflexes, of throwing off the chains of uncritical and self-defeating dependency, of controlling his own energies, of discovering aspects of the world, intense experience in the present moment that is now freer of prefixed perceptions, new possibilities of choice and action, and so on. Yes, psychotherapy can do all these things, but there are many things it cannot do, and they have not been aired widely enough. Often psychotherapy seems to promise the moon: a more constant joy, delight, celebration of life, perfect love, and perfect freedom. It seems to promise that these things are easy to come by, once self-knowledge is achieved, that they are things that should and could characterize one's whole waking awareness. As one patient said, who had just undergone a course in "primal scream" therapy: "I feel so fantastic and wonderful, but this is only a beginning—wait till you see me in five years, it'll be *tremendous!*" We can only hope that she won't be too unhappy. Not everyone is as honest as Freud was when he said that he cured the miseries of the neurotic only to open him up to the normal misery of life. Only angels know unrelieved joy—or are able to stand it. Yet we see the books by the mind-healers with their garish titles: "Joy!" "Awakening," and the like; we see them in person in lecture halls or in groups, beaming their peculiar brand of inward, confident well-being, so that it communicates its unmistakable message: we can do this for you, too, if you will only let us. I have never seen or heard them communicate the dangers of the total liberation that they claim to offer; say, to put up a small sign next to the one advertising joy, carrying some inscription like "Danger: real probability of the awakening of terror and dread, from which there is no turning back." It would be honest and would also relieve them of some of the guilt of the occasional suicide that takes place in therapy.

But it would also be most difficult to take the straightforward prescription for paradise on earth and make it ambiguous; one cannot be a functioning prophet with a message that he half takes back, especially if he needs paying customers and devoted admirers. The psychotherapists are caught up in contemporary culture and are forced to be a part of it. Commercial industrialism promised Western man a paradise on earth, described in great detail by the Hollywood Myth, that replaced the paradise in heaven of the Christian myth. And now psychology must replace them both with the myth of paradise through self-knowledge. This is the promise of psychology, and for the most part the psychotherapists are obliged to live it and embody it. But it was Rank who saw how false this claim is. "Psychology as self-knowledge is self-deception," he said, because it does not give what men want, which is immortality. Nothing could be plainer. When the patient emerges from his protective cocoon he gives up the reflexive immortality ideology that he has lived under—both in its personal-parental form (living in the protective powers of the parents or their surrogates) and in its cultural *causa-sui* form (living by the opinions of others and in the symbolic role-dramatization of the society). What new immortality ideology can the self-knowledge of psychotherapy provide to replace this? Obviously, none from psychology—unless, said Rank, psychology itself becomes the new belief system.

Now there are only three ways, I think, that psychology itself can become an adequate belief system. One of them is to be a creative genius as a psychologist and to use psychology as the immortality vehicle for oneself—as Freud and subsequent psychoanalysts have done. Another is to use the language and concepts of psychotherapy in much of one's waking life, so that it becomes a lived belief system. We see this often, as ex-patients analyze their motives in all situations when they feel anxious: "this must be penis-envy, this must be incestuous attraction, castration fear, Oedipal rivalry, polymorphous perversity," and so on. I met one young person who was nearly driven crazy and perverse trying to live the motivational vocabularly of the new Freudian religion. But in a way this attitude is forced because religion is an experience and not merely a set of intellectual concepts to meditate on; it has to be lived. As the psychologist Paul Bakan penetratingly remarked, this is one of the reasons that psychotherapy has moved away from the Freudian intellectual model to the new experiential model.[29] If psychology is to be the modern religion, then it has to reflect lived experience; it has to move away from mere talking and intellectual analysis to the actual screaming out of the "traumas of birth" and childhood, the acting-out of dreams and hostility, and so on. What this does is to make the hour of psychotherapy itself a ritual experience: an initiation, a holy excursion into a tabooed and sacred realm. The patient imbibes another dimension of life, one previously unknown to him and unsuspected by him, truly a "mystery religion" separate from the everyday secular world; he engages in behaviors that are very esoteric and permit the expression of aspects of his personality that he never thought of expressing or even imagined that he had. As in any religion, the adept "swears by" it because he has lived it; the therapy is "true" because it is a lived experience explained by concepts that seem perfectly to fit it, that give form to what the patient actually is undergoing.

The third and final way is merely an extension and sophistication of this. It is to take psychology and deepen it with religious and metaphysical associations so that it becomes actually a religious belief system with some breadth and depth. At the same time, the psychotherapist himself beams out the steady and quiet power of transference and becomes the guru-figure of the religion. No wonder we are seeing such a proliferation of psychological gurus in our time. It is the perfect and logical development of the fetishization of psychology as a belief system. It extends that system into its necessary dimension, which is immortality and the life-enhancing power that goes with it. This power comes in two forms: from the concepts of the religion and concretely from the person of the guru-therapist. It is no coincidence that one of the very popular forms of therapy today—called Gestalt therapy—for the most part ignores the problem of transference, as though one can shoo it away by turning one's back on it.[30] Actually, what is happening is that the aura of guru infallibility remains intact and provides an automatic shelter for the patient's deep yearnings for safety and security. It is no accident, either, that the therapists who practice these guru therapies cultivate themselves with halo-like beards and hairdos, to look the part they play.

I am not implying dishonesty here at all, merely that men tend to get caught up in the appropriateness of the panoplies they use and need. If one senses therapeutic religion as a cultural need, then it is the highest idealism to try and fill that need with one's heart and soul. On the other hand, even with the best intentions, transference is, willy-nilly, a process of indoctrination. Many psychoanalysts, as we know, try very conscientiously to analyze the transference; others try to minimize it. Despite the best efforts, the patient usually becomes in some way a slavish admirer of the man and the techniques of his liberation, however small it is. We already know that one of the reasons that Freud's influence on ideas was so great was that many of the leading thinkers of our time underwent Freudian analysis and so came away with a personal, emotional stake in the Freudian world-view.

The thing about transference is that it takes root very subtly, all the while that the person seems to be squarely on his own feet. A person can be indoctrinated into a world-view that he comes to believe without suspecting that he may have embraced it *because* of his relationship to a therapist or a master. We find this in very subtle form in those therapies that seek to put man back into contact with his own "authentic self," meaning the pristine powers that are locked inside him. The person is enjoined to try to tap these powers, this inside of nature, to dig down deeply into the subjectivity of his organism. The theory is that as one progressively peels away the social façade, the character defenses, the unconscious anxieties, he then gets down to his "real self," the source of vitality and creativity behind the neurotic shield of character. In order to make psychology a complete belief system, all the therapist has to do is to borrow words for the inner depths of the personality from traditional mystical religions: it can be called, variously, "the great void," the "inner room" of Taoism, the "realm of essence," the source of things, the "It," the "Creative Unconscious," or whatever.

The whole thing seems very logical, factual, and true to nature: man peels away his armor and unfolds his inner self, primal energies from the ground of his being in which he takes root. The person is, after all, not his own creator; he is sustained at all times by the workings of his physiochemistry—and, beneath that, of his atomic and subatomic structure. These structures contain within themselves the immense powers of nature, and so it seems logical to say that we are being constantly "created and sustained" out of the "invisible void." How can one be betrayed by therapy if he is being brought back to primary realities? It is obvious from techniques like Zen that the initiation into the world of the "It" takes place by a process of breakdown and reintegration. This process is much like Western therapy wherein the mask of society is peeled away and the drivenness is relaxed. In Zen, however, it is the primal powers that now are supposed to take over, to act through the person as he opens himself up for them; he becomes their tool and their vehicle. In Zen archery, for example, the archer no longer himself shoots the arrow at the target, but "It" shoots; the interior of nature erupts into the world through the disciple's perfect selflessness and releases the string. First the disciple has to go through a long process of attuning himself to his own interior, which takes place by means of a long subjection to a master, to whom one remains a lifelong disciple, a convert to his world-view. If the disciple is lucky he will even get from the master one of his bows, which contains his personal spirit powers; the transference is sealed in a concrete gift. From all Hindu discipleship too, the person comes away with a master without whom, usually, he is lost and cannot function; he needs the master himself periodically, or his picture, or his messages through the mail, or at least the exact technique that the master used: the head-stands, the breathing, and so on. These become the fetishized, magical means of recapturing the power of the transference figure, so that when one does them, all is well. The disciple can now stand on "his own" feet, be "his own" person.

The fusion of psychology and religion is thus not only logical, it is necessary if the religion is to work. There is no way of standing on one's own center without outside support, only now this support is made to seem to come from the inside. The person is conditioned to function under his own control, from his own center, from the spiritual powers that well up within him. Actually, of course, the support comes from the transference certification by the guru that what the disciple is doing is true and good. Even reconditioning body-therapies like that of the once-noted F. M. Alexander today liberally sprinkle their therapy with ideas from Zen and cite their affinity to people like Gurdjieff. There seems no way to get the body to reintegrate without giving it some kind of magical sustaining power; at least, there is no better way to win full discipleship to a religion than by making it frankly religious.[31]

It is no wonder that when therapies strip man down to his naked aloneness, to the real nature of experience and the problem of life, they slip into some kind of metaphysic of power and justification from beyond. How can the person be left there trembling and alone? Offer him the possibility of mystical contact with the void of creation, the power of "It," his likeness to God, or at the very least the support of a guru who will vouch for these things in his own overpowering and harmonious-appearing person. Man must reach out for support to a dream, a metaphysic of hope that sustains him and makes his life worthwhile. To talk about hope is to give the right focus to the problem. It helps us understand why even the thinkers of great stature who got at the heart of human problems could not rest content with the view of the tragical nature of man's lot that this knowledge gives. It is today well known how

Wilhelm Reich continued the Enlightenment in the direction of a fusion of Freud with Marxist social criticism, only to reach finally for Orgone, the primal cosmic energy. Or how Jung wrote an intellectual apologia for the text of ancient Chinese magic, the *I Ching*. In this, as Rieff has so bitingly argued, these men are of lesser stature than their master the great Stoic Freud.[32]

The Limits of Human Nature

In our earlier discussion of what is possible for man, we said that a person is stuck with his character, that he can't evolve beyond it or without it. If there is a limit to what man can be, we now also must conclude that there is a limit even to what religious therapy can do for him. But the psychotherapeutic religionists are claiming just the opposite: that the life force can miraculously emerge from nature, can transcend the body it uses as a vehicle, and can break the bounds of human character. They claim that man as he now is can be merely a vehicle for the emergence of something totally new, a vehicle that can be transcended by a new form of human life. Many of the leading figures in modern thought slip into some such mystique, some eschatology of immanence in which the insides of nature will erupt into a new being. Jung wrote such an argument in his *Answer to Job;* the answer to the laments of Job was that man's condition would not always be the same because a new man would break out of the womb of creation. Erich Fromm once lamented[33] that it is a wonder that more people are not insane, since life is such a terrible burden; and then he went on to write a book with the title: *You Shall be as Gods.* Gods verging on insanity, one must assume.

Fortunately, there is no need for us to take up the metaphysical aspects of this problem. It is now the center of a passionate and at the same time coolly intellectual review by some of our best critical minds: not only by Rieff, but also by Lionel Trilling and now John Passmore in an important historical-critical work.[34] It can all be summed up in the simplest and sharpest terms: how can an ego-controlled animal change his structure; how can a self-conscious creature change the dilemma of his existence? There is simply no way to transcend the limits of the human condition or to change the psychological structural conditions that make humanity possible. What can it mean for something new to emerge from such an animal and to triumph over his nature? Even though men have repeated such a notion since the most ancient times and in the most subtle and weightiest ways, even though whole movements of social action as well as thought have been inspired by such ideas, still they are mere fancy—as Passmore has so well reminded us. I myself have been fond of using ideas like the developing "spirit" of man and the promise of "new birth," but I don't think I ever meant them to conjure up a new creature; rather, I was thinking more of new birth bringing new adaptations, new creative solutions to our problems, a new openness in dealing with stale perceptions about reality, new forms of art, music, literature, architecture that would be a continual transformation of reality—but behind it all would be the same *type* of evolutionary creature, making his own peculiar responses to a world that continued to transcend him.*

If psychotherapists and scientists lapse into metaphysics so easily, we should not blame theologians for doing the same. But ironically, theologians today are often the most sober about immanence and its possibilities. Consider Paul Tillich: he too had his metaphysic of New Being, the belief in the emergence of a new type of person who would be more in harmony with nature, less driven, more perceptive, more in touch with his own creative energies, and who might go on to form genuine communities to replace the collectivities of our time, communities of truer persons in place of the objective creatures created by our materialistic culture. But Tillich had fewer illusions about this New Being than most of the psychotherapeutic religionists. He saw that the idea was actually a myth, an ideal that might be worked toward and so partly realized. It was not a fixed truth about the insides of nature. This point is crucial. As he so honestly put it: "The only argument for the truth of this

---

* Philip Rieff sobered me up about my loose use of ideas of immanence during a panel exchange a couple of years ago. In a characteristically honest and dramatic way he admitted that he was—like everyone else—a "part man," and he enjoined the audience to admit that we all were, asking what it could possibly mean to be a "whole man."

Gospel of New Being is that the message *makes itself* true."[35] Or, as we would say in the science of man, it is an ideal-typical enjoinder.[36]

I think the whole question of what is possible for the inner life of man was nicely summed up by Suzanne Langer in the phrase "the myth of the inner life."[37] She used this term in reference to the experience of music, but it seems to apply to the whole metaphysic of the unconscious, of the emergence of new energies from the heart of nature. But let us quickly add that this use of the term "myth" is not meant to be disparaging or to reflect simple "illusion." As Langer explained, some myths are vegetative, they generate real conceptual power, real apprehension of a dim truth, some kind of global adumbration of what we miss by sharp, analytic reason. Most of all, as William James and Tillich have argued, beliefs about reality affect people's real actions: they help introduce the new into the world. Especially is this true for beliefs about man, about human nature, and about what man may yet become. If something influences our efforts to change the world, then to some extent it must change that world. This helps explain one of the things that perplex us about psychoanalytic prophets like Erich Fromm; we wonder how they can so easily forget about the dilemmas of the human condition that tragically limit man's efforts. The answer is, on one level, that they have to leave tragedy behind as part of a program to awaken some kind of hopeful creative effort by men. Fromm has nicely argued the Deweyan thesis that, as reality is partly the result of human effort, the person who prides himself on being a "hard-headed realist" and refrains from hopeful action is really abdicating the human task.[38] This accent on human effort, vision, and hope in order to help shape reality seems to me largely to exonerate Fromm from the charges that he really is a "rabbi at heart" who is impelled to redeem man and cannot let the world be. If the alternative is fatalistic acceptance of the present human condition, then each of us is a rabbi—or had better be.

But once we say this, once we make a pragmatic argument for creative myth, it does not let us off the hook so easily about the nature of the real world. It only makes us more uncomfortable with the therapeutic religionists. If you are going to have a myth of New Being, then, like Tillich, you have to use this myth as a call to the highest and most difficult effort—and not to simple joy. A creative myth is not simply a relapse into comfortable illusion; it has to be as bold as possible in order to be truly generative.

What singles out Tillich's cogitations about the New Being is that there is no nonsense here. Tillich means that man has to have the "courage to be" himself, to stand on his own feet, to face up to the eternal contradictions of the real world. The bold goal of this kind of courage is to absorb into one's own being the maximum amount of nonbeing. As a being, as an extension of all of Being, man has an organismic impulsion: to take into his own organization the maximum amount of the problematic of life. His daily life, then, becomes truly a duty of cosmic proportions, and his courage to face the anxiety of meaninglessness becomes a true cosmic heroism. No longer does one do as God wills, set over against some imaginary figure in heaven. Rather, in one's own person he tries to achieve what the creative powers of emergent Being have themselves so far achieved with lower forms of life: the overcoming of that which would negate life. The problem of meaninglessness is the form in which nonbeing poses itself in our time; then, says Tillich, the task of conscious beings at the height of their evolutionary destiny is to meet and vanquish this new emergent obstacle to sentient life. In this kind of ontology of immanence of the New Being, what we are describing is not a creature who is transformed and who transforms the world in turn in some miraculous ways, but rather a creature who takes more of the world into himself and develops new forms of courage and endurance. It is not very different from the Athenian ideal as expressed in Oedipus or from what it meant to Kant to be a man. At least, this is the ideal for a new kind of man; it shows why Tillich's myth of being "truly centered" on one's own energies is a radical one. It points to all the evasions of centeredness in man: always being part of something or someone else, sheltering oneself in alien powers. Transference, even after we admit its necessary and ideal dimensions, reflects some universal betrayal of man's own powers, which is why he is always submerged by the large structures of society. He contributes to the very things that enslave him. The critique of guru therapies also comes to rest here: you can't talk about an ideal of freedom in the same breath that you willingly give it up. This fact turned Koestler against the East,[39] just as it also led Tillich to argue so penetratingly that Eastern mysticism is not for Western man. It is an evasion of the courage to be; it prevents the absorption of maximum meaninglessness into oneself.[40]† Tillich's point is that mystical experience seems to be near to perfect faith but is not. Mysticism lacks precisely the element of skepticism, and skepticism is a more radical experience, a more manly confrontation of potential meaninglessness. Even more, we must not forget that much of the time, mysticism as popularly practised is fused with a sense of magical omnipotence: it is actually a manic defense and a denial of creatureliness.[41]

Again, we are talking about the highest ideal things, which always seem most unreal—but how can we settle for less? We need the boldest creative myths, not only to urge men on but also and perhaps especially to help men see the reality of their condition. We have to be as hard-headed as possible about reality and possibility. From this point of view we can see that the therapeutic revolution raises two great problems. The first is how mature, critical, and sober these new liberated people will be. How much have they pushed in the direction of genuine freedom; how much have they avoided the real world and its problems, their own bitter paradoxes; how much have they hedged on their liberation by still holding on to others, to illusions, or to certainties? If the Freudian revolution in modern thought can mean anything at all, it must be that it brings to birth a new level of introspection as well as social criticism. We already see these reflected not only in academic intellectual awareness but also even in the popular mind, in the letters and advice columns of mass-circulation newspapers. Where, 35 years ago, could you read an advice to the lovelorn that cautioned a girl against her boy friend who refused for moral reasons to make love

† I think Tillich failed to see through one idol in his search for the courage to be. He seems to have liked the idea of the collective unconscious because it expressed the dimension of the inner depth of being and might be an access to the realm of essence. This seems to me a surprising lapse from his customary soberness. How could the ground of being be as accessible as Jung imagined? It seems to me that this concept would destroy the whole idea of The Fall. How can man have the realm of essence "on tap," so to speak; and if he does, doesn't Tillich's understanding of grace lose all its meaning as a pure gift beyond human effort?

to her as she asked him to, because he might be "projecting" onto her his own impotence?

But this brings up the second great problem raised by the therapeutic revolution, namely, So What? Even with numerous groups of really liberated people, at their best, we can't imagine that the world will be any pleasanter or less tragic a place. It may even be worse in still unknown ways. As Tillich warned us, New Being, under the conditions and limitations of existence, will only bring into play new and sharper paradoxes, new tensions, and more painful disharmonies—a "more intense demonism." Reality is remorseless because gods do not walk upon the earth; and if men could become noble repositories of great gulfs of nonbeing, they would have even less peace than we oblivious and driven madmen have today. Besides, can any ideal of therapeutic revolution touch the vast masses of this globe, the modern mechanical men in Russia, the near-billion sheeplike followers in China, the brutalized and ignorant populations of almost every continent? When one lives in the liberation atmosphere of Berkeley, California, or in the intoxications of small doses of unconstriction in a therapeutic group in one's home town, one is living in a hothouse atmosphere that shuts out the reality of the rest of the planet, the way things really are in this world. It is this therapeutic megalomania that must quickly been seen through if we are not to be perfect fools. The empirical facts of the world will not fade away because one has analyzed his Oedipus complex, as Freud so well knew, or because one can make love with tenderness, as so many now believe. Forget it. In this sense again it is Freud's somber pessimism, especially of his later writings such as *Civilization and Its Discontents*, that keeps him so contemporary. Men are doomed to live in an overwhelmingly tragic and demonic world.

The Fusion of Science and Religion

Therapeutic religion will never replace traditional religions with the messages of Judaism, most of Christianity, Buddhism, and the like. They have held that man is doomed to his present form, that he can't really evolve any further, that anything he might achieve can only be achieved from within the real nightmare of his loneliness in creation and from the energies that he now has. He has to adapt and wait. New birth will keep him going, give him constant renewal, say the Christians; and if he has perfect righteousness and faith, and enough of it spread widely enough among his fellows, then, say the Hebrews, God Himself will act. Men should wait while using their best intelligence and effort to secure their adaptation and survival. Ideally they would wait in a condition of openness toward miracle and mystery, in the lived truth of creation, which would make it easier both to survive and to be redeemed because men would be less driven to undo themselves and would be more like the image that pleases their Creator: awe-filled creatures trying to live in harmony with the rest of creation. Today we would add, too, that they would be less likely to poison the rest of creation.[42]

What do we mean by the lived truth of creation? We have to mean the world as it appears to men in a condition of relative unrepression; that is, as it would appear to creatures who assessed their true puniness in the face of the overwhelmingness and majesty of the universe, of the unspeakable miracle of even the single created object; as it probably appeared to the earliest men on the planet and to those extrasensitive types who have filled the roles of shaman, prophet, saint, poet, and artist. What is unique about their perception of reality is that it is alive to the *panic* inherent in creation: Sylvia Plath somewhere named God "King Panic." And Panic is fittingly King of the Grotesque. What are we to make of a creation in which the routine activity is for organisms to be tearing others apart with teeth of all types—biting, grinding flesh, plant stalks, bones between molars, pushing the pulp greedily down the gullet with delight, incorporating its essence into one's own organization, and then excreting with foul stench and gasses the residue. Everyone reaching out to incorporate others who are edible to him. The mosquitoes bloating themselves on blood, the maggots, the killer-bees attacking with a fury and a demonism, sharks continuing to tear and swallow while their own innards are being torn out—not to mention the daily dismemberment and slaughter in "natural" accidents of all types: an earthquake buries alive 70 thousand bodies in Peru, automobiles make a pyramid heap of over 50 thousand a year in the U.S. alone, a tidal wave washes over a quarter of a million in the Indian Ocean. Creation is a nightmare spectacular taking place on a planet that has been soaked for hundreds of millions of years in the blood of all its creatures. The soberest conclusion that we could make about what has actually been taking place on the planet for about three billion years is that it is being turned into a vast pit of fertilizer. But the sun distracts our attention, always baking the blood dry, making things grow over it, and with its warmth giving the hope that comes with the organism's comfort and expansiveness. "*Questo sol m'arde, e questo m'innamore*," as Michelangelo put it.

Science and religion merge in a critique of the deadening of perception of this kind of truth, and science betrays us when it is willing to absorb lived truth all into itself. Here the criticism of all behaviorist psychology, all manipulations of men, and all coercive utopianism comes to rest. These techniques try to make the world other than it is, legislate the grotesque out of it, inaugurate a "proper" human condition. The psychologist Kenneth Clark, in his recent presidential address to the American Psychological Association, called for a new kind of chemical to deaden man's aggressiveness and so make the world a less dangerous place. The Watsons, the Skinners, the Pavlovians—all have their formulas for smoothing things out. Even Freud—Enlightenment man that he was, after all —wanted to see a saner world and seemed willing to absorb lived truth into science if only it were possible. He once mused that in order to really change things by therapy one would have to get at the masses of men; and that the only way to do this would be to mix the copper of suggestion into the pure gold of psychoanalysis. In other words, to coerce, by transference, a less evil world. But Freud knew better, as he gradually came to see that the evil in the world is not only in the insides of people but on the outside, in nature—which is why he became more realistic and pessimistic in his later work.

The problem with all the scientific manipulators is that somehow they don't take life seriously enough; in this sense, all science is "bourgeois," an affair of bureaucrats. I think that taking life seriously means something such as this: that whatever man does on this planet has to be done in the lived truth of the terror of creation, of the grotesque, of the rumble of panic underneath everything. Otherwise it is false. Whatever is achieved must be achieved from within the subjective energies of creatures, without deadening, with the full exercise of passion, of vision, of pain, of fear, and of sorrow. How do we know—with Rilke—that our part of the meaning of the universe might not be a rhythm in sorrow? Manipulative, utopian science, by deadening human sensitivity, would also deprive men of the heroic in their urge to victory. And we know that in some very important way this falsifies our struggle by emptying us, by preventing us from incorporating the maximum of experience. It means the end of the distinctively human—or even, we must say, the distinctively organismic.

In the mysterious way in which life is given to us in evolution on this planet, it pushes in the direction of its own expansion. We don't understand it simply because we don't know the purpose of creation; we only feel life straining in ourselves and see it thrashing others about as they devour each other. Life seeks to expand in an unknown direction for unknown reasons. Not even psychology should meddle with this sacrosanct vitality, concluded Rank. This is the meaning of his option for the "irrational" as the basis for life; it is an option based on empirical experience. There is a driving force behind a mystery that we cannot understand, and it includes more than reason alone. The urge to cosmic heroism, then, is sacred and mysterious and not to be neatly ordered and rationalized by science and secularism. Science, after all, is a credo that has attempted to absorb into itself and to deny the fear of life and death; and it is only one more competitor in the spectrum of roles for cosmic heroics.

Modern man is drinking and drugging himself out of awareness, or he spends his time shopping, which is the same thing. As awareness calls for types of heroic dedication that his culture no longer provides for him, society contrives to help him forget. Or, alternatively, he buries himself in psychology in the belief that awareness all by itself will be some kind of magical cure for his problems. But psychology was born with the breakdown of shared social heroisms; it can only be gone beyond with the creation of new heroisms that are basically matters of belief and will, dedication to a vision. Lifton has recently concluded the same thing, from a conceptual point of view almost identical to Rank's.[48] When a thinker of Norman Brown's stature wrote his later book *Love's Body*, he was led to take his thought to this same point. He realized that the only way to get beyond the natural contradictions of existence was in the time-worn religious way: to project one's problems onto a god-figure, to be healed by an all-embracing and all-justifying beyond. To talk in these terms is not at all the same thing as to talk the language of the psychotherapeutic religionists. Rank was not so naïve nor so messianic: he saw that the orientation of men has to be always beyond their bodies, has to be grounded in healthy repressions, and toward explicit immortality-ideologies, myths of heroic transcendence.‡

We can conclude that a project as grand as the scientific-mythical construction of victory over human limitation is not something that can be programmed by science. Even more, it comes from the vital energies of masses of men sweating within the nightmare of creation—and it is not even in man's hands to program. Who knows what form the forward momentum of life will take in the time ahead or what use it will make of our anguished searching. The most that any one of us can seem to do is to fashion something—an object or ourselves—and drop it into the confusion, make an offering of it, so to speak, to the life force.

‡ It is worth noting that Brown's final point of arrival is the logically correct one, but I personally find his later book very unsatisfying. One wonders why he has to present his new position in such a barrage of aphorisms, such a turbulent hodgepodge of half-veiled thoughts, terse in the extreme, and often cryptic—only to end up in a mystical Christianity of the oldest vintage and a call for the final judgment day. In this, at least, his later book is entirely consistent with the earlier one: natural existence in the frustrating limitations of the body calls for total, all-or-nothing relief, either in unrepression or at last in the end of the world.

References

Note: As the following works of Otto Rank are mentioned frequently, for the sake of convenience they are abbreviated in the references as follows:

PS   *Psychology and the Soul,* 1931 (New York: Perpetua Books Edition, 1961).

ME   *Modern Education: A Critique of Its Fundamental Ideas* (New York: Agathon Press, 1968).

AA   *Art and Artist: Creative Urge and Personality Development* (New York: Agathon Press, 1968).

WT   *Will Therapy and Truth and Reality* (New York: Knopf, 1936; One Volume Edition, 1945).

BP   *Beyond Psychology,* 1941 (New York: Dover Books, 1958).

Excerpts from new translations of other of Rank's works have appeared in the *Journal of the Otto Rank Association,* along with transcriptions of some of Rank's lectures and conversations; this publication is cited as JORA.

I have also cited frequently Norman O. Brown's *Life Against Death: The Psychoanalytical Meaning of History* (New York: Viking Books, 1959) and abbreviated it LAD.

I have also abbreviated often-cited titles of papers and books by various authors after the first complete reference.

Preface

1. Rank, letter of 2/8/33, in Jessie Taft's outstanding biography, *Otto Rank* (New York: Julian Press, 1958), p. 175.
2. LAD, p. 322.
3. F. S. Perls, R. F. Hefferline, and P. Goodman, *Gestalt Therapy* (New York: Delta Books, 1951), p. 395, note.
4. I. Progoff, *The Death and Rebirth of Psychology* (New York: Delta Books, 1964).
5. P. Roazen, *The Virginia Quarterly Review,* Winter, 1971, p. 33.

Chapter One

1. William James, *Varieties of Religious Experience: A Study in Human Nature,* 1902 (New York: Mentor Edition, 1958), p. 281.

Chapter Two

1. S. Freud, "Thoughts for the Times on War and Death," 1915, *Collected Papers*, Vol. 4 (New York: Basic Books, 1959), pp. 316–317.
2. Cf., for example, A. L. Cochrane, "Elie Metschnikoff and His Theory of an 'Instinct de la Mort,'" *International Journal of Psychoanalysis* 1934, 15:265–270; G. Stanley Hall, "Thanatophobia and Immortality," *American Journal of Psychology*, 1915, 26:550–613.
3. N. S. Shaler, *The Individual: A Study of Life and Death* (New York: Appleton, 1900).
4. Hall, "Thanatophobia," p. 562.
5. Cf., Alan Harrington, *The Immortalist* (New York: Random House, 1969), p. 82.
6. See Jacques Choron's excellent study: *Death and Western Thought* (New York: Collier Books, 1963).
7. See H. Feifel, ed., *The Meaning of Death* (New York: McGraw-Hill, 1959), Chapter 6; G. Rochlin, *Griefs and Discontents* (Boston: Little, Brown, 1967), p. 67.
8. J. Bowlby, *Maternal Care and Mental Health* (Geneva: World Health Organization, 1952), p. 11.
9. Cf. Walter Tietz, "School Phobia and the Fear of Death," *Mental Hygiene*, 1970, 54:565–568.
10. J. C. Rheingold, *The Mother, Anxiety and Death: The Catastrophic Death Complex* (Boston: Little, Brown, 1967).
11. A. J. Levin, "The Fiction of the Death Instinct," *Psychiatric Quarterly*, 1951, 25:257–281.
12. J. C. Moloney, *The Magic Cloak: A Contribution to the Psychology of Authoritarianism* (Wakefield, Mass.: Montrose Press, 1949), p. 217; H. Marcuse, "The Ideology of Death," in Feifel, *Meaning of Death*, Chapter 5.
13. LAD, p. 270.
14. G. Murphy, "Discussion," in Feifel, *The Meaning of Death*, p. 320.
15. James, *Varieties*, p. 121.
16. Choron, *Death*, p. 17.
17. *Ibid.*, p. 272.
18. G. Zilboorg "Fear of Death," *Psychoanalytic Quarterly*, 1943, 12:465–475. See Eissler's nice technical distinction between the anxiety of death and the terror of it, in his book of essays loaded with subtle discussion: K. R. Eissler, *The Psychiatrist and the Dying Patient* (New York: International Universities Press, 1955), p. 277.
19. Zilboorg "Fear of Death," pp. 465–467.

20. James, *Varieties*, p. 121.
21. Zilboorg, "Fear of Death," p. 467. Or, we might more precisely say, with Eissler, fear of annihilation, which is extended by the ego into the consciousness of death. See *The Psychiatrist and the Dying Patient*, p. 267.
22. *Ibid.*
23. *Ibid.*, pp. 468–471 *passim*.
24. Cf. Shaler, *The Individual*.
25. C. W. Wahl, "The Fear of Death," in Feifel, pp. 24–25.
26. Cf. Moloney, *The Magic Cloak*, p. 117.
27. Wahl, "Fear of Death," pp. 25–26.
28. In Choron, *Death*, p. 100.
29. Cf., for example, I. E. Alexander *et al.*, "Is Death a Matter of Indifference?" *Journal of Psychology*, 1957, 43:277–283; I. M. Greenberg and I. E. Alexander, "Some Correlates of Thoughts and Feelings Concerning Death," *Hillside Hospital Journal*, 1962, No. 2:120–126; S. I. Golding *et al.*, "Anxiety and Two Cognitive Forms of Resistance to the Idea of Death," *Psychological Reports*, 1966, 18:359–364.
30. L. J. Saul, "Inner Sustainment," *Psycholoanalytic Quarterly*, 1970, 39:215–222.
31. Wahl, "Fear of Death," p. 26.

Chapter Three

1. Erich Fromm, *The Heart of Man: Its Genius for Good and Evil* (New York: Harper and Row, 1964), pp. 116–117.
2. Erich Fromm, *The Sane Society* (New York: Fawcett Books, 1955), p. 34.
3. LAD.
4. Cf. Lord Raglan, *Jocasta's Crime: An Anthropological Study* (London: Methuen, 1933), Chapter 17.
5. LAD, p. 186.
6. *Ibid.*, p. 189.
7. *Ibid.*, pp. 186–187.
8. E. Straus, *On Obsession, A Clinical and Methodological Study* (New York: Nervous and Mental Disease Monographs, 1948), No. 73.
9. *Ibid.*, pp. 41, 44.
10. Freud, *Civilization and its Discontents*, 1930 (London: The Hogarth Press, 1969 edition), p. 43.
11. LAD, p. 118.

12. *Ibid.*, p. 120.
13. Sandor Ferenczi, *Final Contributions to the Problems and Methods of Psycho-analysis* (London: The Hogarth Press, 1955), p. 66.
14. PS, p. 38.
15. LAD, p. 124.
16. *Ibid.*, p. 123.
17. *Ibid.*
18. *Ibid.*, p. 128.
19. *Ibid.*, p. 127.
20. ME.
21. Freud, *A General Introduction to Psychoanalysis* (New York: Garden City Publishing Co., 1943), p. 324.
22. Geza Roheim, *Psychoanalysis and Anthropology* (New York: International Universities Press, 1950), pp. 138–139.
23. Ferenczi, *Final Contributions*, pp. 65–66.
24. Rollo May recently revived the Rankian perspective on this; see his excellent discussion of "Love and Death" in *Love and Will* (New York: Norton, 1971).
25. ME, p. 52.
26. *Ibid.*, p. 53.
27. LAD, pp. 127–128.

Chapter Four

1. Ortega, *The Revolt of the Masses* (New York: Norton, 1957), pp. 156–157.
2. E. Becker, *The Structure of Evil: An Essay on the Unification of the Science of Man* (New York: Braziller, 1968), p. 192.
3. See his two fine papers, "The Need to Know and the Fear of Knowing" *Journal of General Psychology*, 1963, 68:111–125; and "Neurosis as a Failure of Personal Growth," *Humanitas*, 1967, 3:153–169.
4. Maslow, "Neurosis as a Failure," p. 163.
5. *Ibid.*, pp. 165–166.
6. Rudolf Otto, *The Idea of the Holy*, 1923 (New York: Galaxy Books, 1958).
7. Maslow, "The Need to Know," p. 119.
8. *Ibid.*, pp. 118–119.
9. Cf. Freud, *The Future of an Illusion*, 1927 (New York: Anchor Books Edition, 1964), Chapters 3 and 4.
10. Freud, *The Problem of Anxiety*, 1926 (New York: Norton, 1936), pp. 67 ff.

11. Cf. also the continuation of Heidegger's views in modern existential psychiatry: Médard Boss, *Meaning and Content of Sexual Perversions: A Daseinanalytic Approach to the Psychopathology of the Phenomenon of Love* (New York: Grune and Stratton, 1949), p. 46.

12. F. Perls, *Gestalt Therapy Verbatim* (Lafayette, Calif.: Real People Press, 1969), pp. 55–56.

13. A. Angyal, *Neurosis and Treatment: A Holistic Theory* (New York: Wiley, 1965), p. 260.

14. Maslow, *Toward a Psychology of Being,* second edition (Princeton: Insight Books, 1968), Chapter 8.

15. LAD.

16. ME, p. 13, my emphasis.

17. Harold F. Searles, "Schizophrenia and the Inevitability of Death," *Psychiatric Quarterly,* 1961, 35:633–634.

18. Traherne, *Centuries,* C.1672 (London, Faith Press edition, 1963), pp. 109–115, *passim.*

19. Marcia Lee Anderson, "Diagnosis," quoted in Searles, "Schizophrenia," p. 639.

20. LAD, p. 291.

Chapter Five

1. Kierkegaard, *Journal,* May 12th, 1839.

2. O. H. Mowrer, *Learning Theory and Personality Dynamics* (New York: Ronald Press, 1950), p. 541.

3. Cf. especially Rollo May, *The Meaning of Anxiety* (New York: Ronald Press, 1950); Libuse Lukas Miller, *In Search of the Self: The Individual in the Thought of Kierkegaard* (Philadelphia: Muhlenberg Press, 1962).

4. Kierkegaard, *The Concept of Dread,* 1844 (Princeton: University Press edition, 1957, translated by Walter Lowrie), p. 41.

5. *Ibid.,* p. 38.

6. *Ibid.,* p. 39.

7. *Ibid.,* p. 139.

8. *Ibid.,* p. 40.

9. *Ibid.,* p. 140.

10. Kierkegaard, *The Sickness Unto Death,* 1849 (Anchor edition, 1954, combined with *Fear and Trembling,* translated by Walter Lowrie), p. 181.

11. Kierkegaard, *Dread*, pp. 110 ff.

12. *Ibid.*, p. 124.

13. *Ibid.*, pp. 112–113.

14. *Ibid.*

15. *Ibid.*, pp. 114–115.

16. *Ibid.*, pp. 115–116.

17. Cf. Miller, *In Search of the Self*, pp. 265–276.

18. Kierkegaard, *Sickness*, pp. 184–187, *passim.*

19. *Ibid.*, pp. 174–175.

20. *Ibid.*

21. *Ibid.*, pp. 162 ff.

22. Cf. E. Becker, *The Revolution in Psychiatry* (New York: Free Press, 1964); and Chapter 10 of this book.

23. Kierkegaard, *Sickness*, p. 163.

24. *Ibid.*, pp. 164, 165, 169.

25. *Ibid.*, pp. 169–170.

26. *Ibid.*

27. *Ibid.*, p. 165.

28. Becker, *The Revolution in Psychiatry.*

29. Kierkegaard, *Sickness*, pp. 166–167.

30. *Ibid.*, pp. 170–172.

31. *Ibid.*, p. 172.

32. *Ibid.*, p. 173.

33. *Ibid.*, pp. 174–175, *passim.*

34. Freud, *Civilization and Its Discontents*, p. 81.

35. Kierkegaard, *Sickness*, p. 196.

36. *Ibid.*, p. 198.

37. *Ibid.*, p. 199.

38. *Ibid.*, p. 156.

39. Cf. Miller, *In Search of the Self*, pp. 312–313.

40. Kierkegaard, *Dread*, p. 144.

41. *Ibid.*, p. 140.

42. Cf. Miller, *In Search of the Self*, p. 270.

43. Kierkegaard, *Sickness*, p. 199.

44. James, *Varieties*, p. 99.

45. Ortega, *The Revolt of the Masses*, p. 157.

46. Kierkegaard, *Dread*, pp. 140 ff.

47. *Ibid.*, pp. 141–142.

48. *Ibid.*, p. 104.

49. *Ibid.*, p. 145.

50. Cf. R. May, *The Meaning of Anxiety*, p. 45.

Chapter Six

1. Freud, *Civilization and Its Discontents*, p. 43.
2. LAD, p. 188.
3. C. G. Jung, *Memories, Dreams and Reflections* (New York: Vintage, 1965), pp. 149–151.
4. *Ibid.*
5. Quoted in Vincent Brome, *Freud and His Early Circle* (London: Heinemann, 1967), p. 103.
6. LAD, p. 103.
7. Cf. Freud, *The Future of an Illusion*, 1927 (New York: Anchor Books edition, 1964), p. 32.
8. Freud, *Beyond the Pleasure Principle*, 1920 (New York: Bantam Books edition, 1959), p. 61.
9. *Ibid.*, p. 66.
10. C. Rank's penetrating remarks on Freud's theoretical problems, WT, p. 115; and see Brown's discussion, LAD, pp. 97 ff.
11. See *Beyond the Pleasure Principle*, pp. 93, 105, 106 note; and LAD, pp. 99–100.
12. LAD, pp. 101 ff.
13. WT, p. 130.
14. Cf. LAD, p. 109.
15. WT, p. 116.
16. *Ibid.*, pp. 121–122, my emphasis.
17. *Ibid.*, p. 115.
18. See ME, p. 38.
19. Levin, "The Fiction of the Death Instinct," pp. 277–278.
20. E. Jones, *The Life and Work of Sigmund Freud*, abridged edition (Doubleday Anchor, 1963), p. 198.
21. *Ibid.*, p. 354.
22. *Ibid.*, p. 194.
23. *Ibid.*, p. 197.
24. *Ibid.*, p. 194 note.
25. *Ibid.*, p. 197 note.
26. Jones, *Freud*, abridged edition, p. 354.
27. Quoted in Zilboorg, *Psychoanalysis and Religion* (London: Allen and Unwin, 1967), p. 233.
28. *Ibid.*, pp. 232–234, *passim.*
29. *Ibid.*, p. 234.
30. Quoted in Roazen, *Brother Animal, The Story of Freud and Tausk* (London: Allen Lane the Penguin Press, 1969), p. 172 note.
31. C. G. Jung, *Memories*, p. 156.
32. *Ibid.*, p. 157.

33. Paul Roazen, *Freud: Political and Social Thought* (New York: Vintage Books, 1970), pp. 176–181.

34. *Ibid.*, p. 176. Fromm makes a similar point, *Freud's Mission*, p. 64.

35. *Ibid.*, p. 178.

36. Cf. Jung, *Memories*, p. 157.

37. Roazen, *Freud*, p. 179.

38. Jung, *Memories*, p. 156.

39. Jones, *The Life and Work of Sigmund Freud*, 3 volume edition (New York: Basic Books, 1953), vol. 1, p. 317.

40. Quoted in Brome, *Freud*, p. 98.

41. Cf. Brome's intelligent and probing discussion, *Ibid.*, p. 125.

42. Roazen, *Freud*, p. 180.

43. E. Fromm, *The Heart of Man*, pp. 43–44.

44. Jones, *Freud*, vol. 2, p. 55.

45. *Ibid.*, pp. 145–146.

46. *Ibid.*

47. Cf. E. Becker, *The Structure of Evil*, p. 400; and *Angel in Armor* (New York: Braziller, 1969), p. 130.

48. Jones, *Freud*, vol. 1, p. 8 and note "j."

49. Jones, *Freud*, abridged edition, p. 329.

50. Jones, *Freud*, vol. 1, p. 317.

51. Jung, *Memories*, p. 157.

52. Jones, *Freud*, vol. 2, p. 420.

53. *Ibid.* Cf. also Fromm, *Freud's Mission*, p. 56.

54. Quoted in Brome, *Freud*, p. 127.

55. Quoted in Roazen, *Brother Animal*, p. 40.

56. Zilboorg, *Psychoanalysis and Religion*, p. 226.

57. Pp. 133–134, *Psychoanalysis and Faith: The Letters of Sigmund Freud and Oskar Pfister*, (New York: Basic Books, 1963).

58. Zilboorg, *Psychoanalysis and Religion*, p. 242.

59. *Ibid.*, p. 255. See also Puner's excellent analysis of this rigidity: *Freud*, pp. 255–256, *passim*.

60. Jung, *Memories*, pp. 152–153.

61. *Ibid.*, p. 154.

Chapter Seven

1. Camus, *The Fall* (New York: Knopf, 1957), p. 133.

2. Levi, *Of Fear and Freedom* (New York: Farrar-Strauss, 1950), p. 135.

3. See Olden, "About the Fascinating Effect of the Narcissistic Personality," *American Imago*, 1941, 2:347–355.

4. Jung, *Two Essays on Analytical Psychology* (Cleveland: Meridian Books, 1956).

5. *Vancouver Sun*, 8/31/70, "From Champion Majorette to Frank Sinatra Date," by Jurgen Hesse.

6. Freud, *A General Introduction to Psychoanalysis*, 1920 (New York: Garden City edition, 1943), p. 384.

7. See Benjamin Wolstein's excellent critical study: *Transference: Its Meaning and Function in Psychoanalytic Therapy* (New York: Grune and Stratton, 1954).

8. Freud, *A General Introduction*, pp. 387–388.

9. S. Ferenczi, "Introjection and Transference," Chapter 2 in *Contributions to Psychoanalysis* (London: Phillips, 1916); and compare Herbert Spiegel, "Hypnosis and Transference, a Theoretical Formulation," *Archives of General Psychiatry*, 1959, 1:634–639.

10. Ferenczi, "Introjection and Transference," p. 59.

11. *Ibid.*, p. 61.

12. *Ibid.*, pp. 72, 78, 79; in italics in the original.

13. *Ibid.*, p. 68.

14. Freud, *Group Psychology and the Analysis of the Ego*, 1921 (New York: Bantam Books edition, 1965), p. 68. Cf. also T. W. Adorno's important appreciation of this reorientation: "Freudian Theory and the Pattern of Fascist Propaganda," *Psychoanalysis and the Social Sciences*, 1951, p. 281, footnote.

15. Freud, *ibid.*, p. 60.

16. Otto Fenichel, "Psychoanalytic Remarks on Fromm's Book, *Escape From Freedom*," *Psychoanalytic Review*, 1944, 31:133–134.

17. Freud, *Group Psychology*, p. 16.

18. *Ibid.*, p. 9.

19. Fromm, *Heart of Man*, p. 107.

20. Fritz Redl, "Group Emotion and Leadership," *Psychiatry*, 1942, 573–596.

21. *Ibid.*, p. 594.

22. W. R. Bion, "Group Dynamics—A Re-view," in Melanie Klein, ed., *New Directions in Psychoanalysis* (New York: Basic Books, 1957), pp. 440–447.

23. *Ibid.*, esp. pp. 467–468. Bion also develops his argument along the lines of Redl earlier—that there are different types of groups and thus different "uses" of leaders.

24. Paul Schilder, in M. Gill and M. Brenman, *Hypnosis and Related States* (New York: Science Editions, 1959), p. 159.

25. Canetti, *Crowds and Power*, p. 332.

26. Wolstein, *Transference*, p. 154.

27. Freud, "The Dynamics of the Transference," 1912, *Collected Papers*, vol. 2, p. 319; cf. also *A General Introduction*, p. 387.

28. Freud, "The Dynamics of the Transference," p. 315.

29. Freud, *The Future of an Illusion*, 1928 (New York: Doubleday Anchor edition, 1964), p. 35; see the whole of Chapter III.

30. Heinz and Rowena Ansbacher, eds., *The Individual Psychology of Alfred Adler* (New York: Basic Books, 1956), pp. 342–343.

31. W. V. Silverberg, "The Concept of Transference," *Psychoanalytic Quarterly*, 1948, 17:319, 321.

32. Fromm, *Beyond the Chains of Illusion: My Encounter with Marx and Freud* (New York: Simon and Schuster, 1962), p. 52.

33. C. G. Jung, *The Psychology of the Transference* (Princeton: Bollingen Books, 1969), p. 156.

34. Roy Waldman, *Humanistic Psychiatry: From Oppression to Choice* (New Brunswick, N.J.: Rutgers University Press, 1971), p. 84.

35. Jung, *Transference*, p. xii.

36. T. S. Szasz, *Pain and Pleasure: A Study of Bodily Feelings* (London: Tavistock, 1957), pp. 98 ff.

37. Jung, *Transference*, p. 156.

38. ME, p. 178; WT, p. 82.

39. BP, pp. 130, 136.

40. WT, p. 82.

41. A. Angyal, *Neurosis and Treatment: A Holistic Theory* (New York: Wiley, 1965), pp. 120–21.

42. Cf. WT, pp. 82 ff.

43. Freud, *An Autobiographical Study* (London: Hogarth, 1946); cf. also *A General Introduction*, p. 387.

44. Ferenczi, "Introjection and Transference," pp. 38, 44.

45. Cf. Searles, "Schizophrenia and the Inevitability of Death," p. 638; also Helm Stierlin, "The Adaptation to the 'Stronger' Person's Reality," *Psychiatry*, 1958, 21:141–147.

46. E. Becker, *The Structure of Evil*, p. 192.

47. Cf. AA, p. 407.

48. Harrington, *The Immortalist*, p. 101.

49. AA, p. 411.

50. Harrington's marvelous phrase, *The Immortalist*, p. 46.

51. Freud, *Group Psychology*, pp. 37–38.

52. On all this cf. Harold Orlansky's excellent reportage, "Reactions to the Death of President Roosevelt," *The Journal of Social Psychology*, 1947, 26:235–266; also D. De Grazia, "A Note on the Psychological Position of the Chief Executive," *Psychiatry*, 1945, 8:267–272.

53. Cf. Becker, *The Structure of Evil*, p. 328.
54. *Ibid.*
55. WT, pp. 74, 155; BP, p. 195; AA, p. 86; ME, p. 142.
56. AA, pp. 370, 376.
57. Cf. PS, pp. 142, 148; BP, pp. 194–195.
58. AA, p. 42.
59. BP, p. 198.
60. ME, pp. 232–234.
61. BP, p. 168.
62. Jung, *Transference*, pp. 71–72.
63. Melville, *Moby Dick*, 1851 (New York: Pocket Library edition, 1955), pp. 361–362.
64. See my discussion of this in *Structure of Evil*, p. 261.
65. Ferenczi, "Introjection and Transference," p. 47.
66. See also J. A. M. Meerloo and Marie L. Coleman, "The Transference Function: A Study of Normal and Pathological Transference," *The Psychoanalytic Review*, 1951, 38:205–221—an essay loaded with important revisions of traditional views; and T. S. Szasz's important critique, "The Concept of Transference," *International Journal of Psychoanalysis*, 1963, 44:432–443.

Chapter Eight

1. BP, p. 196.
2. G. K. Chesterton, *Orthodoxy*, 1908 (New York: Image Books, 1959), p. 80.
3. See AA, Chapter 2; PS, Chapter 4; BP, Chapter 4, etc.
4. BP, p. 168; PS, p. 192; WT, p. 303.
5. ME, p. 232.
6. WT, p. 62.
7. *Ibid.*, p. 304.
8. ME, p. 232.
9. WT, p. 302.
10. BP, p. 234.
11. Roheim, "The Evolution of Culture," p. 403.
12. ME, p. 44.
13. *Ibid.*, pp. 46 ff.
14. *Ibid.*, p. 43.
15. BP, p. 234.

16. See also Rollo May's contemporary critique on this problem in his *Love and Will.*
17. PS, p. 92.
18. BP, pp. 196–197.
19. Cf. WT, p. 62.
20. Cf. E. Becker, *The Birth and Death of Meaning,* second edition, Chapter 12.
21. WT, p. 287.
22. WT, p. 131.
23. BP, p. 197.
24. WT, p. 304.
25. PS, p. 92.
26. To see how "Christian" is Rank's analysis of sexuality and the other, see Reinhold Niebuhr's outstanding study, *The Nature and Destiny of Man* (New York: Scribner and Sons, 1941), Vol. 1, pp. 233–240.
27. BP, pp. 186, 190.
28. Jung, *The Psychology of the Transference,* p. 101.
29. AA, p. 86.
30. AA, p. 42; WT, p. 278.
31. Cf. E. Becker, *The Structure of Evil,* pp. 190 ff.
32. WT, p. 147.
33. BP, p. 272. Jung saw that Freud's circle itself was a father-religion: *Modern Man in Search of a Soul,* 1933 (New York: Harvest Books edition), p. 122.
34. *Ibid.,* pp. 273–274.
35. *Ibid.,* p. 194.
36. *Ibid.,* pp. 188–201.
37. Cf. Tillich, *Systematic Theology,* Vol. 3, pp. 75–77.

Chapter Nine

1. WT, pp. 251–252.
2. *Ibid.,* Chapter 12.
3. *Ibid.,* p. 195.
4. *Ibid.,* p. 241; JORA, June 1967, p. 17.
5. WT, pp. 73, 155, 303.
6. *Ibid.,* p. 149; JORA, Dec. 1970, pp. 49–50.
7. WT, pp. 148–149.

8. Freud, *Introductory Lectures* III, p. 445; emphasized by Jung, *Psychology of the Transference*, p. 8, note 16.

9. Roy D. Waldman, *Humanistic Psychiatry* (New Brunswick: Rutgers University Press, 1971), pp. 123–124; see also the excellent paper by Ronald Leifer, "Avoidance and Mastery: An Interactional View of Phobias." *Journal of Individual Psychology*, May, 1966, pp. 80–93; and compare Becker, *The Revolution in Psychiatry*, pp. 115 ff.

10. WT, p. 149.

11. BP, p. 50.

12. WT, pp. 146–147.

13. JORA, June, 1967, p. 79.

14. WT, pp. 146–147.

15. *Ibid.*, p. 151.

16. *Ibid.*, p. 149.

17. AA, pp. 376–377.

18. *Ibid.*, p. 372.

19. *Ibid.*, p. 27.

20. WT, p. 93.

21. *Ibid.*, pp. 95, 173.

22. Nin, JORA, June, 1967, p. 118.

23. WT, p. 195.

24. *Ibid.*, pp. 251–252.

25. *Ibid.*, p. 173.

26. Turney-High, *Primitive War*, p. 208.

27. WT, pp. 74, 287.

28. *Ibid.*, p. 288.

29. See the crucial historical paper by James M. Baldwin, "The History of Psychology," *International Congress of Arts and Science*, vol. 5, St. Louis, 1904, pp. 606–623; and Stephan Strasser's most important work, *The Soul in Metaphysical and Empirical Psychology* (Pittsburgh, Pa.: Duquesne University Press, 1962); and PS, Chapter 1, pp. 84 ff., and Chapter 7.

30. PS, p. 192.

31. ME, p. 143.

32. PS, p. 10; cf. also Becker, *The Revolution in Psychiatry*, pp. 120–121.

33. PS, p. 10.

34. See BP, Chapters 1 and 8; PS, Chapters 1 and 7; and see Progoff's excellent summary, *Death and Rebirth*, pp. 221–228, 258–259.

35. ME, p. 143.

36. *Ibid.*, pp. 143, 232.

37. JORA, Fall 1966, p. 42; ME, p. 45; and see O. H. Mowrer's important writings, which were very much resisted by the mainstream

of psychologists, *The Crisis in Psychiatry and Religion* (New York: Insight Books, 1961), esp. Chapter 8.

38. WT, pp. 74, 152, 205, 241, 303–304.
39. *Ibid.*, pp. 92–93.
40. *Ibid.*; cf. also Waldman, *Humanistic Psychiatry*, p. 59 and his outstanding pp. 117–127, which must now represent the definitive reintroduction of the equation of sin and neurosis in modern psychiatry; and cf. Mowrer, *The Crisis in Psychiatry*, Chapters 3 and 4.
41. WT, pp. 93, 304.
42. AA, p. 27; Waldman, *Humanistic Psychiatry*, p. 120. Waldman draws not on Rank but on Adler, to whom Rank is also clearly indebted. After Adler, Karen Horney wrote extensively and with great insight specifically on the dynamics of self-glorification and self-depreciation in neurosis. Particularly important are her discussions of the need for heroic triumph and perfection and what happens to them in the neurotic. See especially her *Neurosis and Human Growth* (New York: Norton, 1950).
43. BP, p. 193; WT, p. 304; ME, p. 141.
44. ME, pp. 142–144.
45. WT, pp. 150, 241; AA, p. 86; WT, p. 94.
46. Chesterton, *Orthodoxy*, pp. 18–29; and cf. ME, p. 47.
47. BP, p. 49.
48. Cf. BP, pp. 166, 197; WT, p. 303; and Becker, *Birth and Death*, second edition, Chapter 13.
49. Freud, "Observations on Transference-love," p. 388.
50. Van der Leeuw, *Religion in Essence*, vol. 2, p. 467.
51. ME, pp. 44–45.
52. Cf. also G. P. Conger's important and neglected book, *The Ideologies of Religion* (New York: Round Table Press, 1940).
53. Cf. Jung, *Psychology of the Transference*, p. 69.
54. ME, p. 232.
55. Becker, *Structure of Evil*, pp. 190–210.
56. AA, p. 429.
57. Jung, *Psychology of the Transference*, pp. 101–102.
58. Jung, *Memories*, p. 288.

Chapter Ten

1. Boss, *Meaning and Content of Sexual Perversions*, pp. 46–47.
2. Alfred Adler, *The Practice and Theory of Individual Psychology* (London: Kegan Paul, 1924), Chapter 21.

3. Straus's excellent thought—"The Miser," in *Patterns of the Life-World*, ed. by J. M. Edie (Evanston: Northwestern University Press, 1970), Chapter 9.

4. M. Boss, *Psychoanalysis and Daseinanalysis* (New York: Basic Books, 1963), pp. 209–210.

5. BP, p. 169.

6. W. Gaylin, ed., *The Meaning of Despair* (New York: Science House, 1968), p. 391.

7. Rank, WT, pp. 126, 127, 131.

8. Cf. Becker, *The Revolution in Psychiatry*.

9. Adler, *Individual Psychology*, p. 252.

10. Boss, *Sexual Perversions*, p. 46.

11. W. Bromberg and P. Schilder, "The Attitude of Psychoneurotics Towards Death," p. 20.

12. Harrington, *The Immortalist*, p. 93.

13. James, *Varieties*, p. 138.

14. Adler, *Individual Psychology*, pp. 256–260.

15. Within psychoanalysis no one understood this functional dualism better than Wilhelm Reich; see the brilliant theory in his early book *Character Analysis*, 1933 (New York: Noonday Press, third edition, 1949), pp. 431–462.

16. Cf. Becker, *The Revolution in Psychiatry*.

17. Chesterton, *Orthodoxy*, esp. Chapter 2.

18. Reich, *Character Analysis*, pp. 432, 450.

19. Adler, *Individual Psychology*, p. 257.

20. Boss, *Sexual Perversions*.

21. Chapter 9, in J. M. Edie, ed., *Patterns of the Life-World*.

22. Freud, "Fetishism," 1927, *Collected Papers*, vol. 5, p. 199.

23. *Ibid.*, pp. 200, 201.

24. Bak, "The Phallic Woman: The Ubiquitous Fantasy in Perversions," *Psychoanalytic Study of the Child*, 1968, 23:16.

25. M. E. Romm, "Some Dynamics in Fetishism," *Psychoanalytic Quarterly*, 1949, 19:146–147, my emphasis.

26. *Ibid.*

27. Jung, *Transference*, Ch. 10.

28. Boss, *Sexual Perversions*, pp. 24, 32, 33, 37, 119, 136.

29. LAD, pp. 132–134.

30. Nancy T. Spiegel, "An Infantile Fetish and its Persistence into Young Womanhood," *Psychoanalytic Study of the Child*, 1967, 22:408.

31. Cf. Greenacre, "Perversions: General Considerations Regarding Their Genetic and Dynamic Background," *Psychoanalytic Study of the Child*, 1968, 23:57.

32. Romm, "Some Dynamics," p. 148–149.
33. S. M. Payne, "Observations on the Ego Development of the Fetishist," *International Journal of Psychoanalysis*, 1938, 20:169.
34. See his "On Obsession."
35. P. Greenacre, "Certain Relationships Between Fetishism and Faulty Development of the Body Image," *Psychoanalytic Study of the Child*, 1953, 8:84.
36. Greenacre, "Certain Relationships," p. 93; see also her "Perversions," pp. 47–62.
37. Cf. Bak, "Phallic Woman," p. 20; Greenacre, "Certain Relationships," p. 80; "Perversions"; "Further Considerations Regarding Fetishism," *Psychoanalytic Study of the Child*, 1955, 10:192.
38. Otto Fenichel, "The Psychology of Transvestism," *International Journal of Psychoanalysis*, 1930, 11:220.
39. A. S. Lorand, "Fetishism in Statu Nascendi," *International Journal of Psychoanalysis*, 11:422.
40. Freud, "Fetishism," p. 201.
41. S. Nagler, "Fetishism: A Review and a Case Study," *Psychiatric Quarterly*, 1957, 31:725.
42. Cf. Becker, *Angel in Armor*.
43. ME, p. 52.
44. *Ibid.*, pp. 199–200.
45. AA, pp. 54–55.
46. PS, p. 43.
47. *Ibid.*
48. F. H. Allen, "Homosexuality in Relation to the Problem of Human Difference," *American Journal of Orthopsychiatry*, 1940, 10:129–35.
49. M. Balint, "A Contribution on Fetishism," *International Journal of Psychoanalysis*, 1935, 16:481.
50. Freud, "Fetishism," p. 199.
51. Boss, *Sexual Perversions*, pp. 50 ff.
52. *Ibid.*, p. 52.
53. *Ibid.*, pp. 41–42.
54. *Ibid.*, p. 74.
55. *Ibid.*, p. 51.
56. Greenacre, "Further Notes on Fetishism," *Psychoanalytic Study of the Child*, 1960, 15:191–207.
57. Greenacre, "The Fetish and the Transitional Object," *Psychoanalytic Study of the Child*, 1969, 24:161–162.
58. Freud, "Fetishism," p. 201.
59. Cf. Greenacre, "The Fetish and Transitional Object," p. 150.
60. Greenacre, "Further Notes," p. 200.

61. *Ibid.*, p. 202.
62. Cf. James Glover, "Notes on an Unusual Form of Perversion," *International Journal of Psychoanalysis*, 1927, 8:10–24.
63. Fenichel, "Transvestism," p. 219.
64. Cf. Bak, "Phallic Woman," p. 16; Fenichel, "Transvestism," p. 214.
65. Fenichel, "Transvestism," p. 219.
66. Bak, "Phallic Woman," p. 25.
67. Fenichel, "Transvestism," p. 219.
68. Greenacre, "Certain Relationships," p. 81.
69. H. T. Buckner, "The Transvestite Career Path," *Psychiatry*, 1970, 33:381–389.
70. Freud, "Fetishism," p. 204.
71. Greenacre, "Further Notes," p. 204.
72. *Ibid.*, p. 206.
73. Romm, "Some Dynamics," p. 147.
74. *Ibid.*, p. 140.
75. Cf. Becker, *Angel in Armor*, Chapter 1.
76. Greenacre, "Certain Relationships," p. 67.
77. Rank, JORA, Dec. 1970, p. 49.
78. Cf. Becker, *Angel in Armor*.
79. Bieber, "The Meaning of Masochism," *American Journal of Psychotherapy*, 1953, 7:438.
80. Zilboorg, "Fear of Death," pp. 473–474.
81. WT, pp. 129–131.
82. Hart, "The Meaning of Passivity," *Psychiatric Quarterly;* 1955, 29: 605.
83. Romm, "Some Dynamics," p. 145.
84. BP, pp. 185–190; cf. also his letter to Jessie Taft, Nov. 9, 1937, p. 240 of Taft, *Otto Rank*.
85. BP, p. 189.
86. Cf. Ansbacher, *Alfred Adler*, pp. 271–273.
87. Cf. D. A. Schwartz, "The Paranoid-Depressive Existential Continuum," *Psychiatric Quarterly*, 1964, 38:690–706.
88. Cf. Adler in Ansbacher, p. 427.
89. Fromm, *Escape From Freedom* (New York: Avon Books, 1941), pp. 173 ff.
90. Bieber, "The Meaning of Masochism," p. 441.
91. Cf. Fromm, *The Heart of Man*, Chapter 3.
92. A. A. Brill, "Necrophilia," *Journal of Criminal Psychopathology*, 1941, 2:440–441.
93. Boss, *Sexual Perversions*, pp. 55–61.

94. Straus, "The Miser," pp. 178–179.
95. Cf. Jung, *Transference*, p. 69; Fromm, *Beyond the Chains of Illusion* (New York: Simon and Schuster, 1962), pp. 56 ff.
96. Letter to Jessie Taft, Sept. 26, 1937, *Otto Rank*, p. 236.

Chapter Eleven

1. Freud, *Psychoanalysis and Faith: Dialogues with the Reverend Oskar Pfister* (New York: Basic Books, 1963), pp. 61–62.
2. *Reich Speaks of Freud*, M. Higgins and C. M. Raphael, eds. (New York: Noonday Press, 1967), pp. 20–21.
3. Cf. esp. pp. 192 and 199 of his *Memories, Dreams, Reflections*.
4. Kierkegaard, *Fear and Trembling*, pp. 49 ff.
5. Cf. Lev Shestov's hard commentary in his classic *Athens and Jerusalem* (Athens, Ohio: Ohio University Press, 1966), pp. 229 ff.
6. Cf. LAD, p. 308.
7. *Ibid.*, pp. 291–292.
8. R. L. Stevenson, quoted in James, *Varieties*, p. 85 note.
9. Which failure he in fact admits on p. 268.
10. Cf. David Bakan's reaffirmation of this Rankian view: *Sigmund Freud and the Jewish Mystical Tradition* (New York: Schocken Books, 1965), pp. 275–276.
11. LAD, p. 270.
12. *Ibid.*, p. 293.
13. *Ibid.*, p. 292.
14. Cf. Becker, *Revolution in Psychiatry*.
15. Cf. LAD, pp. 31, 39.
16. Marcuse, *Eros and Civilization* (New York: Vintage Books, 1962), p. 211.
17. *Ibid.*, p. 216.
18. Rieff, "The Impossible Culture: Oscar Wilde and the Charisma of the Artist," *Encounter*, September 1970, pp. 33–44.
19. *Ibid.*, p. 41.
20. *Ibid.*, p. 40.
21. *Ibid.*, p. 41.
22. Harrington, *The Immortalist*.
23. Quoted in Jacques Choron, *Death and Western Thought*, p. 135.
24. *Ibid.*, pp. 135–136.
25. *Ibid.*, pp. 135–136.

26. Harrington, *The Immortalist*, p. 288.
27. See Rieff, *The Triumph of the Therapeutic: Uses of Faith After Freud* (New York: Harper and Row, 1966).
28. Quoted in Jessie Taft, *Otto Rank*, p. 139.
29. Paul Bakan, in private conversation.
30. Cf. J. Fagan and I. L. Shepherd, eds., *Gestalt Therapy Now* (Palo Alto: Science and Behavior Books, 1970), pp. 237–38.
31. Cf. F. M. Alexander, *The Use of the Self; Its Conscious Direction in Relation to Diagnosis, Functioning, and the Control of Reaction*, with an Introduction by John Dewey (New York: Dutton, 1932); and G. D. Bowden, *F. M. Alexander and the Creative Advance of the Individual* (London: Fowler, 1965).
32. Rieff, *The Triumph of the Therapeutic*.
33. Fromm, *The Sane Society* (New York: Fawcett Books, 1955), p. 34.
34. Passmore, *The Perfectibility of Man* (London: Duckworth, 1970).
35. Tillich, "The Importance of New Being for Christian Theology," in *Man and the Transformation: Papers from the Eranos Yearbooks*, vol. V, ed. by Joseph Campbell, translated by Ralph Manheim (New York: Pantheon Books, 1964), p. 172, also p. 164.
36. For other careful use of concepts and language about the meaning of immanentism see the important books by George P. Conger, *The Ideologies of Religion* (New York: Round Table Press, 1940); and Frank B. Dilley, *Metaphysics and Religious Language* (New York: Columbia University Press, 1964).
37. Langer, *Philosophy in a New Key* (New York: Mentor Books, 1942), p. 199.
38. Fromm, *Man For Himself* (New York: Fawcett Books, 1947), pp. 95 ff.
39. A. Koestler, *The Lotus and the Robot* (New York: Macmillan, 1960).
40. P. Tillich, *The Courage to Be* (New Haven: Yale University Press, 1952), pp. 177 ff.
41. See E. Jacques, "Death and the Mid-life Crisis," pp. 148–149.
42. Cf. J. V. Neel, "Lessons from a 'Primitive' People," *Science*, Vol. 170, No. 3960, Nov. 20, 1970, p. 821.
43. R. J. Lifton, in the Preface to *Revolutionary Immortality* (New York: Vintage Books, 1968). I take this to be the argument, too, of Peter Homans' recent difficult book, *Theology After Freud* (Indianapolis: Bobbs-Merrill, 1970).

INDEX

Absolution, 173
Action blockage, 44
Adler, Alfred, depression, as
      problem of courage, 210
Adorno, T. W., 140
Anal stage, 30–34, 37
Anality, meaning of, 3–34
Anderson, Marcia Lee, 65–66
Agape, Freud on, 153
Agape surrender and role of
      women, 170
Ambiguity, anxiety as function of,
      69
Ambivalence of man, 51
Ambulatory schizophrenia, 78
Anti-heros:
    Charles Manson "family," 6–7
    organized religion and, 7
Anxiety:
    in children: denial of, 54
        effect of earthquakes, 21
    as function of ambiguity, 69
    lure of, 56
    psychotherapy and, 58
    as a teacher, 87–88
Art and Artist (Rank), xi, 171, 173
Art and psychosis, 172
Attitudes toward death, 13–15, 20
    by child, 13–24
Augustinian-Lutheran tradition,
      impotence and death, 88

Automatic cultural man, 74
Automatic instinctive programming
      in man, lack of, 52

Behmen, Jacob, 88
Bergson, Henri, 151
Boss, Médard, 208
Brewster McCloud (film), 32
Brown, Norman, 7, 30, 260–263,
      285
Bunuel, L., 59
Burrow, T., 262

Camus, Albert, 127, 152
Carnal Knowledge (film), 169
Cassavetes, John (actor), 23
"Castrated mother," effect on child,
      38
Castration anxiety:
    "castrated mother," 38
    Oedipal period, 227
Castration complex, 36–39
Causa-sui project:
    child's use of body as, 43
    conceptual ambivalence of,
      119–123
    emotional ambivalence of,
      115–119
Character:
    armor of, 57
    defenses, 57, 61

Character (Con't.)
  development, new psychoana-
      lytic thought and, 61–62
  school of anxiety and
      destruction of, 88
  structure, breakdown of, 75
Characterology, Kierkegaard's,
      70–75
Charles Manson "family," 137–139
Chesterton, G. K., 201
Child:
  and action blockage, 44
  anal play, 31
  attitude toward death, 13–23
  use of body as *causa-sui* project,
      39, 43–46
  body versus symbols, 28–29,
      227
  "castrated mother," 38
  castration anxiety, Oedipal
      period, 223–224, 227
  character defenses, 73, 89, 120
  character orientation, 71
  dependence on mother, 36, 38
  development, 71
  early conditioning, 192
  early relationship with mother,
      191
  Oedipal project, 35
  sexual awareness, 44–45
  sexual guilt, 164–165
  symbolic freedom, 40
  toilet training, 37
Childhood identification, 152
Christ as the focus of Eros, 205
Christian motive of Agape, 152
Christianity:
  as condition for cosmic heroism,
      romantic solution, 159–170
  ideal for mental health, 204

Christianity and Fear (Pfister),
      205
Clockwork Orange, A (film), 32
Collective unconscious, 195
Compulsion neuroses (hysterical
      fears; transference-
      neurosis), 180
Compulsions, 180
Consciousness, physiochemical
      identity, 2–3
Control of nature, 230
Cosmology of good and evil and
      transference object, 212
Cosmic significance, 3–6
Courage, Maslow's theory, 48–49
Creative solution, 171–175
Creator (*see* God)
Creatureliness, as human condition,
      87, 107
Cults and heroism, 12
Cultural hero system:
  and organized religion, 7
  youth and, 6
Cultural illusion and natural
      reality, 188
Culturally normal man, 79
Cultural system, heroism and, 5–6
Culture (*see* Christianity)

Darwin, biological limitations and,
      11
Davidson, Thomas, 151
Death:
  acceptance of, 13
  attitudes toward (*see* Attitudes
      toward death)
  depression, 80, 210
  fear of, 12–24, 57, 148–150,
      180
  in schizophrenia, 218
  knowledge of, 27

and rebirth, 57
religious view of, 68–70, 203
Death and the Mid-Life Crisis
(Jacques), 215
Demoniac rage, 84
Dependency in depression, 213
Depression, 210–217
dependency in, 213
fear of death or life, 210
Depressive psychosis, 78
Disillusionment of modern man,
200
Divided Self, The (Laing), 77
Dramatization and fetish object,
234–244
Dream theory, 98
Dynamics of fetishism, 230,
233–244
self-esteem, 229

Ego, development of, 263
Emotional ambivalence, 115
Enlightenment, 121, 151
Escapes from Freedom (Fromm),
134
Evolution and inner forces, 191
Existential dualism, 77
Existential paradox, 26, 68
Existential philosophy, 53
Experience and Nature (Dewey),
263

Fainting, and Freud, 107–114
Fantasy, 78
Feiffer, J. (cartoonist), 169
Female genitals and fetishism, 223
Ferenczi, S., 130–131
Fetishism, 223, 234–244
Fetishization, 178
Frazer, James, 137

Freud, Sigmund, 102–109, 173
and creatureliness, 94–96
on death, 97–105
libido theory, 98
Oedipus complex, 97
emotional ambivalence of,
115–119
fainting spells of, 109–112
on group psychology, 131–134
primal horde, 135
on hating helplessness, 115
on leaders, 135, 136
and life and death instinct,
98–99
and ontological thought, 151
and psychoanalysis, xi–xiv,
93–124, 174
reinterpretations of: anality,
30–34
castration complex, 37–39
Oedipus complex, 34–37
primal scene, 42, 46
religious views of, 153
on transference, 129
Fromm, Erich, 134, 276
character discussion by Freud,
117–118
diagnosis by Jung, 112

Gang psychology, 140
Gaylin, W., 213
General castration fear, 229
Genius, 109
God, 68, 90, 153, 170, 173, 174,
212
(*See also* Christianity; Freud,
Sigmund; Rank, Otto;
Religion)
God-consciousness, 203
Goethe, Johann, 199, 215

Gorky, M., 127, 148
Group behavior and heroisms, 136, 137
Group psychology, 131–134
Group Psychology and the Analysis of the Ego (Freud), 132
Group responsibility and transference, 135
(*See also* Guilt)
Guilt:
depression and, 79, 213
experienced by man, 179–180
and transference, 139–140

Health, as an ideal, 198–207
Heart of Man, The (Fromm), 134
Hedonism, 268
Hermaphroditic image, 224
Heroic individual, 255–285
Heroism:
anality and castration complex, 47
cosmic, 160–170
cultural system, 4–5
and fear of death, 11, 217
depth psychology of, 9–124
earthly, 4–5
failures, 125–252
human nature, 1–8
impossible, 260–268
justification of, 172
narcissism, 2
personal, through individuation, 171
social hero system, 83
and society, 4
transference, 155
natural function, 158
Historical dimension of neurosis, 190
character and illusion merge, 198

Hocart, A. M., ix
Homicidal communities, 137–139
cheap heroism, 139
magical transformations, 138
urge for heroic self-expansion, 138
Homosexuality, 117–118
Greek, 231, 232
Huizinga, 201
Human aggressiveness and life and death instinct, 98
Human character, 47–66
as defense against despair, 63
and fear of life and death, 53, 180
grand illusion, 56
Human condition, 68
creatureliness as, 87, 107
as neurosis, 198
and transference, 142–158
Human dualism, 76
Human existence, dimensions of, 29
Human nature:
heroism, 1–8
limits of, 276–281
sexuality and dualism of, 41
Humanistic psychology, 151
Humanness, full and part, 58–64
Hypochondria, 226
Hypnosis:
dependent on sexuality, 141
and transference, 129–131
Hypnotic trance, 137
Hysterical fears, transference-neurosis, 180

I Ching (Jung), 276
Illusion, problem of, 186–189
Immortality, 152, 153
Enlightenment view of, 121
Impossible heroism, 260–268

"Inauthentic" men, 73
Independence, avoidance of, 80
Individuality and early
    conditioning, 192
Individuation, 171
    terror in depression, 211
Infant (*see* Child)
Inner Sustainment, 22
Introverts, 82–85

Jacques, Eliot, 215
James William, 88
    on God as life force, 153
Jonah Syndrome, 48–49
Jones, interpretations of Freud,
    113–115
Judeo-Christian renunciatory
    morality, 174
Jung, Carl, 108–109, 206
    collective unconsciousness, 195
    hermaphroditic image, 226
    psychological analysis, 195

Kazantzakis, Nikos, *Zorba the
    Greek*, 21–22
Kierkegaard, Soren, 67–92,
    159–175
    characterology of, 70–75
    on child development, 71
    and demoniac rage, 84
    on development of person, 77
    on neurosis, 205
    on heroism, 91
    on human imagination, 79
    and infinitude, 76
    and introvert, 82
    meaning of manhood, 85–92
    on philistinism, 74
        and normal neurosis, 81
    and Otto Rank: on religion, 174
        on sin and neurosis, 196–198

shut-upness, 71–72
    theorist of psychosis, 75
Kubrick, Stanley, 32

Laing, Ronald, 77
Leader, group response as victims
    of, 137
Levi, Carlo, 127, 139–140
Libido theory, 98
Lie of character, 72–73
Life:
    depression, fear of, 210
    experience, 183
    fear of, 144–148, 180
    schizophrenia psychosis, fear of,
        218
    symbolically and biologically,
        183
Life against Death (Brown), 8,
    30, 260
Life denial, fear of death and, 14
Lifton, Robert Jay, 8
Lopreato, J., 24
Love and sexuality, as modern
    religion, 161, 162
Love's Body (Brown), 285
Luther, Martin, 88

Man:
    absolute tension of dualism, 153
    achievement, 206
    existential dilemma, 25
    free of instinct, 177
    modern, 85, 191
    as theological being, 175
    of truth as reality, acceptance
        by, 189
Mana-personality, 128
Manhood, meaning of, 85–92
Maturity:
    and aging, 215
    anxiety and ultimate, 87

Menopausal depression, 214, 215
Mental health, Christianity as ideal for, 204
Mental illness:
  depression, 210–217
  general view, 208–252
  perversion, 221–224
  schizophrenia psychosis, 217–221
Misery, reality and, 57
Modern ideologies on neurosis, 177
Modern man (see Man)
Montaigne, M., on repression, 20, 23
Motives, ontological, 151, 152, 205
Mystery cults, Eastern Mediterranean, 12
Myth-ritual complex, 199

Nagler, Simon, 229
Narcissism, 2–3
Narcissistic neurosis, 183
Narcissistic omnipotence, 2–3
Narcissistic personality, 128
Narcissistic project:
  anal stage, 37
  castration complex, 37–39
Natural coward, child as, 50
Natural creature guilt, 192
Nature, organismic awareness, 191
Nazi leaders, psychological use of guilt and fear, 140
Nazism, 85
Neurosis, 176–177, 198
  as clinical problem, 183
  creative power, 180, 181
  "cure," 198–200
  and faith, 200
  historical dimension, 190–195
  modern ideologies, 177

and normalcy, 178–179, 187
and sin, 196–198
Neurotic collapse of human ideology of God, 193
Neurotic obsession and primitive religion, 199
Neurotic structure, four layers of, 57
Neurotic symptom, 185
Neurotic type, 177–186
Nexus of unfreedom, 127–158
Nichols, M. (director), 169
Nin, Anaïs, 188
Noch Einmal, problem of Freud's character, 93–124
Normal behavior, refusal of reality, 178
Normal man, 178
Normal neurosis, 81
Normalcy and neurosis, 178–179, 187

Obsessions, 180
Oedipal dynamics, 181
Oedipus complex, 97, 161
Oedipus project, 34–37, 46
Olden, Christine, 128
Omnipotence, 2
Ontological motives, twin, 151, 152, 205
Oral stage, 36–37
Organismic awareness, 191
Organized religion, cultural hero system, 7
Ortega, José, 89

Paradox of man, 69
Partialization, 178
Pascal, B., 27, 29
Peat bog corpses, 108

Penis-envy, 39–42
Perls, Frederick, 213
Personal character, neurosis and, 166
Personal freedom versus species determination, 230–234
Personal relationship and transference, 129
Personality dynamics, 171
Perversion and species determinism, 230–231
Pfister, Oscar, on Kierkegaard, 204–205
"Philistines," 178
"Philistinism," 74, 81
Pieper, Josef, 201
Playboy mystique, 168
Power, fascination of person with, 127
Pre-Oedipal period transference and, 129
Primal horde, 135
Primal scene, 42–46
Primitive religion, neurotic obsession, 199
Programmed cultural heroics, 87
Psychical conflicts, artist and neurotic, 184
Psychoanalysis:
    present outcome, 176–207
    and religion, 175
Psychoanalytic ideas, recasting of, 25–46
Psychological gurus, modern man and, 194
Psychological man, 191
    psychological redemption of, 195
Psychological self-scrutiny, fallacy of, 192

Psychology and religion, 68, 255–285
Psychoses, Kierkegaard as theorist of, 75
Psychotherapy, limitation, 268–276

Rank, Otto, 159–175
    and control of nature, 230
    on Freud, 257
    and man, 175
    and neurosis, defined, 176–207
    psychoanalysis and religion, 175
    and religion, 153, 174
    and Soren Kierkegaard: on religion, 174
    on sin and neurosis, 196–198
Reality:
    and fear, 17
    of human condition, 85
    psychiatry and religion, 67–68
    refusal of, 178–179
Rebirth, 57, 58
Regressive transference, God-consciousness, 203
Redl, Fritz, 135
Reich, Wilhelm, 276
Religion, 68
    as cure of neurosis, 199
    problem of death, 203
    and science, fusion of, 281–285
    society and, 7
Repression, meaning of, 178
Revolutionary Immortality (Lifton), 8
Romantic love:
    procreation and sex, 163
    sadomasochistic relationship, 165
Rousseau, J. J., 62

Salpêtrière mental hospital, Pinel's
    observation on, 190
Santayana, G., 21
Sartre, J. P., 59
Schachtel, E., 145
Schilder, Paul, hypnotic trance,
    137
Schizophrenia, 62–63
    fear of life and death, 218
    infinitude, 78
    symbolic and physical self, 218
    symbolic self, 76
Science and religion, fusion of,
    281–285
Scientific psychology and soul,
    192
Self-consciousness, development of
    animal capable, 191
Self-created man, demoniac rage,
    84
Self-creation, narcissistic project
    of, 37
Self-esteem, 78
    depressive psychosis, 78
    and heroism, 6
    and narcissism, 3
Sexual awareness in child, 44–45
Sexuality and love, as modern
    religion, 161, 162
Sexual naturalism, new cult of
    sensuality, 84
Sexuality:
    hypnosis, dependent on (Freud),
        141
    and modern man, 194
Sin and neurosis, merger of,
    196–198
Social neurosis, 81

Society, religion and, 7
Soul and scientific psychology, 192
Southern California, earth tremors
    in, effect on children, 21
Species determination versus
    personal freedom, 230–234
Spells cast by persons, 127–158
Symbiosis, leader and group,
    139–140
Synthesis of psychoanalytic
    thought, 2–4
Synthesis of thought, human
    science to religion, x

Talent, 185–186
Talion principle, 19
Terror:
    anxiety and, 89
    death and, 11–24
    of self-consciousness, 70
Total personality, cost of repression
    on, 72
Totem and Taboo (Freud), 135
Transference, 127–158, 273
    erotic character of, 141
    fear of death, 148–150
    fear of life, 144–148
    fetish control, 142–144
    higher heroism, 155
    objects, 212
    pre-Oedipal period and, 129
    problem of courage, 142
    problem of value, 203
    reflex of cowardice, 150
Transference-neurosis, 180–181
Transference object, mysterium
    tremendum of existence,
    212

Tribal kings, used as scapegoats by tribes, 137
Trivia, necessity and, 80
Truth, reality and, 189
Twin ontological motives, 151, 152, 205
(See also Man)

Ultimate power of creation, 89
Unconscious mind, 2
Universal guilt, religion and psychology, 194

Van der Leeuw, 203
Victim, group justification of murder of, 138
Vital lie (see Anxiety)

Waldman, Roy, 2–4
Whyte, L. L., 262
Women:
    Agape surrender, 170
    as sexual object, 168–169
Women's liberation movement, 170
"Wrecked by Success" syndrome, 49

You Shall be as Gods (Fromm), 276
Youth and cultural hero system, 6–7

Zorba the Greek (film), 21–22